Miles City
Rollicking Cow Capital of the Montana Frontier

By
Bill O'Neal

EAKIN PRESS ⚜ Fort Worth, Texas
www.EakinPress.com

Copyright © 2025
By Bill O'Neal
Published By Eakin Press
An Imprint of Wild Horse Media Group
P.O. Box 331779
Fort Worth, Texas 76163
1-817-344-7036
www.EakinPress.com
ALL RIGHTS RESERVED

Paperback ISBN 978-1-68179-388-7
Hardback ISBN 978-1-68179-389-4
eBook ISBN 978-1-68179-390-0

ALL RIGHTS RESERVED. No part of this book may be reproduced in any form without written permission from the publisher, except for brief passages included in a review appearing in a newspaper or magazine.

Dedicated to Billy Huckaby

*As a PRCA bareback and bull rider,
he competed in the Miles City Roundup.*

*As an interested spectator, he was entertained by the
World Famous Miles City Bucking Horse Sale.*

*And as a publisher,
Billy has skillfully produced a number of my books,
providing a welcome home for my literary efforts.*

Contents

	Acknowledgments	v
Chapter 1	Introduction to a Frontier Town	1
Chapter 2	Birth of a Frontier Town	6
Chapter 3	General Nelson "Bear Coat" Miles	17
Chapter 4	A Tale of Two Cities	37
Chapter 5	Frontier Violence	56
Chapter 6	Miles City *Demimonde*	76
Chapter 7	From Fire Canoes to Bullwhackers to the Iron Horse	83
Chapter 8	Cattle Town	106
Chapter 9	The Montana Stockgrowers Association	122
Chapter 10	XIT in Montana	138
Chapter 11	Urban Pioneers	151
Chapter 12	Good Times in Miles City	179
Chapter 13	From Remount Depot to the Range Riders Museum	190
Chapter 14	The World Famous Miles City Bucking Horse Sale	201
	Endnotes	213
	Bibliography	225
	Index	232
	Author Bio	243

Acknowledgments

A major research effort for this book was a week spent in Miles City in September 2023. Twenty-eight years earlier I was in Miles City for a briefer time, as part of the research for *Historic Ranches of the Old West*, published by Eakin Press in 1997. During that 1995 research trip I explored Miles City, spending most of a day at the famous Range Riders Museum. When I later decided to focus a book on the frontier period of Miles City, I knew that I would need to spend several days in the Range Riders Museum, which boasts thirteen buildings that feature thousands of items on display.

I contacted Bunny Miller, who has been curator of the museum for thirteen years and who spent years before that assisting her parents, who operated the museum since its inception. I first met Bunny on my 1995 visit to the museum, and after phone calls and correspondence, we were reacquainted on my first day in Miles City in September 2023. I promptly joined the Range Riders Museum, purchased a blue museum cap, and I bought an admission ticket for the week. I did not miss a day without stopping at the museum, taking photos and notes and conferring with Bunny, whose knowledge of the frontier town is encyclopedic.

Nearby, at the WaterWorks Art Museum, I toured the historic 1910 building, and was conducted through the art collection by the museum's executive director, Jenn Hall Tooke. Downtown I visited the Miles City Area Chamber of Commerce, expressing my gratitude for the pamphlets and street maps I had received while preparing for the trip. At the Chamber office I found even more material, along with directions and welcome advice.

On Sunday morning I attended nine o'clock services at the First Presbyterian Church, an impressive example of church architecture completed in 1917. The sanctuary is dominated by a magnificent pipe organ that is original to the building. At eleven o'clock I was in the nearby sanctuary of the First United Methodist Church, where construction began in 1912. At both churches the worship service was followed by a repast in the respective fellowship halls, where I was greeted by a number of congregants, and where I examined and photographed church artifacts that were on display.

Another outstanding example of religious architecture is the three-story Ursuline convent-school, built in 1898-1902 to replace a log building destroyed by fire in 1897. The impressive succeeding structure long served as a Catholic school, which included classrooms, quarters for the teaching nuns, and a top-floor dormitory which housed students from the countryside. I was conducted on a tour by Executive Director Sharon Moore, who brought the picturesque old building back to life with her intimate knowledge of the past of the "Convent Keepers Community Center," as it is known today.

When I visited the Custer County High School, I was directed to Amorette Allison, who is a native of Miles City and a graduate of the school where she now teaches. Indeed, she and her husband live a few blocks away in an historic 1882 residence. Amorette is an enthusiastic and highly knowledgeable local historian, and during an extensive walking tour of the 1921 high school — which has been greatly expanded and modernized – she regaled me with stories of people and places and events of her home town.

At the Custer County Courthouse, Lisa Wagner, Clerk of the Court Recorder's Office, graciously pulled old photos down from the walls so that I could photograph them for the book. Across the street at the Carnegie library (opened in 1902 and later expanded), staff members were cooperative and informative. Indeed, everywhere I went during my work in Miles City I was treated with an eagerness to help a stranger that provided a link from the modern community to the cheerful spirit of the up-and-coming frontier town.

On my 1995 research trip to the area, I explored Medora, nearest town to the nineteenth-centry ranches of the Marquis de Mores and young Theodore Roosevelt. Both Dakota Territory ranchers were members of the Montana Stockgrowers Association, and attended at least one annual meeting in Miles City. At Wibaux, Montana, I saw the home and ranch office of cattle king Pierre Wibaux, who often was in Miles City. From Wibaux I drove to Terry, Montana, and spent the night in the town that was familiar to XIT cowboys. The next morning I met with local historians at the Prairie County Museum. I found out a great deal, and I was especially impressed by the photo collection. I learned about pioneer photographer Evelyn Cameron, and I acquired copies of several of her photos.

I returned from my 2023 research trip with hundreds of photographs. These images were converted into two electronic photo files by Shay Joines, who has come to my aid on several book projects in recent years. I continue to marvel at her technological skills.

One of my granddaughters, Bailey Henderson of Van Alstyne, Texas, is a bright and industrious college student who took on a difficult copying assignment at a needed moment. Bailey also performed other tasks, and I am grateful for her assistance. One of my daughters, Dr. Berri O'Neal Gormley, was of great help with this project from the start. She conducted several fact searches and ordered a number of books that

I needed, before turning to the task of converting my pencil manuscript into an electronic manuscript for the publisher.

At the outset of this project I called publisher Billy Huckaby to see if he might be interested in a book about frontier Miles City. It turned out that Billy was well acquainted with the Miles City Roundup, as well as the World Famous Bucking Horse Sale, from his rodeo days as a young man. He informed me that he would be eager to publish a book about this historic Old West town. Of course, I was elated that I could proceed with this project, confident that it would have a home with Billy Huckaby and his appropriately named Wild Horse Media Group.

Chapter One
Introduction to a Frontier Town

"I can never forget Miles City in '84. As far as fun went, I think I had more there than in any other year of my life . . ."

**Teddy Blue Abbott,
transplanted Texas cowboy**

Miles City was a classic community of the American frontier. This vibrant, rambunctious town came into existence alongside Fort Keogh, one of the largest and busiest outposts of the military frontier. Hundreds of soldiers drank and roistered at the saloons and dance halls and brothels of Miles City. During its first five years of existence, the town relished the presence of post commander Nelson A. Miles, a superb combat officer. Other distinguished military heroes visited Fort Keogh periodically, including famed Civil War Generals William Tecumseh Sherman and Phil Sheridan. Sherman, Sheridan, and Miles each would serve as commanding general of the United States Army. There were Medal of Honor winners garrisoned at Fort Keogh, and one decorated trooper from the Little Bighorn would die in a Miles City shootout.

The transportation frontier was much in evidence on the muddy streets of Miles City. There were horse- and mule-drawn army wagons. Stagecoaches darted in and out of Miles City from Deadwood and other isolated communities. Ox and mule trains labored into and out of town, guided by cursing, whip-popping bullwhackers and muleskinners. Just as rank as the bullwhackers were buffalo hunters and their greasy, blood-smeared hidemen. At times the banks of the Yellowstone were crowded with riverboats, and their crews and captains

Main Street on a busy day in Miles City.
Courtesy Range Riders Museum.

swaggered their way to and from Miles City's houses of merriment. And beginning in 1881, when Miles City was barely five years old, the first railroad reached town and continued westward without a pause. Railroad cars now rumbled continually along the tracks at Miles City, bringing visitors and new settlers and a profusion of goods to the growing community. Almost the entire transportation frontier had paraded through Miles City within just half a decade.

During that time, and for years thereafter, the female inhabitants of the sporting houses drank and laughed their way through countless all-night parties. Nearly three blocks of cribs and brothels faced northeast on Sixth Street, stretching from the Northern Pacific depot almost to Main Street. Mag Burns operated the best known parlor house, and Cowboy Annie and Connie the Cowboy Queen were among the most popular ladies of the evening. From time to time the Miles City red light district was visited by Martha Jane Cannary, known throughout the West as Calamity Jane.

Despite the hard drinking and frequent fistfights, lethal violence was surprisingly rare. Although many men carried

With the Tongue River adjacent to town, and the Yellowstone nearby, flooding was a frequent problem in Miles City. *Courtesy Range Riders Museum.*

sixguns, shootings and knifings seldom occurred. Miles City was not Dodge City, nor was it Abilene or Border Queen Caldwell or any of the other Kansas cowtowns. Miles City did not degenerate into the shooting violence of Tombstone nor Fort Worth nor Tascosa, the Cowboy Capital of the Texas Panhandle with its own Boot Hill. Miles City was a party town, where cowboys and soldiers and other merrymakers just wanted to have a good time. Despite an occasional shooting or knifing, the atmosphere in Miles City remained ruggedly good natured.

One exotic element of the western frontier often was on the doorstep of Miles City during its early years. Native Americans were driven by Colonel Miles and by other relentless soldiers from their traditional lives as nomadic hunters. After submitting to pressure from the army, entire bands — sometimes numbering well into the hundreds — reported to military authority at Fort Keogh or other outposts. Tipi encampments were set up adjacent to Fort Keogh — and therefore near to Miles City — for weeks or months, before the camps packed up and departed to an assigned reservation. For extended periods of time the Native American way of life could be observed and trading could take place.

Most iconic of all, Miles City became a frontier cattle town. In the early years of Miles City, cattle herds — often from Texas — were driven onto the vast open ranges of eastern Montana. With its railroad connection, Miles City saw Texas cowboys at work and at play. Adventurous cowboys from Texas and elsewhere wanted to see Montana. They longed to ride all the way to this northernmost outpost of the cattle frontier. And once in Montana, many cowboys — such as Teddy "Blue" Abbott and 250-pound Bob Fudge — elected to stay. Noted Texas trail boss, O.C. Cato agreed to drive a herd from the XIT in the Texas Panhandle to an enormous lease north of Miles City. Cato remained in Montana, making his home in Miles City, running the XIT, serving as county sheriff and in the Montana State Senate.

Texas longhorn steers were driven to Montana, and when herds crossed the swift-flowing Yellowstone, crowds from Miles City came out to watch. Cowboy attire, equipment, and methods of riding and handling cattle spread rapidly. And rodeo became the most popular sport.

Another favorite sport was cattle rustling. More than 400 cattlemen gathered in Miles City in 1884 to organize the Montana Stockgrowers Association. One young rancher, Theodore Roosevelt, emphatically called for "a war on rustlers," a cry repeated by other cattlemen. Granville Stuart, one of Montana's most noted pioneers and a large cattle rancher, quietly gathered a resolute group who would become known as "Stuart's Stranglers." When they went into action after the Association meeting, almost a score of rustlers were killed in several violent incidents. Stuart was elected first president of the Montana Stockgrowers Association, and the organization thereafter held its annual meeting in Miles City for more than

Rodeo was the favorite sport in Miles City.
Courtesy Range Riders Museum.

three decades. Miles City adapted the nickname "Cow Capital of the World." And when Fort Keogh was converted into the nation's largest remount station, horses became as numerous as cattle in the region. Miles City soon developed a colorful event known today as "The World Famous Bucking Horse Sale."

Thus after Old Milestown came to life in 1876, the community rapidly evolved into Miles City. Miles City then swaggered through a series of frontier phases. But for all of the western adventure and excitement that was packed into its founding years, Miles City has been somewhat overlooked in comparison to Tombstone and Dodge City and Deadwood and other frontier counterparts. By venturing back to the raw beginnings of this Montana community, the following pages hopefully will resurrect to some degree the energetic pioneers and exhilarating activities of their rollicking past.

Chapter Two

Birth of a Frontier Town

"We were a careless, happy people in those days, and the temptation to fraternize and be sociable was improved on every occasion, even if business did have to wait."

— Sam Gordon, pioneer newspaperman

The United States Army served as midwife of Miles City. The future cattle town was born in the wake of a military debacle which stunned the American people and created a public outcry for action.

News of the "Custer Massacre" — often described as the worst defeat ever inflicted on the frontier army[1] — became widespread during July 1876, just when Americans were exuberantly celebrating the nation's centennial. "FIRST ACCOUNT OF THE CUSTER MASSACRE," headlined an extra edition of the *Bismarck Tribune* on July 6, 1876, eleven days after the Battle of the Little Bighorn was fought in the remote Northern Plains. *The Tribune* announced that their chief correspondent, Mark Kellogg, was among those killed with Custer. "NO OFFICER OR MAN OF 5 COMPANIES LEFT TO TELL THE TALE," proclaimed one sub-headline. The last of a deck of headlined queries posed a key question: "What Will Congress Do About It?"[2]

Congress, faced with a public furor, rapidly acted to approve military requests. These requests previously had been submitted by Gen. Phil Sheridan, commander of the vast Division of the Missouri. During the early 1870s, as trouble worsened with the Sioux, Cheyenne and other tribes of the Northern Plains, General Sheridan lobbied for more reservations and for troop

The American people were about to celebrate the US Centennial when word came of the debacle of Custer's Seventh Cavalry at the Little Big Horn. *Author's Collection.*

expansion in his division. General Sheridan also wanted to establish two new forts at strategic points. One would be located at the mouth of the Little Bighorn River — eleven miles, as it turned out, north of the site where Custer and his command would meet destruction. Sheridan wanted the other new military base to be erected at the confluence of the Tongue and Yellowstone rivers — where the future town of Miles City would subsequently grow.

The army had known about the Tongue and Yellowstone location since June 29, 1806, when Lt. William Clark led a contingent of the Corps of Discovery into camp at the site during the return journey of the Lewis and Clark Expedition. As the explorers made their way back from the Pacific coast, Captain Meriweather Lewis and a few men explored a northerly route, while Lieutenant Clark followed the Yellowstone and found its junction with the Tongue River. The two groups of explorers reunited on August 11, 1806, at the confluence of the Missouri and the Yellowstone, reaching St. Louis six weeks later. The Tongue and Yellowstone location already was a

The US Army learned about the strategic site of the confluence of the Tongue and Yellowstone rivers when Lt. William Clark chose the location as a camp for his explorers on June 29, 1806. *Courtesy National Archives.*

favorite campsite of Native American bands, and soon it became a stopping point for white traders and trappers.

There was a major military exploration of this area in 1873. The Yellowstone Expedition of more than 1,500 men and 275 mule-drawn supply wagons marched along the Yellowstone River as an escort for Northern Pacific Railroad surveyors. Col. David S. Stanley commanded the expedition and Lt. Col. George Armstrong Custer was second-in-command. Twice Custer's Seventh Cavalry and other units clashed with large war parties of Sioux and their allies, led by Sitting Bull, Crazy Horse, Gall, and Rain-in-the-Face. At the end of the expedition, Colonel Stanley's recommendation included the establishment of an army base at the confluence of the Tongue and Yellowstone Rivers. One reason for this recommendation was that the riverboats *Josephine* and *Key West* had steamed up the Yellowstone carrying troops and provisions, which encouraged General Sheridan to intensify his drumbeat for placing an outpost at this useful location.

Three years later, in July 1876, after learning of the stunning defeat of the Seventh Cavalry, Congress acted with unaccustomed dispatch, and the order for developing a new fort at the Yellowstone-Tongue site was signed on August 28, 1876.[3] Col. Nelson A. Miles, a bold field commander who, during the Civil War, had risen from the rank of lieutenant to major general, was ordered to Montana to lead a column against the victorious Sioux and Cheyenne, and to command the new outpost.

Like almost all Civil War officers, Miles had been reduced in rank by the shrunken post-war army. As a colonel he commanded the Fifth Infantry, even though cavalry units dominated the Indian wars of the West. But during the Red River War of 1874-75, Miles pushed the Fifth relentlessly across the Texas Panhandle in pursuit of Comanche bands, and he instilled pride in his infantrymen that they could perform as successfully as cavalry units.

Lt. Col. George Armstrong Custer and the Seventh Cavalry first probed the eastern Montana wilderness during the Yellowstone Expedition of 1873. *Courtesy National Archives.*

Miles and his wife Mary, while posted in 1875 at Fort Hays, Kansas, had become friends with Lt. Col. George Armstrong Custer and his lovely wife, Libbie. But by 1876 Miles was in command at Fort Leavenworth when orders came to join the general pursuit in Montana. Miles was elated by this opportunity, and he promptly led five companies of the Fifth toward the Yellowstone with more soon to follow. "I had a well-drilled and splendidly-disciplined regiment, experienced in Indian campaigning . . . ," recalled Miles. "I did not feel the least hesitancy in taking it up into that country." Miles dispatched Lt. Col. J.N.G. Whistler to select a location for the base.[4]

With the regimental band playing "The Girl I Left Behind Me," along with "one of the national airs," the column marched to the train depot at Fort Leavenworth. Miles and his men were transported by rail to Yankton in Dakota Territory, where they boarded a large steamboat. The river steamer had to stop frequently to replenish the wood supply for the engines. Colonel Miles took advantage of such stops to disembark and drill his men, or to hold strategic conferences with his officers. A sad day came at Fort Abraham Lincoln, headquarters of the recently-decimated Seventh Cavalry. There now were twenty-seven officers' wives who were widows, including Libbie Custer, and Colonel Miles paid his respects to the bereaved women.[5]

When the expedition reached the north-flowing Tongue River, the "Tongue River Cantonment" was established on the low plain where the two rivers joined. The supplies and provisions were off-loaded and work on a crude, ramshackle post was begun. As was customary, most of the labor on the cantonment was provided by the troopers: the Fifth Infantry Regiment, along with six companies of the Twenty-second Infantry.

But Colonel Miles simultaneously launched preparations for a winter offensive, ignoring warnings that it was "utterly impossible for white men to live in that country and endure the extreme cold . . ." Miles was confident of the toughness of the soldiers under his command: "if the Indians could live there the white man could also, if properly equipped . . ."[6]

Colonel Miles procured about thirty horses "for mounting some of the infantry to act as couriers and messengers." Miles tried out every new piece of equipment and weaponry the war department considered for adoption. He enlisted experienced frontiersmen and friendly Indians in putting together a company of scouts. Noted scouts including Luther "Yellowstone" Kelly and "Buffalo Bill" Cody.

The rudimentary structures of the Tongue River Cantonment — also called the "Tongue River Barracks" and the "New Post on the Yellowstone" — continued to take shape around a small parade ground. Cottonwood trees lined the banks of the rivers, so log buildings were erected, along with picket construction (logs placed vertically into the ground). These structures were not intended to be permanent, so roofing often was brush or sod or canvas. There were no fortifications — no blockhouses or stockade walls.[7]

Across the entire American West, the introduction of an army post to a frontier region brought economic transformation. Soldiers needed fresh vegetables and meat, and cavalry horses and draft animals required grain and hay. Army privates earned only thirteen dollars per month, and paymasters usually did not reach frontier outposts but once every two months or more. Sutlers on the military bases were directed to limit the sale of liquor. But soldiers wanted to drink and they lusted for more earthy entertainment. Saloons sprang up just outside the military reservations, and so did "hog ranches" — houses of soiled doves that received their unappealing nickname because of the quality of the women. With their clientele consisting mostly of poorly paid troopers, the prostitutes who plied their trade at "hog ranches" were past their physical prime, or perhaps they had never been attractive, even as young sporting ladies.

As soon as it was learned that a large cantonment was to be established where the Tongue River flowed into the Yellowstone, civilians who dispensed pleasure gravitated to the site. There would be hundreds of soldiers stationed at the Tongue River Cantonment, along with a substantial number of teamsters and scouts and other civilian employees. Indeed, at times the men at this "semblance of civilization," as Miles called the outpost, numbered from several hundred to one thousand.[8]

Colonel Miles did not seem to be bothered by the hog ranches, but he despised the "enemy" that his men consumed whenever possible: "r-u-m." "At the cantonment," explained Miles, "there were two or three traders that had come up the river in the autumn with a stock of goods. They had many things for sale that the soldiers required. Fur caps, woolen underclothing and other useful articles . . . ," he continued. But "a stock of liquors" proved disruptive.

"I tried to regulate this liquor traffic in different ways, such as confining the soldiers to malted liquors, beer and wine; allowing only a certain number of drinks in a day; and of various other methods . . ." Most of the soldiers, of course, evaded the restrictions of the commanding officer. While in the field without liquor, "we had the best discipline and not the least trouble." But once back at the cantonment, "there were disturbances and breaches of discipline" leading to courts martial and desertions. On occasion "my men dropped dead in going from a saloon to camp," collapsing in a drunken stupor and freezing to death. Miles grumped that whenever "the soldier found themselves in the vicinity of a saloon, trouble was sure to follow."

One of the three original traders at the cantonment sold "concoctions of 'high wines' and drugs." Miles learned that this individual manufactured gin and different drinks in a cellar, "and sold them at every opportunity to these unfortunate [but obviously thirsty] soldiers under the name of 'liquors,' though they were rank poison."[9]

Fort Keogh was named after Capt. Myles Keogh, who died with Custer at the Little Big Horn. *Courtesy National Archives.*

Colonel Miles had a stake driven a couple of miles east of the cantonment and ordered the growing number of civilians to depart the Tongue River Barracks and settle themselves beyond the stake. Knowing that there were promising business possibilities with the large population at the cantonment, and that there would be safety from hostile attack because of the nearby presence of hundreds of soldiers, the "coffee-coolers" (civilians who loafed around the cantonment) promptly moved past the staked marker, as directed. Tents went up immediately, along with shacks and log cabins. Two saloons and a dance hall opened for business, and soon there were houses of merriment. The hardscrabble little community was called "Milestown," and Colonel Miles and members of his staff soon were invited to a banquet. The menu consisted "of approximately 90 per cent wild game, eight per cent liquor, and two per cent 'trimmings.'" Major F.D. Pease, seated at one end of the table, toasted Colonel Miles as "our future president."[10]

Clearly there were no hard feelings against the commanding officer who had summarily evicted "coffee-cooler" civilians from the cantonment. "We were a careless, happy people in these days," reminisced newspaperman Sam Gordon, an early settler who cherished the pioneer experiences of Milestown,

Captain Keogh's horse, *Comanche*, suffered several wounds — including protruding arrow shafts — during the Battle of the Little Big Horn. Warriors rode off with the cavalry horses, but the injured *Comanche* was left behind and became the only survivor of the Custer battle. *Comanche* was adopted as a permanent mascot by the Seventh Cavalry. *Courtesy National Archives.*

"and the temptation to fraternize and be sociable was improved on every occasion, even if business did have to wait."[11]

"The life we lived was conducted strictly on first principles;" explained Gordon, "each to his trade, calling or pursuit and no interference with others and it is astonishing how fairly the game was played."

Gordon was aware that in the early days Milestown had a rough reputation, but he insisted that: "We were a pretty well-behaved community," even though there were "some delightful shindies [scrimmages, brawls] when the 'Diamond R' gang . . . ran afoul of a bunch of swaddies from [Fort] Keogh feeling their oats, but it was all fists and boots and never a shot fired or a knife used."[12]

Actually, there was indeed an occasional shot fired and at least one throat cut and even a lynching. But as Gordon pointed out, "It was a man's town at first . . ." There was gambling and

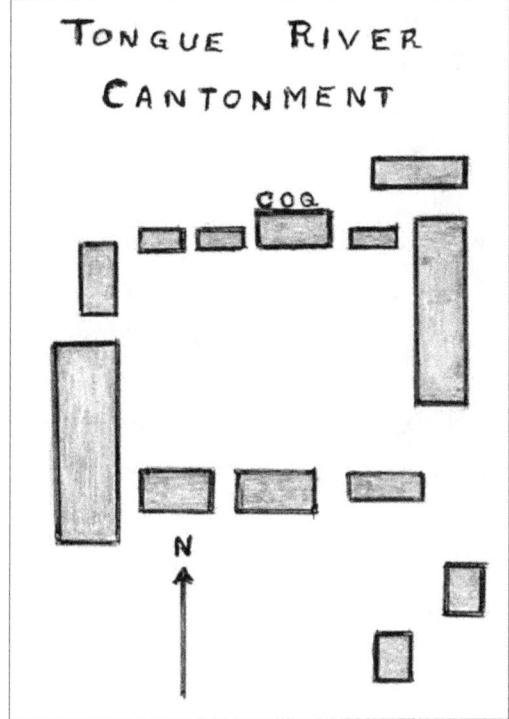

Drawing of the Tongue River Cantonment, adapted from the research of Herbert M. Hart. The north line of structures was Officers Row, with the largest of the four buildings the COQ built for Colonel Miles. *See Old Forts of the Northwest, p. 179.*

drinking and dancing, but gunplay and outlawry were minimal. However, as in most frontier communities, "inquiry into one's antecedents or private business was discouraged."[13]

Within a year's time a major construction project to the west of the Tongue River Cantonment began to produce Fort Keogh, named after Captain Myles Keogh, who had died fighting at the Little Bighorn. Captain Keogh's mount, a warhorse named *Comanche*, was the only survivor from Custer's five-company command. The sturdy animal sustained multiple wounds, which probably was the reason he was not taken by a warrior. But he was nursed by men of the Seventh Cavalry, and *Comanche* became a regimental mascot.

Fort Keogh was quickly built into a large post of substantial buildings, and so "midnight requisitioning" took place at the initial cantonment. The ramshackle structures at the cantonment were taken apart by civilians and used for shacks at Milestown. But the movement of the military base caused a location shift for Milestown. The nondescript but lively community moved to the north bank of the Tongue River, with a Main Street which ran from the river bank westward. A couple of cross streets — Park and Sixth — soon were fronted by several one-story buildings. The Tongue River had to be crossed, first by a ferry, and later by a military bridge, in order to reach Fort Keogh a couple of miles to the southwest. [14]

The original Milestown was not entirely abandoned. Now called Old Milestown or Old Town, some buildings of the first community continued to be occupied by diehard settlers until about 1900. But from the start of its existence, Milestown often had been referred to as Miles City, the label given by the post office. The first post office had been located at the Tongue River Cantonment, and even then correspondence was addressed to Miles City. A post office soon opened on Main Street, and the name Miles City became permanent, even as the relocated frontier community developed into a compact little town that was on the grow.

Chapter Three
General Nelson "Bear Coat" Miles

"You are ahead of every one else who has taken a hand in the Indian campaigns north of the Platte."
— General John Pope to Colonel Miles

Nelson A. Miles in winter clothing.
Courtesy National Archives.

Miles City was destined to become a lively and historic wolf howl of a frontier town, and the community appropriately took its name after a remarkable man of the frontier. Col. Nelson Miles arrived in a wilderness devoid of settlers and immediately launched construction of a major military supply base, while simultaneously making every effort to invade hostile territory in forbidding weather. He harbored no doubts about the likelihood of success.

"While the work of constructing the cantonment was going on and preparations were being made for an active winter campaign," he recorded, "I went with a small escort over the country from the mouth of the Tongue River to Fort Buford at the junction of the Missouri and Yellowstone, in order to reconnoiter and find the best route by which to bring [wagon or pack] trains from that supply depot."[1]

As a commanding officer, Col. Nelson A. Miles was brimful

of purpose, an energetic and well-organized multi-tasker. Having just arrived at the site of a proposed wilderness outpost, he promptly began construction, while at the same time organizing, "an active winter campaign." Soon entrusting these two major efforts to able subordinates, Colonel Miles personally rode out with an escort on a far-ranging reconnaissance mission. As if these activities were not enough, Miles dispatched scouts "to obtain the best information in regard to the position and disposition of the hostile forces . . ."[2] There would be no waste of time tolerated by Colonel Miles.

Nelson Appleton Miles was born on August 8, 1839, on a family farm near Westminster, Massachusetts. The youngest of four children, he was descended from veterans of King Philip's War and the American Revolution. His parents were religious and patriotic. But a small farm offered no outlet for the driving ambition which motivated Miles throughout his life. In 1856 an uncle who was a prosperous merchant obtained a clerk's position for the teenaged Nelson in Boston. Recognizing his lack of education, Miles spent his "leisure" hours in regular attendance at lectures, night school, and in pursuit of a broad reading program.[3]

By 1860 he concluded that civil war was inevitable and that success in combat could provide opportunity for the fame and position he craved. Miles began to study military volumes, and he joined a small group which employed a French veteran to provide instruction in drill. When the War Between the States erupted Miles raised $3,500 to organize a company of infantry. Denied the captaincy of his troop by an ungrateful governor, Miles resentfully accepted a lieutenant's commission in the Twenty-second Massachusetts Volunteers. He had learned a bitter lesson about the value of friends in high places. Throughout his career he would exploit every conceivable

"Bear Coat" Miles stands at center in broad-brimmed hat. To his immediate left is two-time Medal of Honor winner Lt. Frank D. Baldwin. Mounted at left is scout "Yellowstone" Kelly. *Courtesy National Archives.*

contact to promote his advancement.

But during the Civil War, courage, aggressiveness, and a gift for utilizing terrain vaulted him to high rank. He experienced heavy combat duty, and his performance at Antietam won him a colonelcy. Miles was wounded four times, including a throat wound at Fredericksburg and a stomach wound at Chancellorsville. His exploits at Chancellorsville eventually earned him a Medal of Honor. Soon after the battle, the twenty-four-year-old officer was promoted to brigadier general. He fought at Spottsylvania, Cold Harbor, Petersburg, and Appomattox. At war's end he was in charge of a distinguished prisoner, Jefferson Davis.

By then Miles held the rank of major general of volunteers. But in order to continue his military career, Miles had to accept a colonelcy in the regular army. He was determined to reach the top of the frontier army, and his marriage in 1868 to Mary Sherman, niece of General William T. Sherman and of Ohio Senator John Sherman, gave him invaluable contacts.

The following year Colonel Miles assumed command of the

Fifth Infantry Regiment at Fort Hays, Kansas. Soon the Fifth was transferred to Fort Harker, then to Fort Leavenworth, although the ambitious Miles chafed at the exclusion of his regiment from the frontier campaigns that promised glory and promotion to Custer, Mackenzie, Crook, and other rival officers. At last, in 1874, Miles was assigned by General Sherman to lead a column in the Red River War. Miles received his initiation into Indian warfare, and he carried along a newspaper correspondent to insure personal publicity. At the end of the campaign he was made guardian of the German sisters, four girls rescued from captivity after having witnessed the deaths of four other family members. Miles secured the diversion of $10,000 from Cheyenne annuities, and over the years he saw that the girls' needs were met.[4]

Miles had been impressive in his first Indian campaign. A tall, handsome officer, he was bold and brave in combat. But there were less attractive traits. He was vain and ruthless in his personal ambitions. He acquired friends principally for their value as contacts. He was loathe to give credit to other officers, and was deeply jealous of West Point graduates. Miles earned considerable enmity because of harsh criticisms of other officers, and throughout his career he was embroiled in one feud after another. But for a decade and a half — including almost five years as commander at Fort Keogh (first known as the Tongue River Cantonment) — he was a skillful and implacable Indian fighter who successfully employed infantry in warfare otherwise dominated by cavalry.

In the summer of 1876, Colonel Miles established the Tongue River Cantonment while preparing for a pursuit of Chief Sitting Bull and any other hostile band in the region. By October 1876 Miles was leading 394 heavily-clad riflemen slogging through the snow in winter temperatures which dropped as low as fifty-

Sitting Bull, famed war leader, devout holy man, and a skilled opponent of Col. Nelson Miles. *Courtesy Museum of the American Indian.*

five degrees to sixty degrees below zero — and once even to sixty-six degrees below. One night warriors tried to raid the army pack animals, but with his customary thoroughness Miles had seen that the herd was hobbled and well guarded. Nonetheless, reported Miles, "they did succeed in perforating the tent, in which I was sleeping, with rifle balls."[5]

But Miles soon became convinced that "winter was the best time for subjugating these Indians . . . I felt sure that simply to hibernate and allow the Indians to occupy the country [would permit] them to believe themselves masters of the situation . . . My opinion was that the only way to make the country tenable for us was to make it untenable for the Indians."[6]

Colonel Miles meticulously "equipped my command as if I were organizing an expedition for the Arctic regions . . ." Exerting every effort "to keep the train and riding animals in full flesh," they were fed an "abundance of corn . . . and plenty of hay" during winter campaigns. Most of the officers and men had participated in winter marches on the high plains of Texas, and needed little prompting to apply "themselves zealously to their equipment in every possible way." Winter uniforms were composed of "strong woolen clothing." And the soldiers "cut up woolen blankets" for warm underclothing. Miles made sure they were issued mittens "and with arctics or buffalo overshoes."

Some men acquired buffalo moccasins, "and frequently cut up grain sacks to bind about their feet. "They made woolen masks that covered the entire head, leaving openings for the eyes and to breathe through, and nearly all had buffalo overcoats."[7]

"When the snow was deep they frequently marched in single file, the leading man breaking the road until weary, then falling out for another to take his place and returning to the rear of the column . . ." Miles was proud of how mobile his men were during the worst winter months, from October until February. "They crossed the principal rivers, the Missouri, the Yellowstone and the Tongue, with heavily-loaded wagons and pieces of artillery on the solid ice." With Miles and his troops in the field, there would be no peaceful respite in Native American winter camps, with grass-fed war ponies at their weakest.[8]

In one winter march after another, Miles and his toughened soldiers pinned down their hard-pressed enemies. And so, on October 21, 1876, Miles confronted Sitting Bull and a superior force estimated at as many as 1,000 warriors near Cedar Creek. Miles steadfastly formed his heavily-clad "walk-a-heaps" in line of battle. Sitting Bull and Miles conferred between the lines but could come to no agreement. Miles was draped in a huge outer garment trimmed with bear fur, and the Sioux warriors permanently dubbed him "Bear Coat." When Sitting Bull was informed that he and his followers would have to settle on reservation agency lands, the chief "declared the God Almighty made him an Indian and did not make him an agency Indian either, and he did not intend to be one."[9]

An exasperated Miles finally stated "that in fifteen minutes, if he did not accept the terms offered, we would open fire and hostilities would commence." The Sioux reacted with "the wildest excitement," noted Miles. "The prairies were covered with savage warriors dashing hither and thither making ready for battle."

When Miles' column advanced, warriors fired the grass. Despite being outnumbered, the soldiers maintained volleys and discharged their single artillery piece to good effect. At one point the command was surrounded, but Miles formed a hollow square and, utilizing every reserve, broke the Sioux attack. Miles was proud of the performance of his men. "The engagement demonstrated . . . that there was no position that [the Indians] could take from which the infantry could not dislodge them."[10]

When darkness fell Miles corralled the wagons in a nearby valley, and the men dozed beside their rifles. Throughout the night sentries fired at warriors who crept near the camp. The Battle of Big Dry River resumed the next morning. After circling the soldiers briefly, the warriors withdrew. Miles pursued, and a running fight developed. The warriors retreated southeast down Bad Route Creek, abandoning equipment, horses, and tons of winter supplies. After a forty-two-mile chase, the Sioux reached the Yellowstone and crossed to temporary safety. More parleys ensued, and 2,000 Indians finally agreed to go to their agencies, although Sitting Bull and 400 followers slipped away. Miles, of course, insisted that he could have recaptured Sitting Bull if he had been given mounted troops like his rival, George Crook.

Encouraged by his success on the battlefield, Miles rapidly returned to the Tongue River Cantonment and "immediately reorganized" his command for continued pursuit of warriors. Cheyenne raiders ran off 250 head of cattle from the cantonment herd, and Miles promptly took up the chase with 434 men. There were five companies of the rugged Fifth and two troops of the Twenty-second Infantry, along with a scouting force led by Yellowstone Kelly. Each day Miles rode ahead of the main force,

Luther Sage "Yellowstone" Kelly, noted scout for Col. Nelson A. Miles. *Courtesy National Archives.*

accompanied by a few scouts and officers and soldiers.

This extended trek took place in November, December, and January, with a "severe snowstorm" and "intensely cold" nights. Miles pressed the chase, hoping to be led to the camp of Crazy Horse. A dawn raid by daring warriors resulted in the death of one soldier. But on January 7, 1877, Miles' advance guard captured several Cheyennes. Three hundred braves tried to rescue these captives in an evening attack. The assault was turned back, but the soldiers spent a frigid night with hostiles close enough to camp to talk to the captives.[11]

At daybreak several hundred warriors aligned against the soldiers. But Miles unlimbered his two field pieces, turned back several charges by the warriors, and finally, at precipitous Wolf Mountain, launched an attack in force. Fighting raged until a Cheyenne medicine man named Big Crow was shot dead. The demoralized warriors fled down a valley as a blinding snowstorm swirled around the combatants. "The backs of these retreating warriors presented a most delightful picture," stated a relieved Miles, whose badly outnumbered men had engaged in "very close and desperate" fighting.

Despite five hours of heavy firing by both sides, casualties were light. But Miles pointed out that it had been demonstrated "that we could move in any part of the country in the midst of winter, and hunt the enemy down in their camps, wherever they might take refuge." Miles learned that a Montana blizzard was described as "snow blowing in every direction at the same moment of time." During these winter movements, Miles was quietly amused when his men would sing, "Marching Through Georgia."[12]

Six weeks after the Battle of Wolf Mountain, nineteen "chiefs and leading warriors", at the head of a large body of Native American families, came to the cantonment to discuss peace terms. Miles firmly insisted that these plains families settle upon government agencies. When the principal leader, Little Chief, reluctantly agreed to "place ourselves at your mercy," Miles felt "a thrill of joy through my heart . . . as I realized our work had been accomplished." Even Crazy Horse agreed to submit to agency life.[13]

But Sitting Bull and his immediate followers defiantly clung to their old way of life, crossing the border into Canada. And a chief named Lame Deer, who commanded a band of fewer than sixty lodges, "declared that they would never surrender, and would roam where they pleased . . ." An interpreter told Lame Deer that soldiers would come out to bring him in, but the chief retorted "that he had good scouts and that no white man could get near his camp or capture his people."

But Colonel Miles put together a mixed column of cavalry and infantry: four troops of the Second Cavalry, two companies of the Fifth Infantry, and four companies of the Twenty-second Infantry. Miles led this formidable force from his base on May 2, 1877. On May 5 the column left the Yellowstone and marched up the Tongue River. "When we went up the Tongue River," testified Miles, "the snow was a foot deep and the river frozen over." Leaving three infantry companies with his wagon train of supplies and ammunition, Miles led the balance of his command toward Lame Deer's village, in the valley of the Big Muddy Creek.[14]

At daybreak on May 7, a detail of mounted infantry and scouts charged the Sioux pony herd, stampeding the animals up the valley before rounding up a band of about 450 horses and mules. The Native Americans, harshly awakened by shouting, galloping cavalrymen, fled up the valley. Fourteen warriors were killed, but four troopers also were slain, and several others were wounded.

Lame Deer and another prominent warrior, Iron Star, were brought to Colonel Miles while the fighting still raged. Hoping to stop the battle by extracting a surrender, Miles grasped the hand of Lame Deer. But when a scout brandished his gun, Lame Deer wrenched free and snatched up his own rifle. The chief leveled his weapon at Miles, who reflexively yanked his reins, dug in his spurs, and ducked in the saddle. The slug whistled past Miles and slammed into an enlisted man, inflicting a fatal wound. Nearby soldiers shot Lame Deer, and as Iron Star tried to help him escape the chief popped away with a revolver. Both warriors were gunned down by carbine and rifle fire.

Infantry units soon reached the site of battle, and Miles directed them to select Indian ponies for their own use. Later in the day the prairie was filled with bucking horses and inexperienced foot soldiers tumbling to the turf. The Fifth Infantry was humorously dubbed the "Eleventh Cavalry" (there were only ten cavalry regiments in the post-Civil War army) because of their equestrian experiment. The fifty-one lodges of Lame Deer's camp "was one of the richest I had ever seen," remarked Miles. The soldiers were permitted to take whatever they wanted in the way of buffalo robes, horse equipment, and smaller items, before "the remainder was burned."[15]

About one month later one of the first steamboats to come upriver after the winter thaw brought the colonel's wife, Mary Sherman Miles, and little daughter, Cecilia, along with Mary's sister, Elizabeth Sherman. "They were the first white women to come and make their permanent abode in that wild western country," reflected Colonel Miles. "We could only afford them a soldier's welcome, as we were living in tents and in the cantonment bivouac."[16]

Fortunately a cabin built of cottonwood logs had just been completed for the commanding officer of the post. Only five days after the July 11 arrival of the Miles family, Generals William T. Sherman and Alfred Terry debarked from another riverboat. On July 16, a dress inspection and a reception were held in honor of the army's commanding officer, and after a regimental review General Sherman presented Medals of Honor to thirty troopers. A week later Generals Sheridan and Crook came to the post and also were feted with military honors. Prominent citizens from Miles City were guests and eyewitnesses, and these impressive activities became news around town.[17]

Meanwhile the ladies, along with the officers' wives who soon arrived on other riverboats, cheerfully embraced their western adventure. "The outdoor exercises which they were able to enjoy, such as horseback-riding, hunting and sailing on the Yellowstone, together with the novelty of their new life, made it a pleasure and a romance," observed Miles. It had been a year since Miles had seen his wife and daughter, and other officers also had experienced long family absences. Miles reflected that "this was the beginning of civilized and domestic life in that vicinity. The presence of women added a charm and a ray of sunshine to the life of the soldier."[18]

By the fall of 1877 Chief Joseph of the Nez Perce had led about 800 of his people from their home in the Wallowa Valley

Chief Joseph, the articulate statesman of the Nez Perce tribe, finally was cornered by Colonel Miles en route to escape in Canada. His tribal remnant camped near Fort Keogh. *Courtesy National Archives*

of northeastern Oregon, executing a fighting retreat of more than 1,100 miles from a U.S. Army contingent led by General O.O. Howard. The Nez Perce had been ordered to leave their ancestral lands, but Chief Joseph conducted a march toward Montana, hoping to cross into Canada and unite with Sitting Bull and his Sioux. Chief Joseph and his Nez Perce fought skillfully, even though they were reduced in number to a little over 600 as they approached Canada.

Colonel Miles followed the Nez Perce campaign through newspaper accounts. But in mid-September, 1877, a courier brought a request from General Howard to join the pursuit of the Nez Perce. Galvanized into action, Miles supervised an all-night effort to ready a large column. Miles led his men into the field at dawn on September 18, and hurried the column northwest. General Howard, meanwhile, deliberately delayed his pursuit. Overestimating their safety, the Nez Perce slowed their pace to rest the women, children, and wounded, then camped at Bear Paw Mountain, a day's ride from the Canadian border. Miles' scouts discovered them there on Sunday morning, September 30. Miles drove his column toward the camp, an eight-mile march through a cold rain.

When the army arrived unexpectedly, the Nez Perce women

already were taking down the camp. Three companies of the Seventh Cavalry cut left toward the rear of the position to stampede the pony herd. The mounted Fifth Infantry began the battle as a reserve force, but soon joined in the charge as a withering fusillade slammed into the Seventh. Joseph's warriors hastily formed a line on a bluff, then held their fire until the troopers were within 200 yards. Staggered, the Seventh fell back, dismounted, and managed to hold their position until reinforced by the Fifth. But the Second Cavalry was successful in rounding up the pony herd, although Nez Perce mounted on more than 100 horses broke through and headed for Canada, forty miles away.[19]

For the remaining Nez Perce escape was impossible, but the braves retreated and dug in near the village. Chief Joseph, caught out of camp when the attack began, sprinted through the soldiers' line to lead the defense. Dismayed at the punishment inflicted upon his men, Miles ordered more deliberate tactics. His soldiers began to ring the camp, and Lt. Henry Romeyn was directed to lead three companies in a dismounted charge from the southwest. But Nez Perce riflemen mauled the attack force, and Romeyn was drilled through the chest. A handful of troopers fought their way to the edge of the village, but Joseph led a counterattack. Within moments the soldiers were repulsed, leaving their dead inside enemy lines.[20]

During the day's fighting Miles suffered nearly seventy casualties. The warriors shrewdly concentrated their fire on officers and non-commissioned officers: three captains, three lieutenants, ten sergeants, and two corporals were shot. All three first sergeants of the Seventh were slain, and merely one officer of the three troops of "Custer's Avengers" remained unhurt.

Miles worried that escaped Nez Perces might bring Sitting

Tipi encampments were common near Fort Keogh as tribes awaited final settlement on reservations. Citizens ventured out from Miles City for sight-seeing and trade. *Courtesy Range Riders Museum.*

Bull and an overwhelming force of Sioux reinforcements down from Canada. But as darkness fell, Miles resolutely tightened his ring, hoping to keep the Nez Perces trapped until relief could arrive from the south. (Although Sitting Bull had no intention of crossing the border back into the USA, on the third day of the siege apprehensive scouts reported that the Sioux chieftan was approaching. This "war party turned out to be a buffalo herd.")[21]

A heavy snow fell that night and the next day. Miles called for a parley, and Chief Joseph entered Miles' tent under a white flag. But Miles rather treacherously confined the chief — until Nez Perce warriors captured Lt. Lovell H. Jerome and exchanged him for their leader.

When the column's supply train arrived, Miles was able to tighten his cordon and open fire with artillery. The Nez Perces pulled back to the shelter of ravines and stubbornly fought on.

On the night of October 4, however, General Howard arrived. The glory-hungry Miles feared that the general, whom Miles had served as an aide during the Civil War, would receive final credit for the victory, but Howard allowed Miles to accept Chief Joseph's surrender.

Chief Joseph delivered his famous "I will fight no more forever" statement, then turned over 400 Nez Perces. That night White Bird slipped away to the north with a number of followers. In all, about 300 Nez Perces managed to reach Sitting Bull in Canada. Without the timely arrival of Miles and his column, Chief Joseph would have made a complete escape.[22]

In the summer of 1878 Colonel Miles organized a "reconnoitering" party, comprised of his family, a few other civilians, ten officers, and 100 enlisted men. The soldiers were all veterans who had distinguished themselves, and a primary purpose of the expedition was to vacation in Yellowstone Park.[23]

After nearly a fortnight of travel and sightseeing, word arrived that Bannocks had gone on the warpath in Idaho and were heading toward the park. Miles promptly sent his non-combatants to the nearest post, Fort Ellis, then marched with seventy-five crack soldiers to head off the hostiles. He assigned forty men to block Boulder Pass, then led the balance of his force to Clark's Fork Pass. Along the way he engaged seventy five Crows to serve as scouts.[24]

Miles pushed his little command and arrived at Clark's Fork Pass a day ahead of the Bannocks. The warriors unknowingly pitched a camp six miles from Colonel Miles' concealed detachment, and after that he carefully moved closer. A hard rain was falling and the Bannocks huddled in their blankets.

By 4 a.m. Miles and his men had crept to within 500 yards of the camp. A skirmish line was formed in the darkness, with the Crows positioned on the right. At daybreak the force crept to 100 yards' distance, then attacked.

The stunned Bannocks panicked. Several jumped into a nearby river and made it to the other side. The remaining warriors were devastated. Eleven braves were slain, and by 6:00 a.m. the remainder had surrendered. Captain Andrew Bennett and a scout died. Miles sent back the captives, reassembled his party, and resumed his Yellowstone excursion.[25]

Miles led another recreational outing in October 1879. A typical expedition from frontier forts was a hunting trip into country teeming with wild game. Miles rode at the head of eight other officers, a dozen enlisted men, and five Native American scouts in a hunt through the valley of the Rosebud. "We were gone six days and had great success," recorded Miles. "During that time we killed sixty large deer, three antelopes, one mountain sheep, five elks, seventeen buffaloes, seventy prairie chickens and six ducks. At that season of the year the nights were cold, and the game, if properly dressed and hung up, would freeze solid during the night." The hunting party returned to Fort Keogh with ten heavily-loaded wagons. "There was a feast for the whole garrison of four hundred men." [26]

The military exploits of Colonel Miles were related in the favorite Miles City watering hole of the soldiers, the Cottage Saloon, which was the first building on the right as the road from the fort became Main Street. The stories also were told in other saloons and in stores around town. The citizens of Miles City proudly realized that their community was named after one of the most relentless and resourceful Indian fighters in the U.S. Army. Miles traveled to Helena, the capital of Montana Territory, to bolster his position with Governor Benjamin F. Potts and other territorial officials.

Soon a demand grew among the citizens of Miles City and Montana Territory for the federal government to create

Gen. William T. Sherman was one of several famous military leaders who stopped over at Fort Keogh, and who met citizens of Miles City. *Courtesy National Archives.*

a separate Department of Montana, with Colonel Miles as commander. But Miles already directed the Department of the Yellowstone, anchored by Forts Keogh and Custer. General Sherman and Secretary of War George W. McCrary refused to make the effort to establish another department in the area.[27]

Instead, General Sherman detached Miles to preside over a newly-established equipment board which would meet in Washington, D.C., during the winter of 1878-79. Mary Sherman Miles and daughter Cecilia left for the East in October 1878, while Colonel Miles followed a month later. Always interested in the latest equipment and weaponry, Miles convened the committee six days a week, beginning in January 1879 and continuing until the first of April. Everything from new rifles to uniform improvements, from increased pay for enlisted men to mountain howitzers to new cork helmets, was examined and discussed. Committee members investigated production centers in New York, Philadelphia, and Rock Island, Illinois.[28]

Miles made or renewed numerous contacts during his months in Washington, but he clashed with those who opposed his equipment requests. He gave speeches and was interviewed by newspapers. When he and his family returned to a rapidly expanding Fort Keogh, the Colonel and Mrs. Miles headed a lively social life at the post. And in a gratifying trip back East, he delivered the commencement address in June 1880 at the U.S. Military Academy at West Point. Miles had never attended the Academy, of course, but his stellar military achievements made his appearance noteworthy.[29]

His self-promotion, however, remained incessant and without tact, and he clashed increasingly with his superiors, even uncle-in-law, William T. Sherman. But Miles' qualifications were so undeniable that when a vacancy occurred in 1880 he finally received his long-sought star. Miles departed Fort Keogh in 1881 — having commanded the outpost during the first half-decade of its existence — to receive his brigadier's commission in ceremonies at the nation's capital.[30]

With his promotion came command of the Department of the Columbia, with headquarters at Vancouver Barracks, Washington. General Miles commanded the vast Department of the Columbia from 1881 to 1885. He remained busy upgrading the organization, equipment, and training of the department, and by traveling, most enjoyably, to Alaska. In 1882 General Miles and Mary had a son, Sherman Miles.

In 1886 Geronimo and a few warlike Apaches escaped custody after having been corralled by General Crook. General Miles was sent to the trouble spot. He placed guard details at water holes and mountain passes, organized

Gen. Phil Sheridan was another renowned military hero who journeyed to Fort Keogh. Sheridan had lobbied for a military post at the confluence of the Yellowstone and Tongue rivers. *Courtesy National Archives.*

a system of pursuit posses, and established a network of thirty heliograph stations. The elusive Apaches were hounded relentlessly, and Geronimo and a handful of followers finally surrendered. When a public subscription for an engraved sword for Miles fell far short of the needed amount, the General quietly paid the difference, then basked in presentation ceremonies at Tuscon.³¹

In 1890, having received a second star, Major General

Gen. Nelson A. Miles attired in dress uniform and his Medal of Honor. *Courtesy National Archives.*

Miles was promoted to command the Division of the Missouri. By mid-September 1890 Miles and his family were headed East, where his new station would be in Chicago. There was a nostalgic stopover at Fort Keogh, where Miles, Mary, and their children and other members of their party were memorably entertained. Miles City, now a bustling cowtown, provided part of the crowd. The entertainment climaxed with a ball at the fort, with music from the regimental band.³²

A few months later General Miles led troops in quelling violence during the murderous Ghost Dance troubles. He was appointed commanding general of United States armies in 1895. Three years later, during the Spanish-American War, General Miles skillfully executed a nineteen-day campaign to seize Puerto Rico. Following mandatory retirement in 1903, Miles lost his wife to heart failure. But he busied himself from his home in Washington with horse riding, golf, and chess. When the United States entered World War I, the seventy-seven-year-old Miles eagerly volunteered for duty, but his services were respectfully declined.[33]

In 1925 now eighty-five, Miles took his grandchildren to the Ringling Brothers Circus. While the "Star-Spangled Banner" was being played he was felled by a fatal heart attack. After an elaborate funeral, which he would have appreciated, Miles was buried at Arlington National Cemetery.

Chapter Four

A Tale of Two Cities

"For a large part of the trade, the town depends on the garrison at Fort Keogh."

— Journalist F.M. Wilson

Miles City did not become a frontier "city" until the Tongue River Cantonment was replaced by Fort Keogh. Not until the ramshackle wilderness cantonment was expanded into a major military installation did Old Milestown grow from a nondescript camp town into a robust, distinctive community of the Old West. The fortunes of Miles City were bound inextricably with the growth of Fort Keogh. When the principal construction of Fort Keogh was completed, the new post was the largest in Montana Territory, and during the years of its greatest military activity, it was one of the biggest army bases in the entire West. Indeed, in terms of population and structures, the military city of Fort Keogh was larger and more substantial than pioneer Miles City. Throughout the frontier decade of 1876-1886 the story of Fort Keogh and Miles City truly was a tale of two cities.[1]

From the first arrival of troops in 1876, the Tongue River Cantonment was a busy post, and crude log buildings were added constantly. The original military reservation was 100 sections, which covered 64,000 acres of land. The Tongue River Cantonment label began to be replaced by "Fort Keogh" on the Post Roll in October 1877. Fort Keogh was designated the official name by the War Department on November 8, 1878. (Because Native Americans called the swift-flowing Yellowstone "Elk River," the army base to them became "Elk River Fort.") Colonel

Miles selected a site on higher ground more than a mile west of the original cantonment for the permanent buildings of Fort Keogh.[2]

War Department plans called for a diamond-shaped parade ground. A rectangular parade ground customarily was used, but more buildings than usual were planned for Fort Keogh. Fort D.A. Russell, located outside Cheyenne, the Territorial Capital of Wyoming, was another large post which utilized a diamond-shaped parade ground to fit more officers' quarters and barracks around the parade.

Plans for Fort Keogh included twenty-one buildings that would face the parade ground. At the western tip of the diamond would be the COQ (Commanding Officers' Quarters), flanked by a total of thirteen officers' quarters. Facing the two officers' rows were six sets of company barracks and the post headquarters building. A regimental headquarters was erected behind the post HQ. Thirty-nine structures were planned for placement outside the parade diamond. These buildings would include cavalry stables, a large hospital, bakery, granary, guard house, and big warehouses for quartermaster stores and commissary provisions.[3]

Captain Charles Stuart Heintzelman of the Quartermaster Corps was placed in charge of constructing Fort Keogh as well as Fort Custer to the west, situated only eleven miles from the Custer battlefield. Captain Heintzelman was a graduate of West Point, Class of 1867.[4] Heintzelman was a meticulous planner who carefully organized the tools and materials and equipment that would be needed. He also was authorized to hire hundreds of civilian construction "mechanics," who would be divided between the two projects. Manual labor was provided by troopers who were not campaigning in the field.

Captain Heintzelman arrived by steamboat during the

A Tale of Two Cities 39

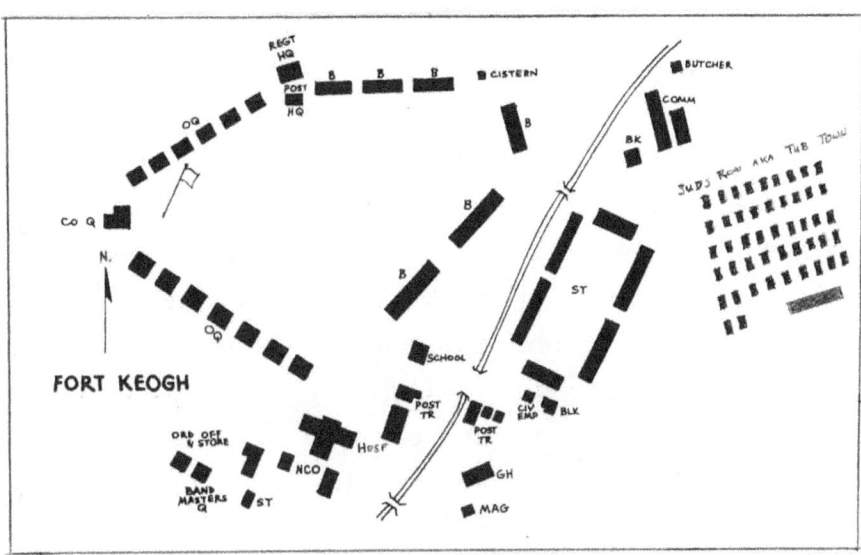

Diagram of Fort Keogh, adapted from the research of frontier fort expert Herbert M. Hart and the illustrations of Paul J. Hartle, as well as Plan of Fort Keogh by Lt. Edward Maguire, Corps of Engineers, 1878. Note the diamond shape of the parade ground. *Old Forts of the Northwest*, 179-181, and Plan of Fort Keogh, M.T., surveyed and drawn by Lt. Edward Maguie, Corps of Engineers, 1878, reproduced in Hoopes, *This Last West*.

Diorama of Fort Keogh, on display at the Range Riders Museum. Half of Officers' Row may be seen in the center; the Commanding Officers' Quarters are at upper right; and the remainder of Officers' Row begins at upper right. Two two-story troop barracks with latrines are clearly visible, and so are two stables at left. The large white building at upper left is the post hospital. *Photo by the author.*

"June rise" of the rivers in June 1877. Steamboats continued to bring men and building supplies, dropping off workers and materials at Fort Keogh. By October 1877 construction began in earnest. The Quartermaster Corps already had standard blueprints on file for most of the buildings at Fort Keogh. Almost all structures would be solid but simple frame affairs, with no plumbing or wiring. Measurements were precise for each building, so locations were laid out carefully around and beyond the parade ground.

A sawmill was set up in a cottonwood stand next to the Yellowstone for rough cut lumber, while riverboats brought in finished lumber, along with 138 kegs of nails. There were twenty-one bundles of window sashes and eighteen crates of window panes. Construction crews opened boxes of drills, augurs, spikes, putty, screw drivers, gear wheels, and several types of pulleys. With an abundance of materials and equipment, as well as large numbers of workmen, construction was rapid. As soon as an officers' residence or a barracks building was completed, old structures at the cantonment were abandoned in favor of new quarters. All thirteen of the two-story officers' quarters were duplexes, while five of the six company barracks were two-story.

The barracks of different sizes cost from $20,800 for a two-story structure housing three troops to $3,000 for a single-story company barracks. The COQ cost $3,300, while the thirteen officers' quarters totaled $39,000. The headquarters office and the granary each cost $2,000, while the bakery was built for $1,000. The commissary warehouse was $2,500 and the quartermaster storehouse was $2,200. Cavalry stables, located just east of the parade ground, cost $10,000. Captain Heintzelman reported that materials for Fort Keogh cost $51,130.90, labor expenses were $57,975.72 and transportation charges added up to

$74,192.81. Fort Keogh was completed in 1878 at a total cost of $183,300.43. The entire congressional appropriation for Fort Keogh and Fort Custer combined was a little over $200,000, but funding was provided to complete Fort Custer, which also was a sizeable installation. As time passed there was need for various additional outbuildings, and enough of these smaller structures were erected to run the total to about 100 buildings at Fort Keogh.[5]

A major collection of log buildings east of the parade ground comprised "Soap Suds Row," also called "Suds Row" or "Tub Town." The wives of enlisted men worked as company laundresses to supplement the meager salaries of their husbands — indeed, some wives took in civilian washing from nearby Miles City. The Tub Town quarters for married soldiers numbered between forty-eight and sixty-five units, and dwellings stood only about fifteen feet apart along a military plat of streets for Soap Suds Row. Yards were small, and the children of Suds Row often numbered more than one hundred. And when one of the wives burned trash too close to her neighbor's home, there was a vehement squabble between the women which compelled the Officer of the Day to station an off-duty private as a guard. Also adding to the soap opera

Fort Custer was built 15 miles from the Custer Battlefield. Left to right is Officers' Row (note the bandstand in front of the COQ, fourth building from left). Behind Officers' Row is a drop-off down to the Bighorn River. Cavalry troops are exercising on the parade ground. *Courtesy National Archives.*

Officers' quarters at Fort Keogh were duplexes, with bedrooms upstairs. The Range Riders Museum rebuilt one of the few remaining OQ duplexes with donations, grants, and a great deal of volunteer labor. *Photo by the author.*

of Suds Row was a Mrs. Jennie Logan, who was the subject of complaints in August 1879 that she was "much too friendly with several Sergeants."[6]

Most of the enlisted men at Fort Keogh were single and therefore quartered in the spacious frame barracks buildings. Colonel Miles saw to it that "the upper story of a large storehouse was turned into a hall for entertainment, pianos and comfortable furniture appeared, the valuable library of the Fifth Infantry was unpacked, and the fine band of the same regiment contributed to make of the post an oasis of civilization." The post library, of which Colonel Miles was justifiably proud, contained 1,208 volumes, and by 1879 there were subscriptions to sixteen periodicals and "many eastern papers." An average of ninety-five patrons per day visited the library.[7]

On Sundays the library was utilized as a chapel. Father Eli Washington John Lindesmith was a Catholic priest from

Ohio who was sent by his bishop to Washington D.C. to be commissioned an Army Chaplain. Subsequently he traveled by rail to Bismarck, then by steamboat to Fort Keogh, where he was welcomed by Colonel Miles. En route Father Lindesmith saw his first Native American, and later he would send a buffalo robe to Pope Leo XIII in Rome. Father Lindesmith found a large number of congregants at Fort Keogh, because many immigrants from Catholic countries enlisted in the army to learn the English language and otherwise establish themselves in the USA. Numerous non-Catholics also attended services. Assigned to spacious quarters in an officer's duplex next to the COQ, Father Lindesmith converted one of his rooms to a private chapel, where a post carpenter built an altar and a cabinet for vestments and supplies. Here Father Lindesmith held weekday masses and received the faithful for sacraments. He also taught school, with classes held in the library/chapel. Noting the soldiers' affinity for liquor, Father Lindesmith

Dining room in the left side of the OQ duplex.
Photo by the author.

promoted a "Total Abstinence Society." At one point enrollment reached 536 "members," but there may have been considerable backsliding, because the saloons of Miles City continued to do a roaring business.⁸

Aside from the post library, other amenities available to the garrison at Fort Keogh included billiards, amateur theatricals, Mother Goose parties, and Christmas trees for the children — as well as the most constant form of entertainment, the regimental band. An officer was nominally in charge of the band, but for the first several years that Fort Keogh existed, Kenneth Price, an Englishman who enlisted at New York City, served as "Principal Musician and Bandmaster, Fort Keogh Band." A bandstand was erected in front of the COQ. The Regimental Band played throughout the day for drills, musters, guard mounts, and dress parades, as well as special occasions for visiting officers and

The regimental band was enormously popular. Christian Barthelmess, at left in this photo, conducted the band. *Courtesy Range Riders Museum.*

other dignitaries. Bandmaster Price also headed the "Fort Keogh String Band," which played for officers' hops and concerts. The band was fully equipped with instruments which included cornets, alto horn, bass horn, French horn, clarinet, piccolo, trombone, tambourine, and both snare and bass drums. The band often played concerts in town, and townspeople were welcome to come to the fort to enjoy the music. Beginning in 1880 the band played summer concerts on the parade ground daily at two o'clock and each evening, and in Miles City townspeople would drift out from the stores and saloons to listen to the distant musical strains. After the Ghost Dance troubles of 1890-91, 600 soldiers returned to Fort Keogh, marching in formation down Main Street with the band leading the parade with impressive martial music.[9]

Father Elias Washington John Lindesmith was assigned to a duplex, and he converted one room into a small chapel where mass could be conducted. He was the post chap-lain, but he also served Catholics in Miles City. *Courtesy Range Riders Museum.*

Meanwhile, Father Lindesmith brought his ministry into Miles City. On August 22, 1880, not long after his arrival, Father Lindesmith conducted a mass for the public in the log courthouse on Main Street. After mass was celebrated in the courthouse on eight occasions, a log cabin on Main Street was rented and mass was conducted there thirty-seven times. More than a score of Catholic citizens offered their homes, and Father Lindesmith recorded thirty-four times that he held mass at private premises. Property was acquired at the northeast corner of Tenth and Main, and in 1881 Father Lindesmith became one of the first three trustees of Sacred Heart Church in Miles City. He was instrumental in bringing six Ursuline nuns as teachers to the Sacred Heart Convent.

While continuing to serve as chaplain at Fort Keogh, he was active in the community — part of his daily routine was to have coffee in the MacQueen House, the largest hotel in Miles City. The congregation grew rapidly, and in 1886 one of the parishioners, Ed Flynn, added thirty feet to the twenty-seven by forty-foot church. In 1891 Father Lindesmith returned to his native Ohio (he had been the first Catholic priest ordained in Ohio). Serving in Ohio for the remainder of his life, he died in 1922 at the age of ninety-four. But for more than a decade, 1880-1891, Father Lindesmith was one of the most productive urban pioneers in the development of early Miles City.[10]

George M. Miles came even earlier than Father Lindesmith to the military base at the confluence of the Yellowstone and Tongue rivers, and like the priest, Miles soon became a key citizen of Miles City. A nephew of Nelson A. Miles, George was born in 1854 in Westminster, Massachusetts. He attended the public schools of Westminster and of Worchester, Massachusetts, and in 1874 George graduated from the Massachusetts Agricultural College. The next year George signed on with Colonel Miles to work as a Quartermaster clerk for the Fifth Infantry when military operations began in Montana Territory.

George took passage with the Fifth aboard the riverboat. *H. Durfee* on the journey to the Tongue River Cantonment. Arriving in August 1876, George served at the new base only until the end of the year, when he decided to establish himself in the growing camp town. In May 1877, George Miles was appointed U.S. Commissioner at Fort Keogh, serving until March 1879. He had his seal of office fashioned at the Fort Keogh blacksmith shop, and in 1878 he secured an appointment as Justice of the Peace for Miles City.

Another city father, Charlie Strevell, lived with Miles, and the two ambitious entrepreneurs entered the hardware business. The two men also were directors of the First National Bank. Miles served as vice president of the banking house, which was organized in 1881 and stood next-door to the popular Cottage Saloon on Main Street. In 1880 Miles married Helen Strevell, Charlie's sister and the daughter of a noted Miles City attorney and judge, Jason Strevell.[11]

George and Helen Strevell Miles became devout and generous members of the First Presbyterian Church, which organized in 1879 and held services in the old log courthouse on Main Street. By this time George Miles had entered the livestock business. In 1877 Miles and Captain (later Major General) Frank Baldwin purchased a band of 1,007 sheep for $2,000 in gold. By the next year the flock had grown to 1,500 sheep, and 5,000 pounds of wool were shipped downstream on the *Batchelor*.

Miles continued to run sheep, and in 1879 he brought horses to a ranch he established about fifteen miles from town. In 1883 he partnered with his father-in-law and another cowman in a cattle operation, the Circle Bar. That same year Miles was elected to the Custer County Board of Commissioners. He remained active as a businessman, rancher, political leader, and a mainstay of the Presbyterian Church for decades. A family residence he erected in 1899 today is on the National Register of Historic Buildings.

Captain Frank Baldwin, like other officers at Fort Keogh, kept a sharp eye out for business opportunities. Officers with family means were influenced by Colonel Miles, who had invested successfully at early stations and who, by the time he reached Fort Keogh, had amassed considerable wealth. Frank Baldwin was an impressive officer who twice had earned the Medal of Honor, once for exploits during the Civil War and a second time during the Red River War where he served with Colonel Miles. Baldwin and his wife, Alice, and their only child, a daughter, were stationed at Fort Hays, Kansas, when Colonel Miles and Lieutenant Colonel Custer also were there.

Captain Baldwin borrowed $1,000 to speculate in Kansas land. The venture was unprofitable, causing financial pressure for the family, but when Baldwin reached the virgin frontier of Montana he collected enough capital to try his hand with George H. Miles in a flock of sheep.

By the end of the Spanish-American War, Baldwin was a colonel, and he fought with his usual distinction in the Philippines. He retired in 1906 as a major general, establishing a home in Denver. During World War I the old veteran served as adjutant general of Colorado, then lived quietly until his death in 1923 at the age of eighty. One of only nineteen men to be awarded two Congressional Medals of Honor (before the practice was limited to a single award), General Baldwin was buried in Arlington National Cemetery.[12]

William N. MacQueen generally was referred to as "Major" MacQueen, but he no longer was connected to the army when he arrived at Fort Keogh in 1880. Major MacQueen was sent by a St. Louis firm as a post trader at Fort Keogh. Shortly after arriving, MacQueen also entered a partnership in a lumber business, with the yard adjacent to the trackway and depot of the advancing Northern Pacific Railroad. Operating as post trader and postmaster at Fort Keogh, Major MacQueen acquired the two-story Inter-Ocean Hotel, located only a short walk from the depot and Church's Livery Stable. An Inter-Ocean Hotel was the finest hostelry in Cheyenne, capital city of Wyoming, and elsewhere. But with excellent business in Miles City, MacQueen changed the name to MacQueen Hotel in 1886 and invested in major expansion and interior improvements. Also known as the MacQueen House, the sprawling frame structure hosted the annual meeting of the Montana Stockgrowers Association while becoming a Miles City landmark. Appropriately, Major MacQueen also purchased a cattle herd to graze on the open range. The Major came to Fort Keogh to function as post trader, but he immediately recognized beckoning opportunities and became an important figure during the cowtown period of Miles City.[13]

Major Paul Borchardt was a German immigrant who volunteered for the Union Army at the beginning of the Civil War. Enlisting as a lieutenant, he served in the Quartermaster Corps and rose to the rank of major. Major Borchardt worked as a sutler with columns in the field and at Fort Pease in Montana in 1875. The next year he was on the scene when the Tongue River Cantonment was established and he was appointed to a sutler's post.

Major Borchardt also was an original settler of Milestown, opening a general merchandise store with two partners. They brought in a load of goods on a riverboat in 1877, and Borchardt also herded twenty-five head of cattle to range near Milestown. Major Borchardt and D.W. Ringer were appointed Commissioners of Custer Country. Borchardt was selected as Chairman and charged to rent a building and provide chairs for county officers. Opening a store on the northeast corner of Fourth and Main, he also became the third postmaster of Miles City, with the post office located from 1881 to 1886 at "Borchardt's Corner." His general store carried meerschaum pipes, stationery, books, nuts, candies, clocks, notions, "and well-selected stock of holiday goods." Officers' wives came to

Miles City to shop during holiday seasons, and "Borchardt's Corner" was a must stop. In the second story of his original building, Borchardt ran a dance hall. Major Borchardt was a popular and busy citizen in early Miles City.[14]

Most of the officers at Fort Keogh were educated men (West Pointers, at a time when few Americans completed or even attended college). Many were from prosperous families, and the wives were cultivated women. These men affiliated with the Masonic Lodge or other fraternal orders as they were organized in Miles City. Officers and their families attended the churches of Miles City: Catholic (organized in 1879), Methodist (1877), Presbyterian (1879), Episcopalian (1890), Baptist (1892). Children from Fort Keogh attended school in Miles City, riding in a wagon driven by an enlisted man.[15]

From Fort Keogh the Tongue River had to be crossed to reach Miles City. At first a ferry was used, before Major T.H. Logan

A ferry was used to cross the Tongue River into town.
Courtesy Range Riders Museum.

Major T.H. Logan, an experienced engineering officer, built the first bridge across the Tongue River. *Courtesy Range Riders Museum.*

supervised construction of a wooden bridge that connected the military reservation with the foot of Main Street. In 1886 a flood destroyed the bridge, causing a revival of the ferry until an iron bridge was erected. Major Logan established a cattle ranch using the THL brand on 500 head. He purchased town lots and placed prefabricated rent houses on his property. Major Logan also dealt in retail goods. Lieutenants Hunter Liggitt and Edward Casey, in 1887 and 1890 respectively, also brought small cattle herds. Major James Brisbin, a thrice-wounded Civil War veteran, purchased cattle and soon became a director of Miles City's First National Bank.[16]

Officers and their wives were invited to social activities in Miles City. They reciprocated with invitations to parties at Fort Keogh. The Fourth of July always was a fun celebration. Most elaborate of all on every military post was the birthday party for General George Washington. In 1880 an officers' "hop" was staged every Tuesday night, with dance music provided by the Fort Keogh String Band. Friends from Miles City were invited, and military ambulances (the four beds in each vehicle were folded to provide seating) were sent to town to transport civilian guests to the post. In 1882 the "Jolly Boys" dancing club was formed at Fort Keogh and the group staged a grand ball every Wednesday evening.[17]

"Almost any occasion was made a reason for a ball," observed Josef James Warhank, the historian of Fort Keogh. "Fort [Keogh] had an Army-wide reputation as a party post." [18]

Warhank described numerous fun-filled activities, and the *Yellowstone Journal* of Miles City reported on the frequent dances and parties, pointing out that "citizens of the City would often join in the fun at Fort Keogh." Warhank commented that, "The soldiers and their families never rested long between the searches for ways of having fun."[19]

While Fort Keogh became known as a party post, Miles City steadily developed its identity as a party town. The two adjacent communities complemented each other as good-time-towns – one military and the other civilian, with a great deal of interaction between the two populations.

The close association with a major military base had positive effects on fledgling Miles City, as noticed by a newspaper reporter from Bozeman in 1879. Miles City was only a couple of years old, but journalist F.M. Wilson was impressed. "On the south bank of the Tongue River, surrounded by a grove of magnificent cottonwoods stands the town of Miles City," he described to his readers. "We had expected to find a place such as Bismarck was in 1873, a collection of log and canvas buildings with a preponderance of saloons, gambling and dance halls, but in this we were disappointed."[20]

Wilson would have found what he expected had he come in 1876 to 1877 to ramshackle Milestown. But when the town relocated, the incoming residents seized the opportunity to upgrade their new community. Instead of picket construction with sod or canvas roofs, "the buildings are principally

Troop maneuvers were conducted in the countryside. Note the supply wagons.
Courtesy National Archives

substantial frame structures, neatly painted and well kept. Some are of hewn logs, but the canvas element is entirely lacking." Indeed, brick buildings soon would be constructed along Main Street.

"We were fairly surprised at the amount of business done, the large and complete stocks of goods kept by the merchants and the population of the place. Already the town has 700 inhabitants... The heaviest line of goods is kept by Broadwater, Hubbel and Company, who have a fine two story building and a large warehouse in both of which every inch of spare room is closely packed with merchandise... Paul McCormick and Company also have a fine two-story building, neatly painted. Their store contains a little of everything, from confectionery to bed quilts, and in the labyrinth of supplies which owned the shelves and counters, we notice clotheslines, neckties, watered ribbons and fine robes. Savage and Ninninger have a varied assortment of goods beginning with groceries and running up through clothing, fire arms and ammunition, terminating finally in . . . liquid comfort for the inner men.

"J.J. Graham, who formerly held a responsible position in the Paymaster's corps of the Army, discovered this to be one of the busiest points in the west and consequently resigned his position, and has occupied a two-story building with a fine stock of groceries, clothing, wines, liquors, cigars and gents furnishings . . ."

At this point the reporter began describing "much that is evil in this young city," an entertaining topic which will be more useful in a later chapter of this book. Reporter Wilson next turned to a pressing need of Miles City: "Lumber with which to erect suitable buildings," but which could not be adequately met by the government sawmill near Fort Keogh. But of course, local entrepreneurial leaders already had recognized this

One of the earliest views of Miles City was a watercolor by Pvt. Hermann Stieffel, a trooper in Company K of the Fifth Infantry. Private Stieffel, although not a trained artist, painted a view from across the Tongue River in 1878. The watercolor measured about nine inches by nineteen inches. A ferry is noticeable at left, and at right angles to the river runs Main Street. From mid-view going left to right are saloons and other businesses along Park Street. The Miles City Preservation Committee and the Custer County Historical obtained permission from the Forbush Memorial Library in Westminster, Massachusetts, hometown of Nelson A. Miles, to place an enlarged copy of the watercolor in Riverside Park, with the assistance of the local Lions Club. *Photo by the author.*

opportunity. "Messrs Broadwater, Hubbel and Company, with commendable enterprise, have determined to erect a sawmill at once. During the winter, logs will be out on the headwaters of the Tongue River and driven down the stream early in the spring, a distance of about 100 miles."

Wilson concluded his observations: "For a large part of the trade, the town depends on the garrison at Fort Keogh. Some idea of the large amount of money disbursed at this post may be had from the fact that this season the government purchased 3,200 tons of oats and corn, 5,800 tons of hay and 7,500 cords of wood. The grain was brought from the east, but the coming season a large portion of it will be raised in the {Yellowstone} Valley."

The population estimate of 700 for 1879 that was given to reporter Wilson probably was a slight exaggeration. The Census of 1880 recorded 629 residents in Miles City, and in 1890 the official population had grown to 956 — an increase of more than fifty percent. But two-year-old Miles City in 1879 clearly was a town on the grow. And a rapidly growing frontier town might be expected to experience a few growing pains.

Chapter Five
Frontier Violence

"We have 23 saloons in our town, and they all do a good business. We are to have one church soon."

— *Yellowstone Journal*, **March 13, 1880.**

A major element of the drama and excitement of the frontier West was unbridled violence. Nothing is more dramatic than life and death conflict, and when that conflict is carried out by men in big hats and boots, armed with revolvers and repeating rifles — or by men wearing war paint and feathered headdresses — there is a special appeal about such turbulent events.

Certainly no motion picture scene announced frontier violence more vividly than two fast-draw gunfighters marching toward one another on a dusty street. Or two groups of gunfighters confronting each other at a local landmark (such as a corral). And of course there were countless drunken confrontations inside saloons and dance halls of the Old West. Even if guns were not drawn, saloon brawls offered plenty of rough action.

During the first several years of its existence, Fort Keogh served up a great deal of campaigning and fighting against Sioux and Cheyenne and Arapaho warriors. In between campaigns, when Fort Keogh combat soldiers were on the post in large numbers, many men spent evenings in the saloons and dance halls and bordellos of Miles City. After a few drinks the combative nature of the soldiers took over, and they fought each other or any civilians who were present. As mentioned in Chapter Two, participants in the saloon "shindies" brawled, scuffled, kicked and slugged with fists and boots.

Western motion pictures portrayed countless gunfights, but movie fans also responded to well-choreographed saloon brawls. *Dodge City* (1939), starring Errol Flynn, staged the most exciting saloon fight ever lensed, and Western movies thereafter tried to match this explosive barroom adventure. Three years later two of the greatest of all Western stars, John Wayne and Randolph Scott, squared off in a Nome saloon and nearly tore the place apart in the fourth of five versions of *The Spoilers* (1942). Showing skilled boxing moves, Wayne finally knocked out Scott. In the western classic *Shane* (1953), Alan Ladd and a burly Van Heflin licked an entire ranch crew after an epic slug fest in a log saloon. *North to Alaska* (1960) features John Wayne once more in the soggy streets of Nome. Early in the film Wayne romps his way through a rugged but exhilarating saloon brawl, and the climax of the movie is a mud-soaked street fight.[1]

Dodge City, starring Errol Flynn and released in 1939, staged the most exciting saloon fight ever filmed. *Author's collection.*

In many of the most enjoyable cinematic saloon brawls, no gunshots were fired and no participants were killed. This scenario mirrored the frequent saloon fights which broke out in the barrooms of Miles City. "To be sure these affairs were disturbances of the peace, but what could one night watchman do, had he been inclined to mix in, which he wasn't." Pioneer journalist Sam Gordon, who was a young man when Miles City was in its "picturesque youth," enjoyed reflecting back on "those strenuous days" of the frontier town.[2]

Gordon admitted "that we were a tough town, but our toughness was largely exuberance of spirit bred of freedom from the ordinary restraints and responsive to the call of the 'wild.'" And so, if off-duty soldiers became "offensive . . . the bullwhackers and the mule skinners of the 'Diamond R' could always be mobilized for an argument with the 'sojers.'" Barroom brawls simply were part of a typical evening spent in the saloons of frontier Miles City.[3]

Journalist Sam Gordon grew up with Miles City, and he later admitted "that we were a tough town . . ." *Courtesy Range Riders Museum.*

Many of the roughest free-for-alls erupted soon after the paymaster reached remote Fort Keogh. The soldiers received their pay usually once every two or three months. Pockets bulging with coins, most of the troopers headed for the resorts of Miles City. After crossing the Tongue River onto Main Street, the first building on the right was the two-story Cottage Saloon, long the favorite watering hole of the soldiers.

"On these occasions," reminisced newspaperman Sam Gordon, "the patronage was so large and so urgent that there was no time wasted on drawing beer. It was emptied into a couple of tubs behind the bar, and dipped up in the beer glasses in a continuous service; one shift filling the tubs and another emptying them. Such a thing as 'a quiet drink' was impossible while pay day lasted."[4]

Fort Keogh provided mounted escorts for the paymaster. In the early years of the fort there was a need for protection against bands of warriors. But after the Native Americans were confined to reservations, road agents became a threat. In May 1884, as the paymaster coach of Major Charles D. Whipple reached the vicinity of Fort Keogh, a gang of outlaws attacked the party. Sgt. Aquille Coonrod, a Medal of Honor recipient for bravery at Cedar Creek, was killed. Two privates were wounded, along with Mr. Such, Major Whipple's clerk. The road agents soon

The two-story Cottage Saloon, at left on the corner of Main and Park streets, was the favorite watering hole of Fort Keogh troopers and a frequent site of barroom brawls. Sleeping rooms were upstairs. *Courtesy Range Riders Museum.*

broke off their assault, as Major Whipple led his battered party to a nearby ranch. Whipple reached Fort Keogh with thousands of dollars in coin, while a detail of troopers rode in vain to track down the robbers.[5] By any measure, a bandit attack on a paymaster coach defended by cavalrymen certainly ranked as a notable incident of frontier violence.

And the saloon brawls continued in Miles City. In 1887, Col. George Gibson, now in command at Fort Keogh, instituted a "pass" system for men intending to visit town. Each soldier had to obtain a pass, and be inspected for proper attire: full regimentals, gauntlets, and shined boots. Furthermore, a system of patrols was established, led by a commissioned officer, with non-coms patrolling expected trouble spots in Miles City.[6]

The first altercation known to produce fatal gunplay occurred in March 1880. Bill Reece, who arrived in Miles City in 1878, developed a popular saloon located at Main and Park Streets. Reece purchased a building from C.W. Savage for $3,000 and renovations produced a dance floor twenty-five feet by one-hundred feet. Reece's Dance Hall and Sampling Room served champagne, wines, and liquors, while a brass band provided dance music. But on March 20, 1880, while visiting Clara Clifton, a prostitute whose crib was near Reece's Dance Hall, Reece and Dr. Chester B. Lebscher engaged in a quarrel. Both men angrily produced pistols and opened fire. The gunfight ended when Reece went down, struck at least twice in the abdomen. Dr. A.J. Hogg was called in to attend Reece, but he died from his wounds two days later. Meanwhile, Dr. Lebscher was released on grounds of self-defense. Clara Clifton moved to Bismarck, but within two years she was arrested on murder charges following another fatal incident.[7]

The year after the Reece-Lebscher shootout, the Northern Pacific Railroad reached Miles City. The railroad brought

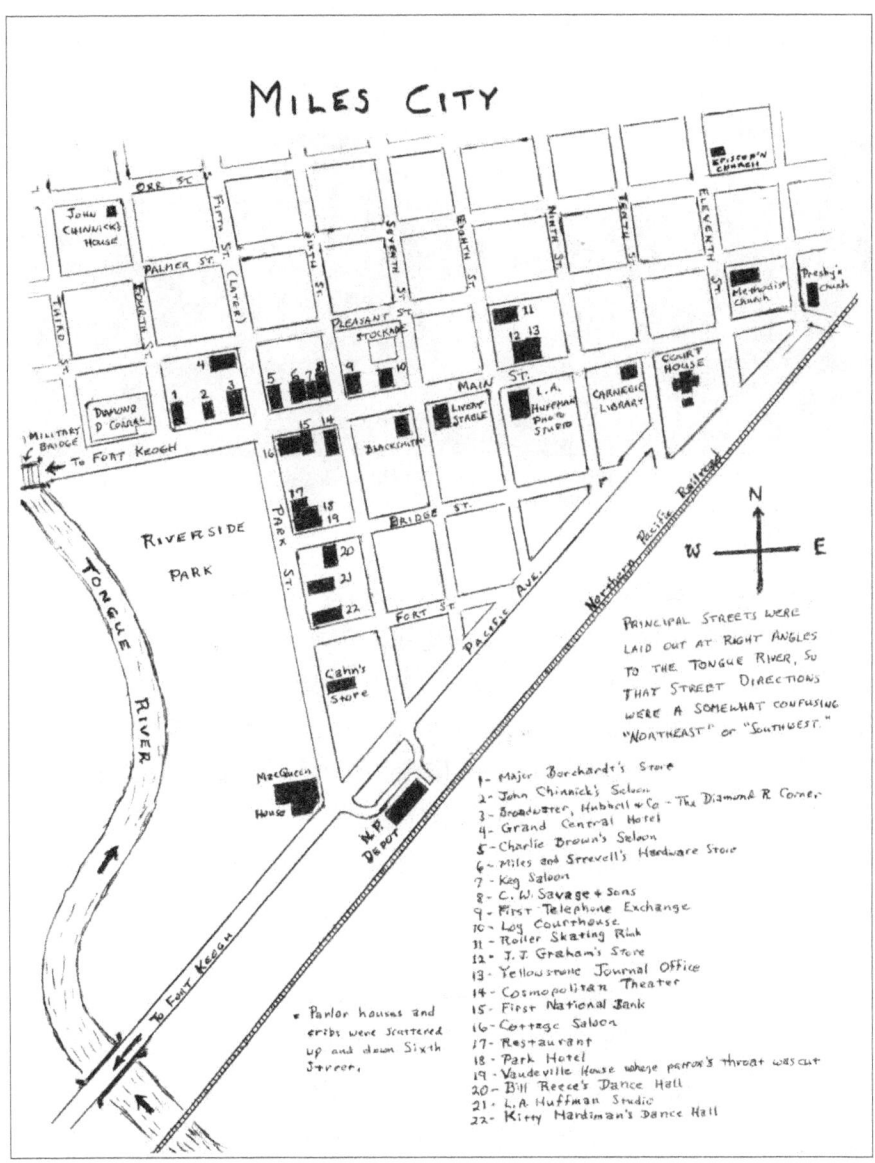

Diagram of frontier Miles City, with a number of notable buildings shaded or labeled. Based on the diagram "L.A. Huffman's Milestown in Brown and Felton, *The Frontier Years."*

The flood of March 1881 inundated Main and Park streets. Charlie Brown's popular saloon is in left foreground, with the famous Cottage Saloon the first building at right. *Courtesy Range Riders Museum.*

prosperity and transformed Miles City into a cowtown. But Sam Gordon saw a downside for his community.

"It was the incoming of the railroad that called the turn on our primitive life and introduced the manners and customs of the older civilization into our little world . . . For one thing it brought in a new class of tough, the city roughneck and booze-fighters, whose kind we had not had because of the splendid isolation we had enjoyed. It was out of this contingent that grew our first and only lynching."[8]

Gordon and everyone else in Miles City welcomed the railroad, "but we were slow to appreciate the new class of citizens, the tramp, the hobo, and the city thug, that it brought to us . . ." He explained that the men of Miles City "elected officials who they knew would not be too officious . . . there seemed to be a tacit understanding to let smaller matters adjust themselves . . . Perhaps it was due to the fact that we were so 'wide-open' that this undesirable element chose to congregate here."[9]

Decent women of the community began to suffer insults

from the newcomers, "while holdups and 'rollings' of drunken soldiers and others were of nightly occurrence." The breaking point came on Saturday morning, July 21, 1883. A saloon denizen named Bill Rigney and a companion, both drunk, staggered uninvited into the home of Bob Campbell. The entire family, plus a boarder named George W. McKay, were eating breakfast when the two drunks appeared "and gave vent to foul language," along with vile insults to daughter Gracie. Campbell and McKay rose to throw out the intruders, and the popular saloonkeeper Charlie Brown passed near and was drawn to the disturbance. Carrying a pickaxe handle with him, Brown knocked Rigney senseless, at which point the other drunk bolted out of the house. The unconscious Rigney was dragged off to confinement at the courthouse.[10]

Throughout Saturday the story of "the invasion of a private house and the offering to insult to the inmates" was told and re-told by "whispering knots of citizens." At midnight about forty determined men approached the jail. Deputy Sheriff Jim Conley, acting as jailer, surrendered his keys. The lynch mob took Rigney from his cell and carried him to the railroad trestle

The long Cosmopolitan Theater (first building on the left) stood on Main Street — until it was burned in retribution for the lynching of Bill Rigney. *Courtesy Range Riders Museum.*

that spanned the Tongue River. None of the vigilantes were ever named, but there were persistent rumors that Rigney had been killed by Charlie Brown's blow, and that the "lynching" was a cover-up.[11]

Rigney's swaying corpse was discovered at dawn. Moments later the Cosmopolitan Theater burst into flames, and within an hour an entire row of frame buildings was burned to ashes on Main Street. Vigilantes assumed that the fire was an act of reprisal and a warning, but the presumed threat only solidified the citizens. A "protective league" was organized, out of which came "a committee of public safety." The committee determined to deport all "suspicious characters." Before the end of this eventful Sunday, the committee held a secret meeting to organize a "patrol" to notify leaders of the "undesirables" to leave town within a matter of hours.[12]

Broadwell, Hubbell & Company — the "Diamond R Corner" is in the foreground facing Main Street. The smaller false front building in the center of the block is John Chinnick's Saloon, gathering place for the town's "toughs." The Post Office is at the end of the street. *Courtesy Range Riders Museum.*

The principal leader "of the toughs" was John Chinnick, who had arrived in Old Milestown by 1877. Chinnick and his wife Nell ran a lively saloon, and when Colonel Miles decreed a move, John promptly loaded a wagon and erected the "G.A.R." Saloon at a prime spot on the new Main Street. (G.A.R. stood for "Grand Army of the Republic," an immensely

The first Custer County Court House, built of squared cottonwood logs, stood on Main Street. *Courtesy Range Riders Museum.*

popular organization among veterans of the Union Army after the Civil War.) Chinnick's saloon became a hangout for the lawless newcomers.[13]

Although Chinnick was ordered on Monday, July 22, to leave Miles City by nightfall, he spent the morning visiting around town in disarming fashion. But at noon he went home where the gang had gathered, and townspeople expected a battle.

Chinnick's home place was on the western outskirts of town. Sam Gordon boarded at Third and Pleasant streets a few hundred yards from Chinnick's house. Gordon began to watch the place through a field glass, observing a congregation of the hardcases who often took meals at Chinnick's. Gordon "observed a sudden commotion," whereupon a messenger raced to town, returning within moments with a doctor. Half an hour later the doctor came back to town with "the startling news that John Chinnick had been accidentally but fatally shot."[14]

Chinnick had decided to fight rather than be run out of town. When he began to strap on a gun, his wife tried to stop him and a scuffle ensued. Most revolvers in the frontier West did not have a safety (and therefore many men carried only "five beans in the wheel," resting the hammer on an empty chamber). While wrestling with Nell, Chinnick's weapon discharged. The law and order citizens would not have to shoot it out with the "undesirables." Chinnick lingered in agony for four weeks, dying on August 20, 1883, at the age of thirty-three.[15]

"Chinnick was a nervy and reckless man," related Gordon. "On the other hand, the committee was composed of men of nerve and determination." But after Chinnick was mortally wounded, his followers "scattered in all directions under the friendly cover of that Monday night and the next day the current of our communal life resumed its accustomed peaceful flow. This event marked the crest of the wave of lawlessness that had been slowly gathering since the incoming of the railroad two years before." Miles City returned to the live-and-let-live attitude which as much as anything kept frontier violence at a tolerable level.[16]

More than a decade later, on November 29, 1893, there was a tragic shooting, involving a decorated hero of the 1876 Battle of the Little Bighorn. Pvt. James Pym was one of fifteen troopers of the Seventh Cavalry who volunteered as water carriers when seven companies of the regiment were pinned down after Lt. Col. George Custer and the other five companies were annihilated on a blazing June day in 1876. As the survivors fought for their lives, everyone suffered thirst, especially the wounded. Private Pym and his comrades courageously scrambled down to the Little Bighorn River under heavy fire. The water carriers lugged cast iron canteens, while they were covered by five sharpshooters in exposed positions. Private Pym was wounded in the ankle during the action. Each of the volunteers was awarded the Congressional Medal of Honor, and the presentation was made in a ceremony at Fort Keogh on

October 5, 1878.[17]

A native of England, Pym joined the British Army as a young man, but apparently deserted and emigrated to the United States. In Boston Pym signed up for a standard five-year enlistment (1874-1879) in the US Cavalry. When his enlistment ended, Pym moved to Minnesota. After marrying, Pym and his bride settled in Miles City, rented a log cabin and opened a restaurant.[18]

Pym acquired a reputation as a man "not to mess with." On one occasion Pym disarmed a hardcase who brandished a revolver at him in front of L.A. Huffman's photography shop. "He took the gun out of the fellow's hand," described Huffman, "tossed it away, knocked his assailant down, kicked him, and told him to leave town and not show his face in it again. The fellow left." [19]

But the Pym restaurant effort failed financially, and when Jim's wife left him he became a problem drinker. At the home of a woman said to be his wife's sister, Pym encountered a cowboy named Miles Alford Tilton. Aware of Pym's reputation, Tilton promptly drew his revolver and fatally wounded the former combat veteran. When the coroner examined Pym's body, his Medal of Honor was pinned inconspicuously to his clothing.[20]

Pym, age forty-one, was buried in the Custer County Cemetery on the outskirts of Miles City. In 1916 another Medal of Honor winner, First Sergeant Henry Hogan, died at the age of seventy-six and was interred at the Custer County Cemetery. Sergeant Hogan twice had been awarded the Medal of Honor, first for gallantry in action during the Battle of Cedar Creek in 1876. The following year, at the murderous Battle of Bear Paw Mountain, Sergeant Hogan braved heavy fire from Nez Perce riflemen to rescue the severely wounded Lt. Henry Romeyn.[21]

By 2009 the two badly weathered Medal of Honor headstones

could barely be read. Retired Army officer Ed Saunders submitted requests to the U.S. Veterans Administration to replace the two gravestones. On Memorial Day of 2010 Saunders and Kurt Homelund, Superintendent of the Eastern Montana State Veterans Cemetery in Miles City, replaced the aged headstones with new markers. Community members turned out to lend support, and the ceremony provided a proud occasion for historic Miles City.[22]

In July 1893, shortly after James Pym was killed in town, a private named Brage was injured during a fight with another soldier. Private Brage was taken back to the post, but he refused to go to the hospital, insisting that he only needed rest. The next morning, however, after leaving the barracks, Brage dropped dead.[23]

Miles City never became an outlaw haunt. The only western badman of any notoriety to spend time in early Miles City was Big Nose George Parrot. Big Nose George was a train and stagecoach robber, a cattle thief, and a murderer. Following a bungled train holdup in Wyoming in 1878, a $20,000 reward was offered for Parrot after two lawmen were ambushed. In February 1879 Big Nose George and some of his gang turned up in early Miles City. They learned that a local merchant, Morris Cahn, regularly took money back east to pay off creditors and to buy merchandise.[24]

Parrot and three of his men planned a robbery at a coulee just outside Terry. Cahn was traveling with a paymaster bound for Fort Keogh and a cavalry escort. But the party became strung out in the rugged countryside near the coulee (thereafter known as "Cahn's Coulee"), and the outlaws got the drop on the escort long enough to steal perhaps $3,600 before galloping away to safety.[25]

Big Nose George and a confederate, Charlie Burris, were

back in Miles City in 1880. The two outlaws became drunk and bragged about killing the two Wyoming lawmen. They were arrested by Miles City deputies Lem Wilson and Fred Schmalsie, then returned to Wyoming for trial. Immediately following an escape attempt in Rawlins, Big Nose George was dragged out of jail and lynched by a mob of 200 men. His corpse was desecrated, with the top of his skull sawed off and skin stripped and tanned and made into shoes.[26]

Miles City did not need to be tamed by a two-gun lawman such as Wild Bill Hickok. But one of the earliest city marshals proved to be one of the most intimidating. Hank Wormwood was a gold prospector who decided in 1878 to take a job as night watchman at Miles City. Soon Hank was a constable, and by 1879 he was town marshal. Hank was tall and he wore his hair long, like an old-time plainsman.[27]

Pioneer photographer L.A. Huffman told of the night when Marshal Wormwood was called to Strader's Saloon, where a drunken soldier was making threats against the lawman. With two dozen other soldiers looking on, Wormwood quietly walked to the swaddy, who had a powerful physique but who was not as tall as the officer. Suddenly Wormwood grasped the soldier's throat with both hands and slammed him against the wall. The soldier gagged as his face turned purple. Marshal Wormwood seized the swaddy's revolver, then forced him into a chair. Leveling a gun at his prisoner, Wormwood warned the other soldiers in the saloon not to interfere as he took his prisoner to Fort Keogh.[28]

Sadly Wormwood, obviously a brave man, died of consumption in 1881 before he could build a reputation as an Old West law officer. Henry was only twenty-nine at his death.[29] But his performance while wearing a badge — a rough physical encounter in a saloon, but no shots fired despite a drawn pistol — fit the usual restrained style of frontier violence in Miles City.

Chapter Six
Miles City Demimonde

*"I suppose these things would shock a lot
of respectable people. But we wasn't respectable
and we didn't pretend to be . . ."*

— Teddy Blue Abbott, cowboy

The term *"demimonde"* entered common usage about the time Miles City became a frontier community. Although originating in France, *"demimonde"* and a related term, *"demimondane,"* held special meaning for the revelers who cheerfully inhabited the saloons and brothels, the dance halls and cribs of Miles City.

Demimonde is a French term referring to women on the fringes of respectable society, and to courtesans supported by wealthy lovers. The term is French for "half-world," and derives from an 1855 play by Alexandre Dumas, *Le Demi-Monde,* dealing with the way that prostitution during that era threatened the institution of marriage. The *demi-monde* was the world occupied by elite men and the women who entertained them and whom they kept. *Demimondane* became a synonym for prostitutes who moved in these circles.[1]

Perhaps it was a stretch to compare the night life of frontier Miles City with the wealthy upper class of France. But Dr. Lorman L. Hoopes, in his detailed account of Miles City, *This Last West,* uses *"demimonde"* and *"demimondane"* freely, and the town's newspapers also found these terms useful and obviously, readily understandable to their readers. It was clear when the *Yellowstone Journal* reported "a portion of the demimonde have been in the habit of going to depot, to meet the trains, at night," that some of the sporting girls were using initiative in seeking out customers as they arrived in town. And who could complain about a "Charity Ball, sponsored by *demimonde* "which helped to raise $100.00 for poor" at Christmas?[2]

The Christmas Charity Ball was held in 1886 at the Roller Skating Rink with "Italian Orchestra" providing dance music and "supper served, 12:30 a.m. by Annie Turner, of restaurant fame; more dancing followed."[3] A decade earlier, when the command of Col. Nelson Miles departed Fort Leavenworth in 1876 for the Cantonment on the Tongue River, Annie Turner followed her customers, leaving Leavenworth and arriving at Milestown in 1877. When Miles City took shape, Annie, an African American madame, erected a single-story cottonwood log building on South Eighth Street. Measuring twenty-five by sixty feet, the parlor house contained a main reception room, saloon, and dance hall, plus an extension in the rear made up of cribs, "tiny one-room shacks where her girls accommodate their clients." In 1882 Annie added another establishment, the "California Restaurant." But after a dance she sponsored in 1882, it was reported that there were "fights plenty." And a couple of weeks later Annie "gave another boisterous fandango last night, at where there were the usual number of drunken fights."[4]

The first parlor house in Miles City was established by Maggie Burns. The Forty-Four House was located on Seventh between Main and Bridge streets. Mag was an excellent businesswoman, and she backed the enterprises of her sweetheart, Bill Bullard, a charter citizen of Miles City. Bullard built a sawmill, served as sheriff of Custer County (1879-1880) and as a bail bondsman, and he opened the Miles City Brewery. Bullard and Mag proved to be a formidable economic duo, and in 1884 she made the largest certificate deposit thus far in Miles City history — $50,000. In 1885 Mag spent $3,500 erecting the "Burns mansion" on Bridge Street.[5]

In the fall of 1884 three N Bar cowboys came into Miles City for a week in town. Teddy Blue Abbott and his two saddle pals quickly found their way to "Number 44", where Abbott was impressed by Mag Burns: "the redheaded fighting son of a gun." Abbott began singing, while the other two banged away on the parlor house piano and a fiddle (which neither could play). Mag protested: "If you leather-legged sons of bitches want to give a concert, why don't you hire a hall? You're ruinin' my piano."[6]

Teddy Blue Abbott stormed outside, saddled his pony *Billy* at a nearby livery stable, and rode back into Number 44 through the front door. Mag slammed the door shut and sent for a lawman. But Abbott rode *Billy* outside through a big open window and galloped down Main Street to the Tongue River ferry. The sheriff ran onto the scene, but the ferryman shouted: "This fellow has a gun the size of a stovepipe stuck in my ribs, and I ain't going to stop."[7]

"It all blew over," reminisced Abbott, "and I came back to Miles City the next night." At Number 44 he became acquainted with Cowboy Annie, who lived at the parlor house. "She was

Cowboy Teddy Blue Abbott enjoyed drinking and indulging in the special pleasures of the Miles City parlor houses — especially at Number 44, operated by Mag Burns and featuring a lady known as "Cowboy Annie." *Courtesy www.findagrave.com.*

the N Bar outfit's girl. They were all stuck on her . . . " Teddy Blue Abbott testified that "Cowboy Annie was the kind who would always dig down and help the boys out." He recalled a night when "we were all together with the girls, drinking and having a good time . . . Cowboy Annie put her gold chain around my neck, and wound her scarf around the crown of my Stetson . . ." She also gave him a pair of white ruffled drawers, which he put on over his pants. "We all paraded down the street, me with my gold necklace and the trimming on my hat and Cowboy Annie's drawers on." Abbott proudly kept the ruffled drawers, and he made up a song "all about Cowboy Annie":

> In Miles City there was a girl with big black eyes —
> and long black hair. With her peachy cheeks and
> Her ruby lips that I love to kiss. Mama —
> Oh, Cowboy Annie was her name.
> And the N-Bar outfit – was her game.[8]

An even more alluring lady of Number 44 was the "Cowboy Queen," Connie Hoffman. Connie was a "leading painted girl" of Deadwood, the raucous gold mining town, during 1879, 1880 and 1882. But like Annie Turner she gravitated to Miles City, as it became a cattle town.

After establishing herself as "Connie the Cowboy Queen," a lovely and popular attraction of the 44 House, she made a move that would have impressed a member of the French demimonde. Connie the Cowboy Queen became the mistress of Sid Paget, a British cattleman who ranged his herd about sixty miles south of Miles City. Paget was an enthusiastic horseman, and since Miles City had a racing track, he provided Connie with her own racing silks — cream and scarlet — as well as horses which were stabled at Charlie Brown's Livery, along with a horse and carriage.[10]

Nannie Alderson was the wife of an area rancher. But when

their ranch home, in their absence, was burned by Indians in 1883, Nannie and her little girl roomed most of the time at the new MacQueen Hotel. There she was presented by considerate ranchers with a baby buggy for walks with her daughter (the buggy would be used in turn by all four of the Alderson children). And there she met Connie the Cowboy Queen.

Mrs. Alderson was a young wife and mother from the Old South, and her father, a Confederate captain, was killed in combat before her second birthday. After she moved with her husband to Montana Territory, he warned her that Miles City "was a pretty hoorah place." But she was a plucky frontier lady, "so I was not surprised by the horses hitched to rails along the store fronts, the wooden sidewalks and unpaved streets, nor was I surprised that every other building was a saloon." When she moved into the MacQueen house, she was not impressed: "It was homey enough . . . , but it was a poorly built, wooden structure: and as the only bath was off the barber shop, I had to bathe in the wash basin . . . The walls were so thin that you could hear every sound from one end to the other, with the result that I overheard several masculine conversations which both fascinated and embarrassed me."[11]

Once every week she took her daughter into the hotel parlor for the morning, while the chambermaid cleaned her room. "One morning . . . ," while she was sewing, "a dark-haired, dark-eyed young woman came into the room. She was striking in appearance and smartly dressed. I had seen her before, and knew she was staying at the hotel . . ." The attractive woman went to her knees and played with the baby. Her name was Connie, and she said that her husband "was on his way up from Texas with cattle." The two women talked about taking the baby on a walk, but the outing never materialized."[12]

Nannie noticed with disapproval that Connie "would go

down to breakfast in the hotel wearing a very beautiful satin Mother Hubbard, hand-painted with flowers, which was hardly appropriate for a public dining room." Connie also "had a habit of going out on the hotel porch after dinner, and talking with the men . . ." Of course, the informal breakfast attire and the after-dinner conversations were normal behavior at a parlor house. Indeed, Connie the Cowboy Queen soon "went straight back to the red light district," reported Mrs. Alderson, who learned Connie's identity from the sister of the MacQueen House proprietor. "It was a most brazen performance," reported Mrs. Alderson, "and scandalized even Miles City."[13]

It is dubious how much Miles City in 1883 was scandalized by Connie the Cowboy Queen or by any of the other women of the town's *demimonde*. Not many of Miles City's early population were married ladies or other decent women, while most of the men enjoyed the company of ladies at the parlor houses and dance halls. "As Mag Burns used to say," quoted Teddy Blue Abbott, "the cowpunchers treated their sporting women better than some men treat their wives."[14]

Mag Burns apparently sold the 44 House to Connie the Cowboy Queen. Connie began to wear a dress embroidered with cattle and horse brands that cost a reported $500. At a Christmas night celebration in 1884 one customer triggered a shot at another celebrant, but the Yuletide gunmen may have been drunk, because no one was hit. Connie changed the name of her establishment to the "Little Club," but the bordello burned down in August 1886.[15]

Another notable member of the Miles City *demimonde* was Kitty Hardiman. By 1879 she owned the "Kitty Hardiman Dance Hall and Saloon" on Park Street. A "magnificent piano" was a feature of the dance hall, and saloon customers were assured an "ample supply" of liquors and cigars. Kitty's establishment was destroyed in a fire of January 7, 1882. She leased the two-story Twenty Seven parlor house on Sixth Street, opening with "a grand supply with music." [16]

A "Madame Greene" opened a dance hall at a property which briefly housed Kitty Hardiman's Dance Hall and Saloon in 1882. Madame Greene's weekly balls proved to be a hit with the Miles City saloon crowds. Teddy Blue Abbott remembered "a very popular *demi-mondaine* by the name of Willie Johnson, who was running Kit Hardiman's honky-tonk..."[17]

In speaking of the Miles City *demimonde*, Abbott related the custom of "marrying" a sporting girl when in Miles City for a week or more. "We all had our favorites after we got acquainted. We'd go in town, marry a girl for a week, take her to breakfast and dinner and supper, be with her all the time. You couldn't do that in other places...," he emphasized. "You couldn't walk around with those girls in the daytime like you could in Miles City."[18] But frontier Miles City, of course, was an easygoing and tolerant town.

"I know of one case where a cowpuncher went in town and gave his sweetheart one hundred dollars, which was all he had in the world, and she kept him all winter," related Abbott. "She lived in a kind of crib behind a saloon, a log shack with just a bedroom and kitchen. He moved in there, and when she had company he slept in the kitchen or in the saloon." Abbott had reflected on these and other happenings. "I suppose these things would shock a lot of respectable people. But we wasn't respectable and we didn't pretend to be..."[19]

Eva Fields was an African American madame who ran a bordello next door to Annie Turner's California Restaurant, but both buildings were destroyed by the fire of August 7, 1886. Fanny French was a successful mulatto madame whose parlor house featured "colored cyprians" and gambling. A fine horsewoman, Fannie French maintained a string of mounts. Perhaps it was in one of these brothels on "coon row" that a African American gentleman known as Israel had a shootout with Dogg Taylor, an African American bartender, over the affections of a Black sporting lady named Cloe. Taylor put a bullet into the leg of his adversary, but Israel's chivalrous effort with a gun won the affections of Cloe.[20]

Another violent episode occurred without warning at Red Ward's Opera House, a two-story brick building at the northeast corner of Park and Bridge streets. Ward's stage usually hosted vaudeville acts which came through town on the Northern Pacific. Like most of the variety theaters in early Miles City, Ward's Opera House featured a low balcony a few feet above the main floor. The balcony was divided into curtained partitions which were visited by scantily clad sporting ladies known as "box rustlers," who tried to sell liquors and personal favors, either behind drawn curtains or in private bedrooms in the rear. One patron of the Opera House was drunk and loud, and when he leaned over the railing of the box, an aggravated passerby reached up and cut the man's throat.[21]

Teddy Blue Abbott was approached by a box rustler at Turner's Theatre. "[S]he had on a little skirt, like a circus girl, and tights that looked like she had been melted and run into them." The box rustler invited him upstairs to buy wine, but five dollars a bottle sounded too steep to the cowboy — even though he was carrying inheritance money and wages in his pistol belt. When she tried to lead him down a dark hall behind the stage, "I thought there might be some kind of a deadfall back there — I was a wise guy — I'd heard those stories."[22]

One evening at Red Ward's Opera House some drunken cowboys in the balcony tossed a loop around a "fat diva" and hauled the husky singer up into their box. She entertained the house by "kicking and emitting unladylike curses." The Cosmopolitan Theatre and Saloon was rebuilt on site in 1882 at Main and Sixth streets. The theater measured sixty-five feet by thirty feet, with boxes above the main floor, in which *demoiselles* (sic) invited one to come up and buy a drink." A large front room facing Sixth Street was a gambling hall: "poker, stud, faro, keno and other games of chance." The stage show usually was "variety comedy," enlivened by a house band. The new version of the Cosmopolitan cost $8,000, but it went up in flames a year later.[23]

When a traveling troupe brought *Uncle Tom's Cabin* to Miles City, the enterprising Charlie Brown hastily converted his lengthy log saloon into a theater. Newspaperman Sam Gordon saw the performance "on a stage constructed of two-inch plank supported on beer cases. The outfit carried its own scenery, such as it was, so that it was possible to give that once famous play a measure of stage glamour, but the nerve-thrilling passage of Eliza over the ice-flooded river had to be cut out, all except the blood-hounds which were held at one side of the stage while they bayed at Eliza, who at the other side flourished a rag-baby as evidence of her safe-crossing and which was no doubt the hound's 'cue' to bark.[24]

Second-rate theatrical and operatic companies began to head west on the Northern Pacific Railroad, stopping off at Miles City with no prior notice but expecting to present "an immediate performance. Any vacant store-room was used . . ." Some of these companies would arrive with no funds, and would have to perform every night for a week to raise enough money to travel to the next town of size. Sam Gordon observed "that the actor people would get pretty chummy with the townspeople, the great craze of the strangers being to ride a cow-pony . . ." With their usual amiability, locals would arrange a horse ride, and "it was always easy to fix them out with a real cowboy escort..." Although there usually were three or four music halls "in full blast every night," the cultural taste of this "man's town... was not notable for its delicacy...."[25]

But if the men of Miles City finally became bored by the indelicate humor and songs at the music halls, or by the aging dramas of second-rate traveling actors and actresses, the saloons and parlor houses always offered drinking and gambling and women. "Poker Nell" was a house dealer and gambler at the Cosmopolitan Theatre and Saloon, and her common-law husband was bartender Harry Bruce. "She knew her cards and was quite a kind woman," reminisced one citizen, who knew her, "and not at all bad to look at...."[26]

Sanborn Fire Insurance maps are available online for the years 1884-1893. Street by street, buildings are outlined and labeled in great detail, including type of construction — frame, brick, log, stone — and interior walls. On one map after another, small buildings are indicated along Sixth Street and vicinity with the explanation, "female boarders." The female boarders,

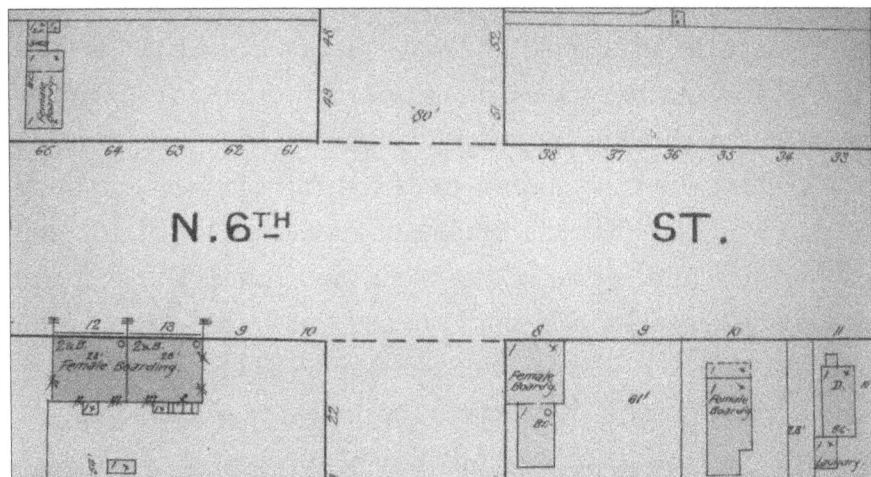

Four of the five Sixth Street buildings on this Sanborn Fire Insurance Map were utilized for "female boarding." (Parlor Houses)

During one of the periodic floods in Miles City, Sam Gordon theorized that "rescue work" was not the primary reason that boatmen rowed after damsels in distress "on the high seas" near a "House of Cheer." *Courtesy Range Riders Museum.*

of course, were sporting ladies who inhabited the parlor houses and cribs of Miles City.[27]

For two decades one of the most famous women of the West was in and out of Miles City, including periods as a "female boarder." Martha Jane Cannary was born in Missouri, probably in 1856, but she became known as Calamity Jane. As a young woman she liked to wear buckskins or leather chaps, topping off her masculine attire with a black slouch hat. The shape of her nose suggests that it might once have been flattened by a fist. She drank to excess, cursed habitually, chewed tobacco, smoked black cigars, worked as a sporting lady — and somehow became the most readily identifiable woman of the Old West.

By 1873 she was working at a bordello near Fort Laramie in Wyoming. In 1875 and 1876 she marched as a teamster with military expeditions, but both times her gender was discovered and she was fired. During the latter year she was thrown behind bars in Cheyenne, and apparently she served other jail terms for disturbing the peace.

Jane ventured to Deadwood in 1876, not long before Wild Bill Hickok was slain there. She claimed a long and intimate — and highly unlikely — association with the famous gunfighter. In Deadwood Jane displayed a classic heart of gold by assuming the unlikely role of nurse. Sometimes working for no pay, she cared for a smallpox patient, a stabbing victim, a dying girl, and a premature baby. A little more in line with her image, Jane also hired out as a bullwhacker, cracking a whip over large teams of oxen.

Martha Jane Cannary, better known as Calamity Jane, restlessly drifted in and out of the red light district of Miles City for twenty years. *Courtesy Range Riders Museum.*

After 1880 she left Deadwood and spent the rest of her life drifting. She first wandered into Miles City in 1882, enjoying the town's Fourth of July celebration but spending a lot of time on a ranch twenty miles west of town. In 1883 she met Teddy Blue Abbott. "She was some sort of madam," said Abbott. "I bought her a few drinks." He put her up to some mischief with a customer, who tried to resist her advances, but Abbott remarked, "she was strong as a bear." In 1885 Calamity

Jane again briefly stayed in Miles City, and she returned in 1894 and again in 1901. During her wanderings Jane lived in shacks and tents and old hotels. The last time Teddy Blue Abbott saw her, she was a sick alcoholic. "I hope they lay me beside Bill Hickok when I die," she told Abbott. She died on August 3, 1903, the twenty-seventh anniversary of Wild Bill's death. And friends arranged to have her buried within twenty feet of Hickok's grave.[28]

Calamity Jane restlessly appeared among the *demimonde* of Miles City for two decades. Annie Turner, "Queen Bee" of the *demimonde* of Leavenworth, established herself in Old Milestown in 1877. Connie Hoffman came from the gold boomtown of Deadwood to become the Cowboy Queen of Miles City. Maggie Burns built Number Forty Four, the first parlor house in Miles City and the headquarters of the lovely *demimondane*, Cowboy Annie. Kitty Hardiman ran her Dance Hall and Saloon on Park Street. There were alluring box rustlers who tempted the customers at the Cosmopolitan and other variety theaters. And members of the Miles City *demimonde* sometimes "married" their favorite cowboy for a week or more. The *demimonde* of the French upper class may have operated on a more sophisticated and luxurious level, but the masculine society of Miles City enjoyed the earthy, frontier version of *demimonde*. *Demimonde* was part of the rough charm of Miles City.

"If you were good to them," said cowboy Teddy Blue Abbott, they'd appreciate it, "and believe me, they had ways of repaying a kindness . . ."[29]

Chapter Seven
From Fire Canoes to Bullwhackers to the Iron Horse

"The coach creaked, jolted, swayed, crawled uphill, made reckless dashes downwards, crossed ice bound streams, performed all kinds of stunts except turning over, halted thrice a day for meals, changed horses frequently and drivers occasionally."

— Rancher John Clay

The transportation frontier was on prominent parade at the adjacent communities of Miles City and Fort Keogh during the late 1870s and the early 1880s. There were freight wagons drawn by horses or mules or oxen, which required the services of whip-popping bullwhackers. There also were stagecoaches, iconic symbols of western travel. Troopers as well as civilians rode horseback, and so did a great many Montana women. The Northwest Pacific Railroad reached Miles City in the fall of 1881, revolutionizing the transportation of freight and passengers in a frontier that suddenly was no longer remote.

But before the railroad, before covered wagons and stagecoaches, there were smoke-belching, sternwheel paddleboats called "Fire Canoes" by the Native Americans. The western version of steamboats proved essential to the creation of Fort Keogh and to the military campaigns of the region, and the most renowned riverboat captain was an admired figure at the fort and at Miles City.

Rivers were the first highways of the northwestern frontier, and the boats which carried men and supplies unlocked the key to the transportation frontier of the Northwest. Lewis and Clark and their rugged companions saw swarms of beaver and other fur-bearing animals, and soon trappers and traders eagerly traversed the Missouri and other great rivers — including the swift-flowing Yellowstone.

Dugout canoes, fashioned from large cottonwood trees, appeared on the western rivers. So did flatboats and Mackinaws, propelled by oars. These craft often were seventy feet in length and could carry ten tons or more of cargo. Keelboats were just as large and utilized not only oarsmen but also poling and sails. Then, from the Mississippi and other eastern rivers came steam-driven paddleboats, even though they were underpowered and drew as much as six feet of water.

But by the 1860s an improved river steamer was undergoing rapid evolution, vessels tailored for the often shallow western

The famous riverboat *Far West* transported wounded troopers from the Little Bighorn to Bismarck, a 710-mile journey in fifty-four hours. The spars at the bow allowed steamboats to "grasshopper" across sandbars. Note that firewood has been cut and stacked for the last leg of the journey. *Courtesy Far West (River boat)," Wikipedia, the Free Encyclopedia.*

waters, for the sandbars, snags, clusters of dead trees, strong currents, ice, and reef outcroppings just below the surface of the rivers. Simple but powerful wood-burning engines gave off a constant clatter as well as the stench of smoke and engine oil. Steam boilers often exploded, or engine fires broke out. Of the approximately 300 riverboats which sank on the Missouri or Yellowstone or other rivers of the Northwest, most were victims of engine malfunction, along with "racks" of deadwood which could rip the bottom out of a steamer.

These shallow-draft riverboats drew as little as fourteen inches of water when unloaded. Loaded they carried 200 tons of cargo or more. To lighten these boats, the decks, bulkheads, support timbers, and almost all of the upper works were constructed of pine or poplar, rather than oak, which is a heavier wood. The western riverboats, therefore, were not as well-constructed, not as large or as handsome as the floating palaces of the Mississippi River. These riverboats distributed the weight of cargo and firewood and passengers upward (although the tall superstructure could be tossed about by high winds on the rivers).[1]

The boat design featured an open-sided main deck just above the waterline. Ten cords or more of firewood were stacked on the main deck, along with barrels and sacks and crates of cargo. Most crew members found a place to sleep on deck, and so did the passengers who paid only a cheap fare, and who had to bring their own food aboard. Next on this multi-tiered vessel was the boiler deck, dominated by cabins which could accommodate about thirty passengers, and which included a main cabin for dining or drinking or cards. At the next level was the hurricane deck, upon which rested the wheelhouse and two small boats on davits.

The riverboat captain often operated the wheel, and a

pilot provided relief at the helm. There was an engineer or, frequently, two, one for each of two engines. Firemen worked four-hour shifts feeding cordwood to the engines. Deckhands and roustabouts (nicknamed "roosters") were constantly on duty, and grabbed sleep and food (responding to the shout "Grubline") when they could. The steward — and perhaps a cabin boy or two — tended the dining room and the passenger cabins.

A vitally important member of the staff was the bartender, who usually paid a fee to operate the liquor concession. Most crew members drank heavily as they performed hard, dirty, smelly, and often dangerous duties. Many passengers also imbibed throughout the journey.

But it should be remembered that the riverboat travelers and the crew members who traversed wilderness streams, who entered lonely but magnificent country — these were men and women who experienced the excitement and the adventure of America's western frontier. For three centuries Americans traveled boldly and with a sense of exhilaration into the frontier West, and they were not easily frightened by discomfort or hardships or perils.

Riverboats usually tied up at night, because the shallow rivers choked with sandbars and driftwood were too dangerous for nighttime travel. Often the boats tied up near a stand of timber or a rack of driftwood. Wood would be cut and carried aboard, and during the evening crew members would fill the fireboxes with freshly cut firewood. At least one or two stops would be made each day at wood yards, where ten cords or more would be purchased. While the wood was being loaded, passengers would walk the gangplank ashore to set foot on new western ground.

In July 1876, in the wake of Custer's defeat at the Little

Bighorn, Col. Nelson A. Miles was ordered to lead his troops from Fort Leavenworth to the area of conflict. After boarding a large riverboat at Yankton, Miles noted with satisfaction: "As we moved up the river... tokens of respect and confidence were shown at every village we passed, and those demonstrations were answered by the cheers and hurrahs of the men..."[2]

During the journey up the Missouri, progress periodically was interrupted by "frequently coming upon a sand bank, owing to the constant changes of that turbulent river." At this point the process of "grasshoppering" was utilized: "the great shafts [spars] in the bow of the boat were lowered, and with the engines the boat was partially lifted off, while the stern wheel was reversed and then another effort was made to find the main current of the waters." But the "weary roustabouts," probably fortified by alcoholic refreshment, seemed to keep their sense of humor.[3]

And Colonel Miles was struck by the camaraderie of his men as they journeyed into a desolate and dangerous wilderness. "In the evening they gathered on the upper and lower decks and amused themselves by listening to the songs of those of their number who were fortunate enough to have fine voices...." With a hint of nostalgia, Miles recalled "a quartette of our men singing the most jolly and rollicking songs that they knew, with a chorus of laughter joined in by their comrades." Any trepidation about soon advancing against recently victorious Sioux and Cheyenne warriors was eclipsed by the adventure of entering a new land aboard a newfangled transportation device. Thus the military frontier met the transportation frontier.

Upon reaching Fort Buford, the steamboat tied up for the night, then at daybreak entered the Yellowstone River, which maintained a powerful current against the boat. Miles observed that "the Yellowstone pours into the Missouri a vast volume of muddy, yellow water . . ." The Yellowstone rises near the Continental Divide in northwest Wyoming and flows north, forming the Yellowstone Lake in today's Yellowstone National Park. Yellowstone Lake is at an elevation of 7,731 feet, but after two downward plunges it flows northeast across Montana 671 miles until joining the Missouri River.[4]

The most famous riverboat captain on the Missouri and Yellowstone rivers was Captain Grant Marsh, an intrepid figure who would become well-known at Fort Keogh and Miles City. Captain Marsh was a tall man with a strong physique and a stern, determined visage. Born in New York in 1834, Marsh was twelve when he became a cabin boy on an Allegheny River steamer. Marsh later worked as a deckhand before becoming a mate and student pilot under Samuel Clemens, who later renamed himself Mark Twain and wrote a classic account of riverboating, *Life on the Mississippi*. With the outbreak of the Civil War in 1861, Marsh was employed on riverboats hauling Union troops and supplies during the Shiloh and Vicksburg campaigns. After 1862, however, Marsh turned his abilities as a river pilot and captain to the lucrative traffic on the Missouri. Gold had been discovered in Montana in 1862, and spectacular profits were available to captains who could bring passengers and freight from St. Louis to Fort Benton. Late in the 1866 season he guided the river steamer *Louella* from Fort Benton to St. Louis with a boatload of miners who carried $1,250,000 in gold. Other risky trips delivered badly needed supplies to lonely military posts.[5]

In 1871 Captain Marsh, Commodore Sanford B. Coulson, and other partners formed the Coulson Packet Company. The firm's fleet of riverboats featured the *Far West*, especially constructed to meet the challenges of the Missouri and Yellowstone and lesser rivers of the northwestern frontier.[6]

The most famous riverboat captain on the Missouri and Yellowstone Rivers was Grant Marsh, who became well-known at Fort Keogh and Miles City. *Courtesy National Archives*

With Captain Marsh at the helm, various riverboats made legendary journeys. But his most acclaimed feat came in 1876, when the *Far West* had been chartered by the army to accompany the columns as a supply boat, troop transport, and floating headquarters vessel during the expedition against the Sioux and Cheyenne. Custer and his immediate command were slain to a man, while there were numerous other casualties as the Seventh Cavalry battled desperately for survival at the Little Bighorn. Captain Marsh piloted the *Far West* to the Little Bighorn and took aboard more than fifty wounded troopers (one man died en route and had to be buried ashore). Marsh then steered through the Bighorn River, raced down the Yellowstone (passing the future site of the Tongue River Cantonment and Milestown) to the Missouri River, then on to Bismarck near Fort Abraham Lincoln, home of the Seventh Cavalry. From June 30 to July 3, 1876, his 710-mile river journey took only fifty-four hours. Marsh was at the wheel of the *Far West* almost the entire journey, and of all of his record-setting feats, delivering the casualties — and news of the Custer disaster — remains his most renowned accomplishment.[7]

During the campaigns of the next few years, Captain Marsh was in constant demand with the army to steer chartered boats into battle areas. As he readied the *Far West* for a mission led by Colonel Miles and the scout, Buffalo Bill Cody, some of the deckhands grumbled about being exposed to danger from ashore. General Alfred Terry brought these complaints to Captain Marsh, who was indignant.

"Well, I'll tell you, General," replied Marsh angrily, "you have always given me a big salary [during this period Marsh was paid $1,200 per month] and the preference over all other steamboat men in government work. So have the other army officers for the last ten years. I consider it a compliment to be called on for this kind of service and I prefer that you consider my boat a soldier and send it where you want it until you get through with it. Anybody among my crew who don't like it, can quit and go ashore."[8]

Captain Marsh left the Coulson Packet Company after the season of 1877 and brought his skills and reputation to the Leighton - Jordan Company, which maintained a warehouse at Miles City. Commanding the sternwheeler *F.Y. Batchelor*, Captain Marsh journeyed to and from Miles City in 1878, 1879, 1880, and 1881. His fame preceded him, and he became a familiar face around Miles City. And while the *F.Y. Batchelor* was tied up at Miles City, the crew members brought their sailors' version of recreation to the local saloons and bordellos.[9]

The greatest of all riverboat men of the northwestern frontier, Captain Marsh generated stories from those who knew him. Buffalo Bill Cody told of riding downriver with Marsh at the wheel of the *Far West*: "with a full head of steam [we] went flying past islands, around bands, over sandbars, at a rate that was exhilarating." Cody heard Nelson Miles ask Marsh if he could land the boat near a large tree within view.

"Yes, sir; I can land her there, and make her climb the tree if necessary," came the confident reply."[10]

Twenty-four riverboats arrived at the military docking

facilities as the construction of Fort Keogh proceeded rapidly. Fourteen paddlewheelers made the journey the next year. But with a large garrison in place, there were only nine riverboats during 1879 and the same number the next year. With the Northern Pacific completed to Miles City in the fall of 1881, only seven steamers arrived, and in 1882, with trains running all year, riverboat traffic declined to just three.[11]

A tangible reminder of the riverboat contribution to the frontier community soon was built on Main Street. In 1880 Jimmy Dance erected a modest hotel near the northeast corner of Seventh and Main. The previous year the river steamer *Yellowstone* had wrecked on the Buffalo Rapids about twelve miles down the Yellowstone River from town. Lumber was salvaged from the wreckage and worked into the two-story "Steamboat Building." And the Range Riders Museum later would display the ship's big bell, which today stands prominently in front of the main building.[12]

During the first few years of its existence, Miles City showcased a memorable frontier transportation activity just before it disappeared. Freight long had been hauled by wagon

Freight wagons were essential for overland transportation.
Courtesy Range Riders Museum.

trains drawn by mules or horses or oxen. When oxen were utilized, these "bull trains" were driven by "bull whackers." Journalist Sam Gordon realized that he was viewing one of the final performances of bull trains and the colorful bullwhackers as these frontiersmen and their great beasts headed to the Diamond R corner, an early Main Street landmark which took up a block catercorner from the Cottage Saloon, the soldiers' favorite. The Diamond R Overland Freight Company was a major freighting enterprise during the 1870s which owned 116 wagons and 700 oxen. When the Diamond R changed hands, the purchase price reputedly was $75,000. There were about seventy employees, including a number of crusty old bullwhackers.[13]

"[I]t was surely a sight," recalled Gordon, "when a 'Diamond R bull-train' pulled into Main Street en route to Fort Keogh from Glendive or Buford, loaded with government freight." Glendive was more than eighty miles downstream on the Yellowstone, and often freight-laden steamboats could not draw closer to Fort Keogh. Fort Buford was located at the confluence of the Yellowstone and Missouri rivers, even farther to the northeast.

This well-known example of a Concord stagecoach, the "Deadwood Stage," is on display in the transportation building of the Range Riders Museum. *Photo by the author.*

"With from eight to twelve yoke of 'bulls' to a team," described Gordon, "hauling two and often three wagons loaded to the top and with a real 'bull-whacker' walking along back by the wheelers, a pageant was paraded . . . of a phase of civilization that was just then passing off the stage. Ranking with the experts in any vocation, the professional bull-whacker in action was a most satisfying sight, and the 'pull' up Main Street was their dress parade."[14]

The stock of the bull-whacker's whip was about six feet in length, with a long lash "and a 'popper' on the end that would bite out a bunch of hair wherever . . . it landed on some poor, patient brute's hide . . ." Western railroads steadily reduced the role of bull trains. And Gordon regarded mule trains as unworthy of comparison with bull trains. "The mule-train was never as interesting or as picturesque as the bull-train....The 'mule-skinner' rode a wheeler and guided his team with a jerk line. Any loafer could do that," concluded Gordon.

He seemed gratified to have watched the finale of the bullwhackers played out in the Yellowstone Valley and on the

A bull train making its way down Main Street to the Diamond R Corner.
Courtesy Range Riders Museum

Main Street of Miles City and at the Diamond R Corral. "Here the faded glory of the 'bull-train' was for a time restored and here it vanished for good . . ."

Gordon wrote with admiration that "it took an artist to pilot a string of bulls along a side-hill road with a top-heavy load . . ." And while he admired the bullwhacker's artistry as a teamster, "It was a dog's life as far as the comforts and amenities went. The menu rarely went beyond black coffee, sour-dough bread and 'sow-belly' fried in a skillet in its own grease thickened with flour, and of camp shelter there was none . . ." Bullwhackers "were too tired at night" to set up a camp, and they moved out early each morning.

Bullwhackers relished displaying their unique skills in front of townspeople along Main Street. "It was a fleeting glory though," admitted Gordon, "for an hour after the train had been parked all hands were too drunk to tell their own names . . ." The Diamond R park was littered with the unconscious bullwhackers as they slept off the effects of their all-too-rapid celebrations.

During the early years of Fort Keogh, army columns were constantly in the field campaigning against Native American warriors and tribal villages. Despite the lack of good roads, wagons played an important role in supplying troops in the field. But when attack while in the field seemed likely, civilian teamsters proved hard to hire. A campaign in October 1876 — soon after the Custer debacle — required five infantry companies and eighty-six supply wagons. With a serious shortage of civilian drivers, Lt. Col. E.S. Otis had to instruct a number of infantrymen as replacement teamsters. Even after the railroad arrived, wagon transport was necessary whenever the troops marched into the field.[15]

Of course, lack of roads slowed the supply wagons.

Therefore, in order to more effectively control the countryside and to facilitate the growth of commerce, the army made a sustained effort to build roads and bridges. The noted scout Yellowstone Kelly selected the road site between Fort Keogh and Deadwood. A road between Fort Keogh and Bozeman was completed during the winter of 1880-81. Company K of the Fifth Infantry, commanded by Medal of Honor recipient Capt. Frank Baldwin, had the standing assignment of maintaining the 110-mile road between Fort Keogh and Fort Custer. A Miles City newspaper referred to the road efforts of the army as the "pick and shovel drill." Most important of all was the long "Fort Keogh Road," which connected the wilderness outpost with Bismarck, D.T., and to the world beyond. Mail deliveries flowed along the Fort Keogh Road, and so did civilian traffic.[16]

The army constructed more than 800 miles of roadway leading in and out of Fort Keogh — and Miles City. The army was tasked with maintaining these roads, and both construction and road maintenance were done at government expense. Through the network of roads in the vicinity, the army played a vital role in bringing civilization to the Miles City area.

Before the railroad arrived, mail deliveries by stagecoaches were essential in connecting Fort Keogh and Miles City with the outside world. Stagecoaches carried passengers from point to point (or "stage to stage", thus the term "stagecoach") as well as light packages of freight, along a prescribed route. But the real moneymaker for stagecoach lines was mail, and there was fierce competition for U.S. mail contracts.

Stagecoaches were used in Europe during the 1600s. In the 1700s stagecoaches ran in the New England colonies and between Philadelphia (the largest colonial city — 40,000 population) and New York (the second largest at 20,000). There were different types of American stagecoach vehicles, but in

Concord, New Hampshire, the Abbott-Downing Company designed and carefully crafted a conveyance ideally suited for the rugged roads of America. In England, coaches were ponderous with a steel spring suspension system. But the rigid metal springs served up a hard, uncomfortable ride, and if a spring broke en route, coaches in the vast West were disabled indefinitely.

In 1826, however, Lewis Downing and his assistant, J. Stephen Abbott, produced the first Concord stagecoach, featuring a breakthrough suspension system. Anchored to iron standards at the four corners of the vehicle frame were "thorough braces," four-inch-wide, six-or-eight-ply belts of thick steer-hide leather. Thoroughbraces formed a cradle upon which the body of the coach was suspended, and which functioned as shock absorbers for passengers.[17]

"Our coach was a great swinging and swaying stage ... an imposing cradle on wheels." In 1861, Mark Twain accompanied his brother on a stagecoach trek from St. Joseph, Missouri, to Carson City, Nevada. Twain reveled in the adventure. "We jumped out and stretched our legs every time the coach stopped [usually to change horses], and so the night found us still vivacious and unfatigued."[18]

Noted rancher John Clay described a winter coach ride through the mountains of Wyoming. The frigid journey took seventy-two hours with "the thermometer marking zero every night." Clay and his traveling companion were "clad in big overcoats and covered with buffalo robes. The coach creaked, jolted, swayed, crawled uphill, made reckless dashes downwards, crossed ice bound streams, performed all kinds of stunts except turning over, halted thrice a day for meals, changed horses frequently and drivers occasionally."[19]

Concord coaches usually were drawn by six horses, and

teams were changed approximately every twelve miles, although some relay stations of out of Miles City were only a few miles apart, probably because of topography — a steep mountain or a difficult stream crossing. Most stopovers took only ten minutes, just long enough to change teams. These stations consisted merely of a cabin and a barn or corral, and were run by a bachelor station hand or two. But every fifty miles or so stood a "home station," a more substantial cabin with a kitchen and sometimes even a sleeping room — with bunks or at least pallets for the floor. Station stops were given picturesque names such as "Frozen to Death" or "Big Porcupine" or, more descriptively "Pompey's Pillar" or "Terry's Landing."[20]

The Fort Keogh Road headed due west cross country from Bismarck and Fort Abraham Lincoln to the confluence of the Powder River and the Yellowstone, a distance of 251 miles. The route then angled southwest alongside the Yellowstone about 40 miles to Fort Keogh and Miles City. The road from Fort Keogh to Fort Custer was 109 miles, while it was 325 miles from Miles City to Bozeman (which required a fare of $42).

Because of the improved and lighter suspension system of the Concord Coach, the framework and body of the vehicle were altered for better balance, along with tall, carefully crafted wheels. There were interior seats for nine passengers: one seat facing inward from the front, another from the back, and a bench in the middle. If more than nine passengers needed to be accommodated, some could sit on top. An iron rail was fitted to the top, either to secure baggage or to provide handholds or footholds for outside passengers. Additional baggage could be carried in the "boot," a compartment across the rear that was enclosed by black oiled leather for weatherproofing. The top of the coach stood eight feet and six inches above ground, and the elevated driver's seat was only two feet from the top, affording visibility and better handling. The running gear was made from hand-forged iron and quality woods. When leaving the factory in Concord, new coaches were brightly painted with multiple coats and polished with spar varnish. A Concord Coach weighed about 2,500 pounds and the purchase price was over $1,000. A smaller vehicle with open sides and a much lower center of gravity was a "Mud Wagon," which carried fewer passengers and less freight.

Despite long distances and cramped legs, the adventure-loving Mark Twain spoke for many other Concord passengers in describing a western ride. "The stage whirled along at a spanking gait, the breeze flapping curtains and suspended coats in a most exhilarating way; the cradle swayed and swung luxuriously; the pattering of the horses' hoofs, the crackling of the driver's whip, and his 'Hi-yi! g'lang!' were music."[21]

The stagecoach became an iconic vehicle of the Old West, and was a background feature in countless Western films. Stagecoaches were part of the street and road traffic in and around Miles City, and the frontier citizens of the town — and of Fort Keogh — always were eager to see the mail arrive, as well as travelers. It was four days from Bismarck to Miles City along the Fort Keogh Road, and of course there were other stagecoach routes as well.[22] In the early years of Miles City, the Concord Coach was a familiar and welcome sight.

The transportation frontier climaxed spectacularly with the completion of transcontinental railroads, each of which had a network of branch lines. America's industrial revolution was well under way before the Civil War, and that titanic conflict sped up industrial progress, at least in the North. During the latter decades of the nineteenth century America experienced a surge of industrialization, and railroads became the nation's greatest industry.

The discovery of gold in California launched serious efforts to build a railroad to the Pacific. During the 1850s the federal government surveyed four possible routes across the West. Selection of one above the others was stymied by the fact that southern congressmen insisted upon a southerly route, while northern congressmen wanted a line that would connect with the railroad network in their section. Although government support of railroad construction, through federal loans and land grants, already had been utilized on eastern railroads, a western line could not be commenced until a route was determined. This impasse finally was solved by the outbreak of the Civil War.

Throughout the war northern congressmen, in the absence of their southern counterparts, were free to pass all manner of legislation that had been delayed by the bitter sectional conflict of the 1850s. In 1862 the *Pacific Railroad Act* was approved by Congress and signed by President Lincoln, an enthusiastic supporter of railroads. Two railroad companies were chartered, each incorporating the magic word "Pacific." The Union Pacific (UP) would lay track westward from Omaha, while the Central Pacific would struggle eastward from Sacramento across the Sierra Nevada Mountains. Companies were organized and equipment was assembled, and construction began in 1864. With the war raging, progress was slow. But when hostilities ended, capital, materials and manpower (the UP employed 10,000 men, America's largest work force, matched by the Central Pacific) became readily available. From generals to sergeants, veteran leaders were available, including men with vast experience with logistics. The driving of the Golden Spike in 1869 announced completion of the nation's first transcontinental railway.

But the nation already had given its congressional blessing

to half a dozen similar projects, including the Northern Pacific (NP). The Northern Pacific Railway Company was chartered on July 2, 1864. Congress granted the Northern Pacific a potential 60 million acres of land to connect the Great Lakes with Puget Sound on the Pacific, thus erecting trackage that would open vast undeveloped areas to farming, lumbering, ranching, and mining, while connecting Oregon and Washington to the rest of the United States.

Laying track into Miles City for the Northern Pacific Railroad in November 1881. *Courtesy Range Riders Museum*

But for six years backers of the Northern Pacific struggled to find financing, and ultimately only forty million of the possible 60 million acres was claimed. Not until February 15, 1870, was groundbreaking finally held, at Carlton, Minnesota, west of Duluth. When the bold financier Jay Cooke became involved in the company there was a flurry of construction. By 1873 tracks were laid to present-day Bismarck, and simultaneously rails also were being laid in the Pacific Northwest. But Jay Cooke over-invested in the NP, and in September 1873 Cooke and Company went bankrupt. The resulting Panic of 1873 triggered one of the nation's worst depressions, and by 1875 the Northern Pacific declared bankruptcy.[23] But in 1874 and 1875 the Seventh Cavalry, operating out of Fort Abraham Lincoln, provided protection to Northern Pacific surveying crews. The NP project was not yet abandoned.

A change of leadership brought capitalist and promoter

Henry Villard to the Northern Pacific presidency in 1881. Villard had developed major interests in the Pacific Northwest, and he was determined to complete the railroad. Ultimately there would be 6,800 miles of track, including branch lines, and even though turbulence would continue at the NP leadership level, by the fall of 1881 tracks were approaching Miles City.[24]

"The railroad — the Northern Pacific — had been coming for several years and in the late fall of 1880 had gone into winter camp at Glendive [more than 80 miles northeast of Fort Keogh on the Yellowstone] and was expected at Milestown reasonably early the next fall."[25] Sam Gordon thus expressed the matter-of-fact attitude held in Miles City toward the railroad. When Miles City came into existence only a few years earlier, the Northern Pacific was stuck nearly 300 miles away in Bismarck. Now it was still stuck, over eighty miles away in Glendive. Once construction resumed in 1881, however, word came to Fort Keogh — and to Miles City, of course — that NP tracks would arrive in November.

"Naturally Milestown set out to celebrate the occasion with befitting ceremony," reminisced Gordon. Miles City always had been a good time party town. A reception committee was organized.

"The reception was a failure," admitted Gordon with astonishment. "The only time . . . that Milestown had failed to pull off a public function with *due eclat*. The committee had done its work well. There were washtubs full of sandwiches, kegs of beer on tap, pails of dill pickles and many other snicks and snacks that we supposed the track crew would relish and certain eminent citizens were even loaded with 'remarks' on the "the potentiality of this significant occasion,' but they never got a chance to uncork."[26]

The hard-working track crew came into sight about noon,

and the crew boss let his men pause long enough to have "a bite and a sup" before being set to work again. So the citizens had to "eat our own sandwiches and drink our own beer." — without listening to "torrents of eloquence" from the lineup of speakers.

The assembled crowd did get to see the military-style precision that had been perfected, then passed on to other rail outfits, by Union Pacific track layers. Materials for a mile of track required forty cars. Union Pacific surveyor William Bell described the process of track laying: "Less than thirty seconds to a rail for each gang, and so four rails go down to the minute! . . . Close behind the first gang come the gaugers, spikers, and bolters, and a lively time they made of it. It is a Grand Arrival Chorus that these sturdy sledges are playing . . . It is in triple time, three strokes to a rail, four hundred rails to a mile . . ."[27]

The Northern Pacific added an element to the track laying. Sam Gordon watched "the big black horse who drew the iron car who knew his business as well as any of the humans he worked

A Northern Pacific steam engine with a 4-4-0 wheel arrangement is pulling a train through eastern Montana. *Author's collection.*

with . . ." The horse was named "Old Nig," and he repeatedly pulled a dump car loaded with two rails and eighteen ties from a supply car to the tracklayers.[28]

The Diamond R had contracted with the Northern Pacific to supply ties. A large sawmill was located at a slough off Seventh Street and adjacent to the Tongue River. This sawmill provided most of the lumber used in construction in Miles City and at Fort Keogh. To satisfy the need for logs for railroad ties, the Diamond R sent a big logging and tie-making crew into the woods up the Tongue River in anticipation of the June Rise in rivers. A boom was erected so that the timber would be funneled toward the sawmill, rather than swept down the Yellowstone. The Northern Pacific built a spur from its main line down to the sawmill.[29]

To celebrate Thanksgiving shortly after the arrival of the NP tracks, the Northern Pacific staged a remarkable feast on November 24. Invitations were sent to prominent citizens by J.B. Clough, Engineer of the Yellowstone Division. The N.P. Engineering Department was noted for its fine cooks and for the excellent cuisine it provided itself — by rail, of course.

NPR
Your presence is desired at Headquarters of Engineering Department, Yellowstone Division, N.P.R.R. at Miles City, November 24th, 1881, to join with the Engineers of the Division at a Thanksgiving Dinner.
Yours cordially
J.B. Clough
Eng. Yellowstone Div.
R.S.V.P.

THANKSGIVING DINNER
At
ENGINEERS HEADQUARTERS
N.P.R.R. MILES CITY
November 24, 1881

SOUPS
Oyster, Vermicella, Vegetable

OYSTERS
Fried, Scalloped, Raw

FISH
Trout, Salmon

MEATS
Roast Turkey, Roast Chicken, Roast Beef
Roast Mutton, Venison, Mountain Sheep
Buffalo Loin, Elk, Chicken Pie

VEGETABLES
Mashed Potatoes, Sweet Potatoes, Squash
Cabbage, Tomatoes, Celery

SIDE DISHES
Peaches, Cherries, Jelly, Plums
Cranberries Apples

PASTRY
Apple Pie, Lemon Pie, Peach Pie
Cranberry Pie, Strawberry Pie

CREAM
Lemon Vanilla

CAKES
Fruit Cake, Pound Cake, Jelly Cake
Sponge Cake, Dough-nuts

FRUITS
Peaches, Apples, Strawberries
Coffee, Tea, Chocolate[30]

The menu of this sumptuous feast, held only a matter of days after the Northern Pacific reached — and promptly forged on past — Miles City and Fort Keogh, was a pleasurable reminder of what a railroad could bring to a frontier community. As Sam Gordon reflected, "our primitive life" and "the splendid isolation we had enjoyed" was at an end, for good or ill" – we never could decide which."[31]

NP President Henry Villard pushed his work force to complete a mile and a half of track per day. By September 1883 the east and west lines neared connection at Gold Creek, a stream between Butte and Missoula where there had been a minor strike in the 1850s and 1860s. Villard the promoter decided to label the Northern Pacific ceremony "Gold Spike at Gold Creek." Four passenger trains were chartered to bring dignitaries from the East, headlined by General Ulysses S. Grant, Civil War hero and former president (1869-1877).[32] Now the Northern Pacific was a transcontinental railway with a host of branch lines.

Even before the Gold Spike was driven at Gold Creek, economic transformation was coursing across eastern Montana and Miles City. Indeed, Miles City was in the process of acquiring what became its most deeply embedded identity.

Chapter Eight
Cattle Town

"The cowpuncher was a totally different class from those other fellows on the frontier. We was the salt of the earth, anyway in our own estimation..."
— Cowpuncher Teddy Blue Abbott

Miles City eagerly embraced the colorful and lucrative role of the cattle town during the 1880s. By November 1881, when the Northern Pacific reached Miles City and thus provided a rail connection with eastern slaughterhouses, cattle towns already were scattered across most of the cow country of the West. In 1867 Abilene, Kansas, became the rip-roaring terminus of the Chisholm Trail from Texas. During the 1870s this most famous of cattle trails gave birth to other lively cowtowns in Kansas, including Wichita and bloody Newton and, during its wild 1880s heyday, "Border Queen" Caldwell, on the Kansas-Oklahoma line. Also during the 1870s and 1880s, Dodge City on the Western Trail earned its designation as the "Bibulous Babylon of the Plains." Farther north on the Western Trail was Ogallala, Nebraska, which boasted its own Boot Hill and Front Street.

These and other railheads welcomed cattle herds to their stockyards and cowboys to their saloons and bordellos. Such a setting was a natural fit for frontier Miles City, as soon as cattle and cowboys and railroad tracks managed to reach Montana.

Slowly at first, and then with rapid acceleration, the required elements of a "cattle town" closed in on Miles City from the west, from the east, and, inexorably, from the south. Cattle first were driven into Montana in small herds from Oregon and

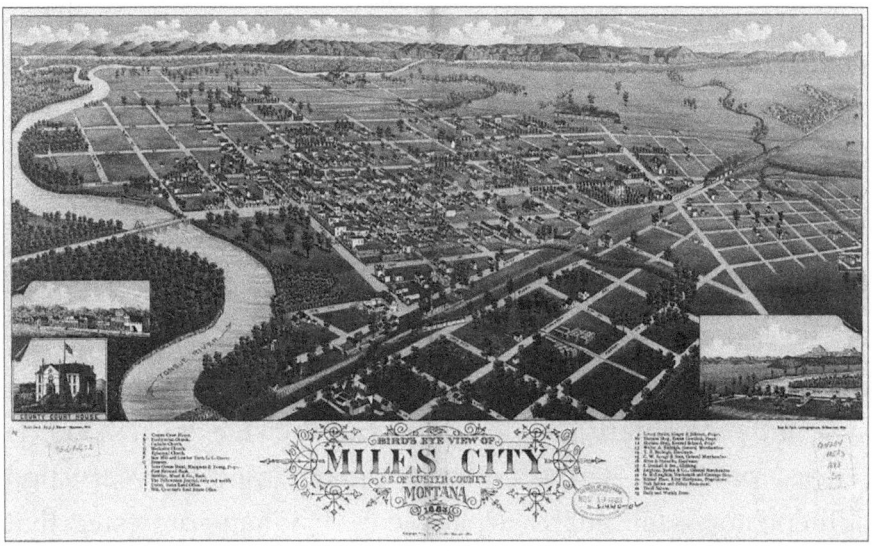

This bird's eye view was produced in 1883, when Miles City was entering its prime as a frontier cattle town. Use of a magnifying glass provides a wealth of detail about the streets and buildings. *Author's collection.*

Idaho, and were nicknamed "Westerners." Cattle ranching was practiced on a limited scale in deep mountain valleys of western Montana, where there was winter shelter and ample water. And in 1868 600 Texas steers were driven into Montana from the south and east, along the dangerous Bozeman Trail by the bold cattle pioneer Nelson Story, who armed his company of drovers with repeating rifles and led the expedition through hostile territory.

The "Beef Bonanza" was at its height in the early 1880s, and by 1883 it was estimated by the US Department of Agriculture that there were 600,000 head of cattle in Montana Territory, as well as 500,000 sheep. As late as 1880 the majority of cattle remained in Montana's western ranges. But by 1883 Texas cattle drives from the south shifted the center of Montana cow country to sprawling Custer County. A popular saying described Miles City as "a circle of 150 miles of the richest grassland around."[1]

One drover remembered that "in 1883 all the cattle in the

world seemed to be coming up from Texas. On the trail we were hardly ever out of sight of a herd . . ." While hunting stray horses he rode to the top of a hill, and "I could see seven herds behind us; I knew there were eight herds ahead of us, and I could see the dust from thirteen more of them on the other side of the river."[2]

Miles City already was in development as a town, and there were astute businessmen in the community who were alert to opportunities. A stockyard was erected on the Yellowstone River side of the Northern Pacific bridge. But the stockyard stood on federal property — the ten-mile square military reservation still encompassed nearly 64,000 acres. Civilians protested that the facility would have to be on military property somewhere near both Miles City and to the railroad tracks. Ultimately a fine stockyard was erected about 750 yards west of the N.P.R.R. bridge across the Tongue River, standing on the Fort Keogh Military Reservation.[3]

Veteran cowpuncher Teddy Blue Abbott stated flatly that "Miles City had the best stockyards and, besides that, it appealed to Wyoming cowmen because they could follow the Tongue River in and have good grass and water all the way."[4]

Abbott was a keen judge of cow country conditions during the heyday of the cattle frontier. Although born in England in 1860, when he was ten he emigrated with his family to the United States. The Abbotts settled near Lincoln, Nebraska, and he began tending to the modest herd of cattle his father acquired. He also earned a little money caring for the cattle of his neighbors. Although still a boy, he was captivated by the cowboy's way of life. Soon he was working "with Texas cowpunchers, the most independent class of people on earth, and breathing that spirit."[5]

While still in his teens, Abbott helped drive a cattle herd

up the Western Trail in 1879 and again in 1881. In 1883 Abbott came up once more driving a large herd into Montana. During these years, he was in and out of Miles City, always enjoying the night life. Once, after being injured doing ranch work, he was sent into Miles City to recuperate. Immediately he felt better, and a memorable eight days in town ensued. In 1884, while working a beef roundup, he learned of the approach of two big herds belonging to the N Bar Ranch. (Niobrara Cattle Company, owned by the Newman brothers of St. Louis). Abbott quit the roundup to accompany the combined herd of 4,000 cattle 300 miles farther north: "It was all new country up there and I would like to see it . . ." Indeed, that seemed to be "every cowpuncher's ambition in the eighties," according to Abbott. "They all wanted to get to the Yellowstone."[6]

The trip did not disappoint the cowboys: "It was a cowman's paradise — big grass, all kinds of game except buffalo, and we had it all to ourselves."[7]

Proud of his status as a cowboy, Abbott was convinced that the proliferation of cowboys in and around Miles City improved the society of the growing cattle town. "Before we got there it was an army post and buffalo hunters' town . . ." The soldiers, of course, remained garrisoned at Fort Keogh, and buffalo hunters and bullwhackers also were still around town when Abbott and other cowboys began to arrive with cattle herds. "Cowpunchers and buffalo hunters was a rough class — they had to be, to lead the life they led."[8]

"The buffalo hunters didn't wash, and looked like animals. They dressed in strong, heavy, warm clothes and never changed them. You would see three or four of them walk up to a bar, reach down inside their clothes and see who could catch the first louse for drinks."[9]

"The cowpunchers was a totally different class from these

other fellows on the frontier," pointed out Abbott with a touch of self-satisfaction. "We was the salt of the earth, anyway in our own estimation, and we had the pride that went with it. That was why Miles City changed so much after the trail herds got there; even the women changed. Because buffalo hunters and that kind of people would sleep with women that cowpunchers wouldn't even look at, and it was on our account that they started bringing in girls from eastern cities, young girls and pretty ones. These girls followed us up [the trails], and we would meet old pals in new places."[10]

While cowpunchers were busy upgrading the quality of sporting ladies in the bordellos, businessmen of Miles City developed the commercial needs of a cattle town. Aspiring ranchers needed capital to build open range spreads, both large and small. As early as 1878 A.R. Nininger & Co., a general merchandise store located at the northwest corner of Main and Sixth, provided a safe to keep sums of money and valuables as a service to customers. More banking services were offered in 1879, and by 1880 C.W. Savage organized the Miles City Bank in an addition to the existing building. Nininger served as bank president, Savage as vice president, and Alexander Hardy was cashier. The bank was organized with a capital of $100,000. In 1882 the Stebbins-Post-Mund Bank opened on Main Street, soon occupying a large brick building. Stubbins-Mund & Co. also operated banks in Billings and Livingston, Montana; in Deadwood, Central City and Spearfish in Dakota Territory; and in Buffalo in Wyoming Territory. By 1884 the Miles City enterprise was incorporated for $100,000 and was named, fittingly, the Stockgrowers National Bank. Another suitably named enterprise was the Merchants & Drovers Bank, although the name was changed in 1882 to the First National Bank. The authorized capital was $250,000, while the president was

Miles City businessman Joe Leighton and the vice-president was charter citizen George H. Miles. Located next door to the famous Cottage Saloon, the First National Bank soon moved into a two-story brick structure.[11]

Hotels tried to attract customers with labels such as the Drover's House, built near the N.P. Depot in 1882, and the Ranchman's Hotel, a two-story brick structure which opened in 1884 at the southeast corner of Main and Sixth. But the largest and most notable hostelry in Cowtown Miles City opened in 1882 as the Inter Ocean Hotel (a popular name which was used, for example, by the most prominent downtown hotel in Cheyenne). The big frame structure was built by Major William MacQueen who soon renamed it the MacQueen Hotel.[12]

The MacQueen Hotel was located at the end of Park Street, just across from the N.P. Depot. The hotel faced northeast. A two-story veranda dominated the northeast front, and extended partway down the long southwest side. The owner constantly expanded the hotel, which was the largest in Miles City and which, like the cattle town, continued to grow. A deep brick

The MacQueen House from Park Street.
Courtesy Range Riders Museum.

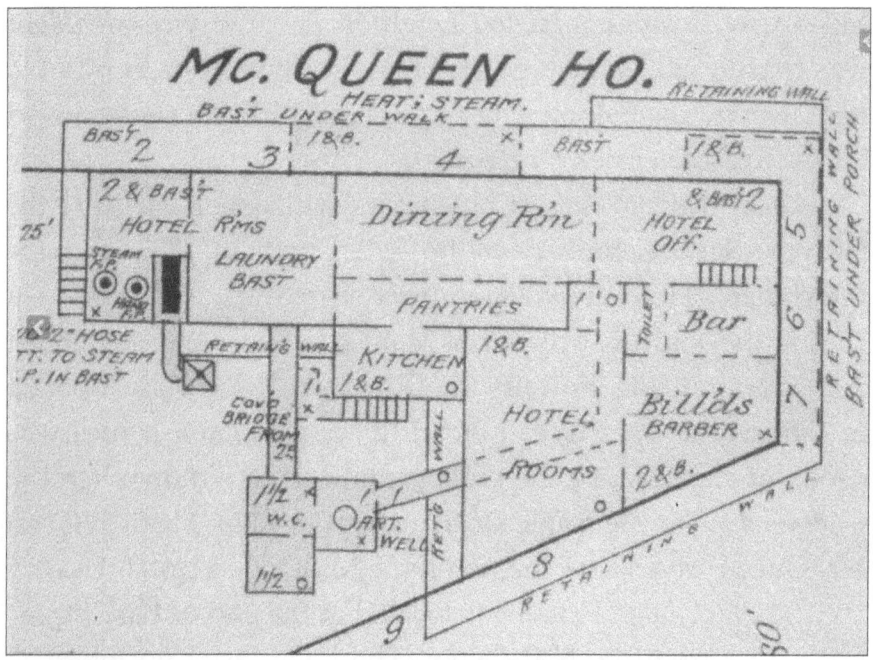

The Sanborn Fire Map detailed the layout of the first floor of the MacQueen House. *Enlargement of Sanborn Fire Insurance Map of Miles City.*

basement was built beneath a new addition, and the main floor billiard hall became a reading room when the billiard tables were moved to the big basement. There was an artesian well on the premises, along with a bath house, which was adjacent to the hotel barber shop. The dining room measured forty feet by seventy feet, and for appropriate occasions was converted to a ballroom. By 1886 there were eighty-six guest rooms, each with small heater and an electric bell and carpet. There were folding beds, marble-topped dressers, tables and commodes. The hallways featured red velvet carpet and tall, gilded, framed mirrors. The MacQueen Hotel became the social center of Miles City, hosting countless dinners and dances, and serving as headquarters of the annual meetings of the Montana Stockgrowers Association.[13]

An essential element that made up a cattle town, that gave it flavor and liveliness, was cowboys. And as one cattle herd

MacQueen House stationery envelope.
Author's collection.

after another was driven to the eastern ranges of Montana, more and more cowboys galloped into Miles City to carouse in the saloons and bordellos. They announced their presence by spurring their cow ponies hell-for-leather down Main Street, whooping and firing their six shooters into the air.

"A lot of the saloon men didn't care much for all the shooting," recalled Teddy Blue Abbott. "And in later years it got to be the custom for the fellows to take off their artillery when they came to town. They would leave it at the livery barn with their horse and outfit."[14]

In one recollection, Abbott may have revealed why there was so seldom lethal shooting inside the saloons of Miles City. "I carried a chip on my shoulder for years, and I got into my share of fights," he admitted. He had been wearing a sixgun since he was a teenager, and at first he thought he wanted to kill someone. But his saloon fights never went beyond fisticuffs. "Because I was always so happy when I was drinking. I loved everybody and everybody seemed to love me . . . I was looking for fun, and that I believe was the case with nine-tenths of them." Looking for fun — that was the primary motivation of most recreational activities in Miles City, and that seems to be why the level of violence rarely went beyond fists or boots.[15] Indeed, cow town businessmen often employed law officers to restrain gunplay on the assumption that Eastern cattle buyers would shy away from rawhide communities where they might be shot.

The *Bozeman Avant-Courier* observed that "Miles City was a wide open town that was very permissive of the frontier good times, but would not tolerate major violence . . . The whole community worked together to keep lawlessness to a minimum. The hard cases were dealt with severely, and this succeeded in an atmosphere of good times and horse-play where all could come to town and let go; otherwise, the holier-than-thous and the unmerciful law and order types would have taken over and driven all away to seek fun elsewhere."[16] Gun violence therefore played only a limited role in the new Montana cowtown.

Miles City would find itself permanently branded by the cowboy culture that invaded the community in the 1880s. The frontier long had attracted adventurous youngsters, and now adolescents and young men eagerly signed on to become cowboys on northbound trail drives. Booted and spurred, clad in big hats and chaps and bandanas, cowboys were high-spirited, proud, and tough.

Cowboys possessed the majestic feeling of height and power and superiority of mounted men throughout history, but their work was hard and dangerous. Cattle drives bristled with hazards, particularly treacherous river crossings (especially the hard-flowing Yellowstone) and stampedes. Longhorns were quick, ornery beasts capable of inflicting harm upon men and horses. Cowboys had to ride, rope and master athletic skills to handle these cantankerous creatures.

The risks, of course, held appeal for young men and boys and even many women. So did the big hats and the high-headed riding boots and the brightly colored bandanas. All of these items had a purpose. The broad-brimmed hat offered protection from sun, rain, hail, sleet, and snow. The crown could double as a water bucket or grain bag for the cowboy's horse. A bandana served as a dust filter, especially for cowboys riding "drag" at the rear of a herd. A cattle herd generated considerable body heat, and days often were hot in Texas, so a bandana could be dampened and worn beneath the hat crown to cool the head. On frigid days in Montana a bandana could be pulled up as a face cover. In case of a horse wreck or other injury, a big bandana could be used as a sling or as a tourniquet. And during an evening on the town, a bright bandana could be knotted in clever fashion to add a touch of cowboy (or cowgirl) decoration.

By the 1880s Texas cowboys were familiar figures on the streets and in the saloons and brothels of Miles City. *Courtesy National Archives.*

Cowboys on a trail drive or working a roundup needed several horses in their "string." These animals were tended by a "horse wrangler" in a *remuda*, a word derived from Spanish and meaning "remount" or "extra horses." A similar term on the northwestern ranges was "cavvy" (from *caviada*). In the frontier northwest "buckaroo" often was substituted for cowboy. *Vaca* was the Spanish word for cow, and a *vaquero* worked cows, so a slight mispronunciation produced the term "buckaroo."

The cowboy's (or buckaroo's) workbench evolved into a large stock saddle descended from the Spanish war saddle. The broad saddle horn in front was used to wrap the loose ends of *la reata* — "the rope," later anglicized to "lariat." *Dar la Vuelta*, or "to throw over," described the movement, a phrase anglicized to "dally." Cowboys would dally the end of the lariat around the saddle. "Dally" — "remuda" — "lariat" — "cowpuncher" — and many other terms were new to Miles City. Much of the terminology already had been introduced to Montana, but with the flood of herds — and cowboys — from Texas, the terms and attire quickly became commonplace. And the cultural exchange was two-way- Texas cowboys had not heard of "shindies" or "swaddies," or "honyockers" or "coffee-coolers" until reaching Miles City and Fort Keogh.

The sudden demand in Montana for heavier saddles featuring a broad saddle horn spawned a vigorous new industry in Cowtown Miles City. Individual craftsmen began to build saddles in one-man shops scattered around town, often located in the side blocks between Main Street and the railroad tracks.

In 1883 a twenty-one-year-old saddlemaker named Al Furstnow arrived in Miles City from Cheyenne. Furstnow worked for about a year at the Goettlich Harness & Saddlery Shop on Main Street before moving on to a shop in Omaha. Soon he was back in Cheyenne, then moved to California before returning in 1894 to Miles City. After working briefly for the Robbins and Lenoir Saddlery, he recognized how the business was flourishing in Miles City, and in August 1894 he opened Furstnow's Saddle Shop. Soon rancher Charles E. Coggshall purchased a half-interest, and by 1896 Coggshall and Furstnow purchased another local shop, thus adding materials and workmen. Furstnow and Coggshall continued to expand, until the partners split into two firms in 1899.

Now competitors, Furstow and Coggshall adapted assembly line manufacturing techniques they had observed in eastern factories, while assigning master saddlemakers to personalize design and decoration. Dozens of craftsmen worked in each of the two shops. Coggshall supervised the development of the Montana Saddle Tree, as well as other innovations. By 1910 Furstnow was producing 800 saddles per year, and he moved into a new building having employed Al Moreno, a talented

Miles City became a major producer of the cowboy's workbench, heavy duty saddles. These and many more saddles are on display at the Range Riders Museum. *Photo by the author.*

In 1916 craftsmen at the Miles City Saddlery built 1,937 saddles. *Courtesy Range Riders Museum.*

stamper from California.

Meanwhile, Clem Latham, a Coggshall employee, acquired two partners. Latham and his partners bought out Charles Coggshall and, in 1909, formed the Miles City Saddlery Company. By then Fort Keogh had been demilitarized, but the vast military reservation and remaining buildings had been converted to the U.S. Army's largest remount station. The Boer War (1899-1902) generated enormous demand for cavalry and draft horses, as did the outbreak of the Great War (1914-1918). As many as forty saddlemakers found employment in Miles

City during this peak period, and every man who could sit a horse was hired by the Remount Station. In 1916 the Miles City Saddlery produced a record 1,937 saddles. Many of these handsome saddles are on display today at the Range Riders Museum and in the History Room at the Miles City Saddlery building on Main Street.

Cowboys enjoyed galloping into town to begin an evening or, better still, several days and nights of recreation in Miles City after a long cattle drive or several months spent on an outlying ranch. When two cowboys raced down Main Street to see who had the fastest cow pony, or when two or three cowboys from different outfits challenged each other to see who was the quickest calf-roper, or when the best riders tried to find who could stay longest aboard a bucking horse, cowboy competitions developed into sport. Such challenges often took place on the Fourth of July, the most popular of all frontier holidays. And the subsequent riding and roping "events" took place in the street — the first step toward rodeos, derived from

Rodeo in Miles City on the Fourth of July, 1903.
Courtesy Range Riders Museum.

Miles City Roundup, 1919.
Courtesy Range Riders Museum.

the old *vaquero* term, *rodear*.

Western communities began to stage cowboy competitions in the 1880s, the very years that Miles City developed into a cattle town. Pecos, in West Texas, celebrated the Fourth of July in 1883 by penning longhorn steers on the courthouse square and inviting area cowboys to rope and to race their horses. The next year Payson, Arizona, began staging "August Races," which also featured cowboy roping contests. On May 1, 1885, a "grand cowboy tournament" was held at Caldwell, Kansas, and cowboy Charles Siringo was awarded "a fine silver cup" for his steer-roping performance. In Arizona the Prescott Frontier Days began on July 4, 1888, and today proclaims itself the "oldest continuous rodeo."[19]

Although cowboys first raced their horses on the streets of Miles City, a racetrack soon was laid out on the edge of town. On the Fourth of July ranch families came into Miles City and parked their wagons in a circle to form a crude arena. Bucking horses were "eared down" by a cowboy in front who bit the animal's ear as a distraction while the hopeful rider mounted the bronc. Later, bucking chutes were built, along with a roofed grandstand. Miles City soon organized a parade to precede the riding and roping events. The community had a brass band, and cowboys — as well as cowgirls — rode in ranch attire in the parade. Mounted Native Americans, also in colorful garb, added to the march, and so did trick ropers. By 1913 the parade and the increasingly organized rodeo events had acquired an official name, the Miles City Roundup. The Roundup quickly became the most popular event of the year in Miles City. Now Miles City had an annual rodeo, and the community boasted everything necessary for a cattle town.[20]

But in years to come there developed an even more spectacular livestock event than a rodeo, and the celebration would acquire a title even more eye-catching than its rodeo label. The "World Famous Miles City Bucking Horse Sale" would permanently identify the Montana community with roots back to a Wild West of hard-riding cowboys, of ranchers and cowgirls, of good times with a western flavor.

Chapter Nine
The Montana Stockgrowers Association

"A true 'cow town' is worth seeing - such a one as Miles City, for instance, especially at the time of the annual meeting of the great Montana Stock-raisers Association."
— Theodore Roosevelt

When Miles City became a cattle town during the early 1880s, open range ranches simultaneously came into existence throughout the grasslands of eastern Montana. In 1882 50,000 head of Montana cattle were sold to eastern markets, in addition to three million pounds of wool. By 1883 there were "approximately six hundred thousand head [of] range cattle, M.T." plus sheep and horses. Also in 1883 the *Miles City Press* listed twenty-seven "large-cattle herds, on ranges tributary to Miles City." This list ranged from 600 to 700 head all the way to 60,000 head (owned by M.H. and W.A. Murphy), 45,000 head on Goose Creek (owned by L.S. Grinnel), 40,000 head on the Powder River (owned by Brown, Hallett and Co.), and 20,000 head on the Powder River (owned by Freuen Cattle Co.).[1] The other twenty counts listed also were rounded off, and thus were at best estimates — generous estimates — of the growth of open range ranching during the early boom years.

With vaguely counted herds all over eastern Montana, these open range operations were plundered by rustlers. Montana pioneer Granville Stuart organized, with partners, the DHS Ranch at the base of the Judith Mountains in 1879. Near the DHS, managing partner Stuart soon "discovered one rancher whose cows invariably had twin calves and frequently triplets, while the range cows in that vicinity were nearly all barren and would persist in hanging around the men's corral." Stuart and other cattlemen visited the ranch and threatened "to hang the man if his cows had any more twins."[2]

But by 1883, cattle and horse thieves regularly raided Montana's open range outfits. Indeed, throughout the entire West stockmen recognized the need to organize themselves against stock thieves, while also attempting to coordinate open range roundups and other ranching practices. The Cattle Theft Association, formed in 1865, was the first of several New Mexico associations formed to battle rustlers. In Silver City the Southwestern Stockman's Association was established in 1881. At the 1884 meeting of the Northern New Mexico Stock Growers Association, there were 125 ranchers in attendance. That same year the Central New Mexico Cattlegrowers Association was founded in Albuquerque. In 1886, in Hillsboro, the Sierra County Cattle and Horse Protection Association was established, one of several county associations formed in New Mexico.

In Colorado the Stock Growers Association employed stock detectives to deal with thievery, as well as supervising branding and attempting to protect Colorado ranges from Texas cattle. Founded in 1867, the organization's name was changed to the Colorado Cattle Growers Association. In northeastern Colorado the Williams River Cattle and Horse Growers Association surely had an easier task than its northwestern Colorado counterpart, the Brown's Park Cattle Association, which operated in one of the most popular outlaw hideout regions in the West.

Forty Texas ranchers, increasingly alarmed at cattle thievery, met in Graham in 1877 to establish the Stock-Raisers Association of Northwest Texas. (Scornful of the relatively mild term "rustlers," association members preferred "damn cattle thieves.") As the organization grew in effectiveness and membership, the name was changed to the Cattle Raisers

Association of Texas, then to the Texas and Southwestern Cattle Raisers Association.

The Wyoming Stock Growers Association had its origins as a countywide organization in 1871, but grew to become the most powerful stockmen's association in the West. By 1885 there were 363 dues-paying members. The WSGA employed stock detectives and maintained a stock-exchange in Cheyenne. At abandoned Fort Fetterman, the old post hospital was utilized for injured cowboys and other ranch employees. In Cheyenne the luxurious WSGA Cheyenne Club was modeled on the gentleman's clubs of eastern cities. And when the Wyoming Territorial Capitol Building was erected, the offices of the Wyoming Stock Growers Association were just down the hall from the Governor's Office.

Therefore, when the ranching frontier exploded across eastern Montana, ranchers of the area had numerous examples of how to organize against stock thieves, as well as how to deal with roundups and how to delineate grazing areas. Groups of ranchers met in the early 1880s, and the Eastern Montana Protective Association convened in Helena on August 15 and 16, 1882. The following year, the Eastern Montana Stockgrowers Association organized in Miles City on April 17, 1883. It was reported that 279 members were present, and Miles City responded to the visitors with bunting and banners throughout the town. A parade was staged, led by a brass band from Fort Keogh. Dancing and other entertainment was provided.[3]

Another group, the Montana Stockgrowers Association, featured cattlemen from western Montana and originated in Helena. By April 1884 the MSGA and the EMSGA had decided to merge under the name Montana Stock Growers Association. Granville Stuart reported that 429 stockmen gathered on April 20, 1884, in Miles City. "The citizens' welcome was as cordial as it had been the previous year and the same splendid entertainment offered," related Stuart.⁴

There were growing concerns that the enormous ranges in eastern Montana were becoming overcrowded, and that "tick fever" from Texas had become a menace. There were important organizational matters to arrange. But the most pressing item was to combat rustlers.

Granville Stuart recognized a strong sentiment among the ranchers "to make the penalty for stealing so severe that it would lose its attraction." Two ranchers from western Dakota Territory, an ambitious Frenchman titled the Marquis de Mores and Easterner Theodore Roosevelt, vigorously urged "a rustler's war."⁵

Stuart counseled a less obvious approach. "I openly opposed any such move and pointed out to them that the 'rustlers' were strongly fortified, each of their cabins being a miniature fortress." Stuart went on to warn that "every man of them was a desperado and a dead shot," and that a fight would result in heavy casualties, along with murder trials for the death of any suspects. Although many younger members still wanted to raid the rustlers, the association voted to take no action.⁶

Granville Stuart, pioneer cattle rancher of Montana and presumed leader of "Stuart's Stranglers." *Courtesy Montana Historical Society, Helena.*

But Stuart and other determined ranchers cleverly were setting up the rustlers, while avoiding any public commitment to violent activities. Learning that at the Miles City convention the MSGA had decided not to make any decisive move, the "jubilant" rustlers "returned to their favorite haunts and settled down to what promised to be an era of undisturbed and successful operations."[7]

The thieves were busy on unsupervised ranges during the MSGA's roundup, but they were being watched by stock detectives. The rustler opponents met at Stuart's cabin on the DHS Ranch after the close of the spring roundup. Although Stuart's role in subsequent events is hazy, the fourteen vigilantes who sallied forth became known as "Stuart's Stranglers."

On June 25, 1884, two rustlers stole seven horses from the string of a cowboy working for J.A. Wells. Rancher Bill Thompson gave chase, fatally wounding one thief, then capturing the other man after a chase of six miles. Incarcerated in a stable, the rustler was seized by vigilantes that night and hanged. On July

Rancher Theodore Roosevelt advocated "a rustler's war" at the 1884 meeting of the Montana Stockgrowers Association in Miles City. *Courtesy Roosevelt Nature and History Association, Medora, N.D.*

3, word reached the DHS that known rustler Sam McKenzie had been sighted nearby with two stolen horses. The entire DHS crew was mobilized, and soon a bound McKenzie was brought to the bunkhouse. After dark he was taken outside and hanged, and the next day the swaying corpse was "the center of an admiring concourse of flies."[8]

After hearing of McKenzie's lynching, two other rustlers rode the next day into Lewistown, several miles south of DHS headquarters. Arrogantly spoiling for trouble with Fourth of July celebrants, Red Owen and Rattlesnake Jake Fallon drunkenly ignited a shootout in Lewistown's only street. One citizen was killed and another wounded, but both outlaws were gunned down by an angry populace. Before the shooting stopped, Rattlesnake Jake had been hit more than nine times, while Red Owen took eleven wounds, "any one of which would have proved fatal."[9]

On that Fourth of July, the "vigilance committee" divided into two groups and sought out more desperados. One group confronted rustlers Billy Downs and California Ed at their hideout at the confluence of the Missouri and Musselshell rivers. Evidence at the hideout included butchered meat, a pile of fresh cowhides, and twenty-six horses with familiar brands. Downs and California Ed were hanged in a grove of cottonwoods. The second group of vigilantes found Brocky Gallagher and Red Mike driving a stolen band of horses across the Missouri River. After a ten-mile chase, they were overtaken and hanged.

The vigilantes then decided to assault the principal outlaw stronghold on the Missouri, fifteen miles east of the Musselshell. A large log cabin, loopholed for defense, sat adjacent to a stable and corral, and a tent made of wagon covers was located one hundred yards away beside the riverbank. On the night of July 8 five vigilantes surrounded the cabin and three others covered the tent, while a ninth man held the horses. The vigilantes opened fire at dawn, when a man emerged from the cabin. Six desperadoes scrambled out of the tent: one escaped clean; the "boss outlaw," John Stringer, was cornered and went down fighting; and four men concealed themselves in the brush, later to fashion a log raft and drift downriver. The five men inside the cabin resisted stoutly, until the building was set ablaze. As the outlaws burst out of the burning cabin, they were shot down.

The next morning the four men on the raft were captured by the military, then turned over to a deputy U.S. marshal. However, at the mouth of the Musselshell a party of masked vigilantes took the prisoners from the deputy. Two log cabins stood nearby, only a few feet apart. A log was placed between the cabins, supported by each roof, and the four rustlers were hanged from the log. Then the cabins "caught fire" and burned to the ground, cremating the four corpses.[10]

Nineteen rustlers had been killed, and stock theft in the area declined immediately. The vigilantes deliberately kept their identities obscure, but they were dubbed "Stuart's Stranglers," and Stuart was elected next president of the Montana Stockgrowers Association. "Once I heard a woman accuse him of hanging thirty innocent men," related Teddy Blue Abbott, who had married one of Stuart's daughters. "He raised his hat to her and said, 'Yes, madam, and by God, I done it alone.'"[11]

Stuart had not done it alone. He later wrote that there were fourteen vigilantes, "and they were all men who had stock on the range and who had suffered at the hands of the thieves." Stuart insisted that not a single victim "was hanged for a first offense," and he scoffed at talk that cattlemen had hired "'gunmen' to . . . drive the small ranchers and sheepmen off the range."[12] Other rumors exaggerated the number of lynch victims to "thirty innocent men"[13] or even more. Theodore

Roosevelt praised the "clean sweep" of the "'stranglers,' [a] happy allusion to their summary method of doing justice," but he qualified his approval: "several of the sixty odd victims had been perfectly innocent men who had been hung or shot in company with the real scoundrels, either through carelessness and misapprehension or on account of some personal spite."[14] Another rancher placed the "total number of outlaws hung or shot in eastern Montana and western Dakota [at] sixty-three."[15] When Teddy Blue Abbott rode for a rancher prominent in the affairs of the Montana Stockgrowers Association, he liked to joke that he "was working for the Montana Assassination. They knew what I meant."[16]

Granville Stuart bristled at accusations of imported gunmen and arrogant ranchers and innocent victims. "There was not one man taken on suspicion and not one was hanged for a first offense. The men that were taken were members of an organized band of thieves that for more than two years had evaded the law and robbed the range at will." Although Stuart described Montana cattlemen as the most "peaceable and law-abiding a body of men as could be found anywhere," they felt forced to take action because the "civil laws and courts had been tried and found wanting."[17]

One of the deadliest vigilante actions in the history of the cattle frontier had been at least partially planned by a faction of the Montana Stock Growers Association during their organizational meeting at Miles City in April 1884. Certainly the trap was set at Miles City, when the membership in open session voted down a campaign against rustlers, who now felt free to continue and expand their program of livestock theft. The unexpected counterattack by vengeful ranchers produced nearly a score of rustlers who were either shot or hanged and, according to Granville Stuart, "put a stop to horse and cattle stealing in Montana for many years."[18] Certainly organized rustling was curtailed — a triumph for the fledgling Montana Stockgrowers Association.

Members of the MSGA enthusiastically returned to Miles City in April 1885. Theodore Roosevelt observed that "the whole place is full to overflowing, the importance of the meeting and the fun of the attendant frolics, especially the horse-races, drawing from the surrounding ranch country many hundreds of men of every degree, from the rich stockowner...to the ordinary cowboy who works for forty dollars a month. It would be impossible to imagine a more typically American assemblance," the future president remarked about his fellow ranchers, " . . . and on the whole it would be difficult to gather a finer body of men . . ."[19]

Working behind the scenes to bring the ranchers and their wives and area cowboys into Miles City were members of the Miles City Club. In the fall of 1883 at a meeting in the dental office of Dr. C.S. Whitney, a dozen young businessmen and professionals organized the Miles City Club as a "Social resort," according to pioneer newspaperman Sam Gordon. A second-story suite of rooms was rented in the Stebbins Block on Main Street. Membership grew rapidly, and the club offered its facilities as "a place of pleasant sojourn while in town, to the very considerable number of cattlemen then utilizing our ranges, who coming here as strangers found a cordial welcome in the club and an easy way of getting acquainted with our businessmen."[20]

To Gordon the Miles City Club "took on the flavor of a stockman's organization and its red-letter days were the three days in April of each year when the annual convention of the Montana Stockgrowers Association met here [the yearly meeting quickly expanded from one day to three] . . . On these occasions the club set forth every day of the session a royal banquet of 'roast pig' and appreciate 'trimmings' . . ." On a trip to New York City, Gordon was in the office of a railroad official and mentioned that he was from Miles City. "Miles City," mused the railroad administrator. "That's the place where they have the roast pig, isn't it?" Gordon was "very much pleased that our fame and hospitality had traveled that far . . ."[21]

A special feature of the MSGA meeting each year was the Stockmen's Dance, held for years in the MacQueen Hotel. And there always was a parade and a brass band and decorations. The Miles City Club headed the efforts to offer prime entertainment for the cattlemen — and to keep the annual meeting in Miles City, rather than in competing towns. The Miles City Club continued to grow, in time leasing the entire second floor of the new Leighton block. And in 1904 the Miles City Club moved into the second story of the Wibaux block, in the 700 block of

The MacQueen House from the front. The MacQueen was the largest hotel in town and was filled with cattlemen during the annual convention of the Montana Stockgrowers Association. *Courtesy Range Riders Museum.*

south Main Street.

"There never was but one Pierre Wibaux . . ." admired his foreman, C.O. Armstrong, "and there is no other that can fill his place."

Today his "place" is represented by a statue which overlooks the range where he proved that he was one of the most progressive and successful ranchmen in the West. This remarkable frontier rancher also became a key citizen of Miles City. Headquarters of Wibaux's W-Bar Ranch was over eighty miles northeast of Miles City. But Glendive was only a little more than twenty miles from W-Bar headquarters, and at Glendive there was a Northern Pacific rail connection to Miles City. Wibaux frequently was in Miles City, engaging in business and real estate and becoming a man of affairs in the cattle town.

Pierre Wibaux was born in 1858 in Robaix, France. His father and grandfather owned and operated textile mills and dyeing works, and Pierre received a good education. An adventurous youth, he joined the French Dragoons when he was eighteen. After a year's service, he traveled extensively in Europe, then was sent to England to study the textile industry. There he met and fell in love with Mary Ellen Cooper. He also encountered numerous Englishmen who were excited about the Beef Bonanza of the American West.

In 1882, once again driven by a sense of adventure, Pierre determined to seek his fortune by becoming a frontier cattleman. His father was angry that Pierre was turning his back on the family business, but he gave his son $10,000 as his inheritance. Pierre journeyed to Chicago, a bustling meat-packing center, where he spent weeks at the stockyards absorbing information about desirable livestock qualities, market conditions, and other information about the cattle business.

In Chicago he met another Frenchman eager to cash in on

the range cattle boom, the visionary Marquis de Mores. Wibaux accompanied the Marquis to the Badlands of western North Dakota, near the Northern Pacific Railroad. A short distance to the west, in eastern Montana and western North Dakota. Wibaux found Beaver Valley to be an ideal site for cattle ranching. Varied timber and deep draws offered protection from winter storms; grazing was excellent; and in unusually dry summers, when streams stopped running, spring-fed ponds always contained water.

In June 1883 Wibaux formed a partnership with Gus Grisy, also a native of Robaix. Grisy and Wibaux devised the GW and G Anchor W brands, then announced plans to place 10,000 head of cattle along Beaver Creek. They bought 160 tons of native hay for the coming winter. Property for a ranch headquarters was acquired on Beaver Creek twelve miles north of the community of Beaver, and a log cabin with a sod roof was built.

Wibaux returned to France in the fall of 1883 to raise more capital, from his family and from other French businessmen. Then he went to Dover, England, where he married Mary Ellen "Nellie" Cooper. Returning to Beaver Valley with a bride and investment capital, Wibaux bought out his partner, paying Grisy 10,000 francs ($2,000) and letting him keep 500 head of cattle. Wibaux kept 500 cows, 475 steers, 200 yearlings, and fifty horses. He adopted a W-Bar brand, which gave his ranch its name.

Unlike many open-range ranchers who grazed only steers for market, Wibaux ran mixed cattle from the beginning, and he provided hay for winter feed. Wibaux thus avoided the terrible winter losses which bankrupted other ranchers, and W-Bar cattle emerged from each winter in better condition to be fattened for sale. Indeed, in 1887 Wibaux began raising the first alfalfa in the region. He upgraded his cattle herd with Shorthorn bulls, most notably in 1897, when he purchased 350 in Canada. He improved his horse herd by bringing in Kentucky stallions and Texas mares, hoping to combine Kentucky speed with the toughness of Texas cow ponies.

In 1885 Pierre and Nellie Wibaux moved from their log cabin into a frame ranch house which measured eighty-by-thirty-six feet. A low-roofed porch extended across the north side. The large rooms boasted wallpaper and carved wood, and Pierre's billiard and wine room was a special favorite of visiting ranchers and cowboys. Water for the house and lawn was piped in from a windmill tank, while the washroom featured a sink fashioned from a four-foot-long sandstone. Painted white, the Wibaux home was inevitably called the "White House." Also in 1885 a stone barn was erected.

Shortly after moving into the White House, Nellie Wibaux gave birth to a son, Cyril. During her first Christmas at the ranch, although still living in the log cabin, Nellie donned an evening gown and cooked a turkey, plum pudding, and mince pie. An admirable hostess in the White House, she once rode out to a district roundup to invite the crew to an open house, where she offered beer, wine, and cigars. When Pierre found it necessary to spend the winter of 1886-87 raising capital in France, Nellie presided over the ranch from the White House. When a female servant committed suicide, Nellie persevered in carrying out her duties.

Pierre was as handsome as his wife was beautiful. He fenced and boxed, and was an excellent horseman. His favorite mount was named *Tic-Tac*, but he also enjoyed driving a team of spirited trotters. Wibaux industriously participated in the range activities of the W-Bar, and he traveled widely to investigate market conditions and to pursue sale or purchase possibilities. Because the White House was twelve miles from town, Pierre built an office with sleeping quarters in Wibaux. (The village on Beaver Creek beside the Northern Pacific first was called Beaver, but in 1884, Gus Grisy, who was serving as postmaster, changed the name to Mingusville, after himself and his wife, Minnie. In 1895, however, a petition effort headed by Pierre renamed the town Wibaux.)

Wibaux was out of the country during the destructive winter of 1886-87, but his animals were in good condition and his losses were minimal. Wibaux boldly capitalized on a situation that drove a majority of other ranchers out of business. He realized that the range suddenly was no longer overstocked, and that the death of so many beeves would drive prices upward. Reasoning further that cattle which had survived were especially hardy, Wibaux aggressively purchased remnants of many devastated herds. In one season he made large profits from sales, while adding 16,000 head of cattle to his herd.

By 1890 his herd had expanded to at least 40,000, and for the next several years he branded 10,000 to 12,000 calves annually. It was estimated that at its peak during the 1890s the W-Bar herd numbered 65,000 head of cattle, as well as 300 saddle horses. (In 1889, when Wibaux was offered $60 apiece for any of his horses, he sold his entire herd of 630 head, including colts, then purchased 300 remounts in a subsequent transaction.) Wibaux usually employed twenty-five to thirty riders during the busy months, then kept ten riders through the winter. In order to combat wolves, he maintained fifty to one hundred wolf hounds, and offered a bounty of $5 and $2.50 respectively for the pelts of wolves and pups.

By 1892 Pierre Wibaux and fellow rancher Henry Boice, whose range adjoined the W-Bar, had decided to erect an office building in town, convenient to the railroad, telegraph, and telephone. A long frame structure was built, with a porch across

In 1914, the year following his death, a statue of Pierre Wibaux was erected by his wife and son near his ranch headquarters.
Photo by the author.

the front. In addition to the office, there was a sleeping room and quarters for the caretaker.

It was twelve miles north to W-Bar headquarters, and Wibaux found the building in town so handy that he soon bought out Boice. Wibaux hired a French gardener to landscape the grounds, and soon an elevated tank pumped water into two artificial ponds, one of which contained a grotto and a cupid fountain. Local citizens and travelers alike admired the complex as "The Park." This landmark was placed on the National Register of Historic Places in 1972, and today it is maintained as a museum and park.

During the early years of the twentieth century, homesteaders entered the area in large numbers, and Wibaux began to reduce his ranching operations. His last recorded cattle shipment was in 1905, but by then he was immersed in other business activities. In 1903 Wibaux bought 36,000 acres of railroad land in Beaver Valley for less than a dollar per acre, then sold it the following year for $16 an acre. Primarily he was living in Miles City by this time. He built and was president of the First National Bank of Miles City; he was a major stockholder in the American Bankers Insurance Company; and he owned a mine

Active in Miles City, Pierre Wibaux left a sizable bequest to create a city park. *Photo by the author.*

near Deadwood. His estate exceeded half a million dollars.

But by the age of fifty-four Wibaux had developed liver cancer, and he died in a Chicago hospital in 1913. The next year his wife and son erected the monument which Wibaux had planned. A year later Wibaux Park was created from a specific bequest on the north edge of town, and it has been kept up to date and has served the people of Miles City for more than a century.

Other ranchers in the area also spent time in Miles City and made contributions to the vigorous cattle town. But one ranch in particular — a very large ranch with a legendary background — made a special impression upon Miles City and the surrounding territory. And the manager of the ranch and his family proved to be popular and productive members of the community.

Chapter Ten
The XIT in Montana

"To chase and rope wolves was hard on horses and dangerous for the cowboys, but exciting – just what a cowboy liked!"
— Bob Fudge, XIT cowboy

"He was a man who held an unusual place in affections of the people who formed an acquaintance in the old free-hearted days of the range ... His death will be sincerely deplored in all parts of the west and southwest, especially among live stock men ..."
— Obituary of O.C. Cato of the XIT

There was widespread admiration throughout the cattle frontier for the enormous XIT Ranch sprawling across the Texas Panhandle. In 1879, following legislative groundwork laid in previous years, the Texas Legislature passed a law appropriating 3,050,000 acres of Panhandle rangeland to finance a splendid new state capitol in Austin. From this legislation would emerge the Capitol Syndicate Ranch, better known in western ranching circles as the XIT.

The XIT lands extended from the northwest corner of the Texas Panhandle south for more than 200 miles along the New Mexico border. From 1885 through 1888 the magnificent state house rose in Austin, and as construction work progressed the company received title to their Panhandle lands.

Fencing operations on the vast XIT went on for two years in the mid-1880s. The XIT was enclosed by 575 miles of barbed wire fence. Three hundred carloads of materials were purchased at a cost of $181,000. During the next decade the ranch was divided into ninety-four pastures requiring about 1,500 miles of fence. Some 6,000 miles of wire were used, along with 100,000 cedar posts, five carloads of wire staves, one carload of staples, and an entire carload of hinges for the hundreds of gates. Line riders maintained a constant check on the fencing, and some divisions kept fence wagons in operation at all times.[1]

Such gargantuan operations were typical of the XIT. While stocking the vast range, in 1886 nearly 90,000 head of cattle were purchased and herded to the XIT. During its heyday the XIT maintained herds totaling 125,000 to 150,000 head of cattle. There was a sustained effort to improve the quality of longhorn herds through the purchase of Hereford, Durham, and Polled Angus bulls.

Therefore there was little surprise when the XIT of Texas participated in a new grazing practice in the north country. During the 1880s big Texas ranchers began moving young steers north to be fattened for market on the ranges of Wyoming and Montana. John V. Farwell, XIT managing director, conducted experimental grazing in Montana in 1889. Impressed with the results, he wasted no time enlarging the northern XIT on a larger scale.

In 1890, Farwell established a northern headquarters by buying a small ranch on Cedar Creek in Custer County, Montana, sixty-five miles north of Miles City. Farwell leased two million acres as a finishing range, a superb grassland located "between the rivers" — the Yellowstone and the Missouri. A subdivision was established at the Hatchet Ranch, almost twenty miles north of Terry.[2] (Except for the purchase of the little Hatchet Ranch and the small Cedar Creek spread, all of the XIT land in Montana was leased, while the three million XIT acres in Texas was owned by the Capitol Syndicate.)

From 1890 through 1896, the Texas XIT drove from 10,000 to 20,000 steers annually to Montana. Normally, the XIT sent five herds on the 850-mile journey from the Texas Panhandle to

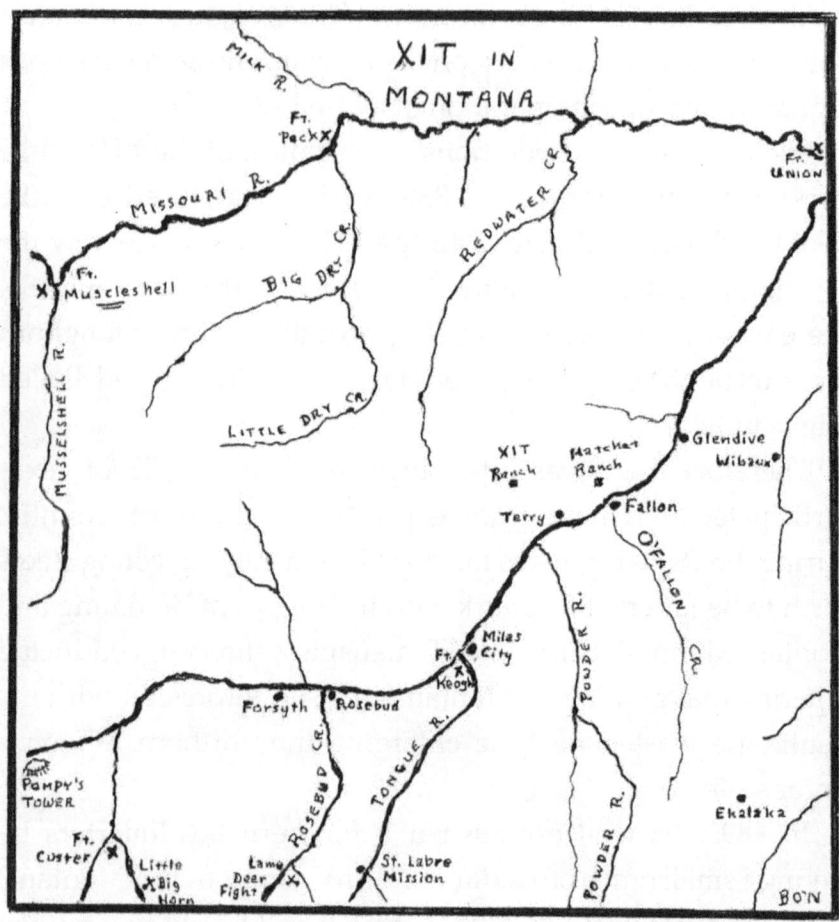

The XIT leased a Montana range reputed to be two million acres. The company owned only two small ranches in Montana: a headquarters unit on Cedar Creek that became known as the XIT Ranch, and a subdivision spread, the Hatchet Ranch. The vast range, called "The Big Open," stretched between the Yellowstone and the Missouri and the Musselshell rivers, but most of the cattle grazed near the Big Dry and Redwater creeks. *Sketched by the author.*

Montana. Each herd usually was composed of 2,500 steers and driven by eight cowboys, a trail boss, a horse wrangler and a cook. The drive took three months, during which time the trail hands were paid $35 a month (XIT cowboys in Texas earned only $25 monthly).[3]

Although most of the trail hands were laid off in Montana, enough men were retained to drive the combined remuda back to Texas. The XIT's most famous animal was *Dunnie*, a buckskin mustang so dependable on night herd that he was used season after season on the long drives. One of the five chuck wagons was used to feed the remuda crew during the two-month return journey, while the four "empties" were hitched together in two pairs and driven back by one team per pair.[4]

While the XIT "double-wintered" steers were bred in the Panhandle, they expanded on the Montana range in loin and frame. Bob Fudge, a 250-pound (or more) Texas cowboy helped drive two herds from Texas and then stayed with the Montana XIT until 1901. Most of the time Fudge was in charge of the

An XIT remuda, commonly called a "cavvy" in Montana.
Photo by Evelyn Cameron, courtesy of Prairie County Museum, Terry, Montana.

XIT chuck wagon. Note Evelyn Cameron and her camera in silhouette.
Courtesy Prairie County Museum, Terry, Montana.

Hatchet subdivision.

Endorsing the policy of finishing cattle on northern ranges, Fudge reported that "when they had been in Montana a year or two, they grew in size and weight to more than double the steer which we brought up the trail from Texas."[5]

In 1890 O.C. Cato was sent up from Texas, to manage the Montana operation. According to Al Denby, one of the first trail hands brought from Texas, Cato was such an expert cattleman that he "could very near tell the color of a cow by looking at her track."[6]

Born in 1858, Osceola C. Cato was raised on the family farm near Waco. The Chisholm Trail crossed the Brazos River at Waco, and young Cato's imagination was captivated by Longhorn steers and the cowboys who handled them. At fourteen he left home to become part of the great adventure of the age.

After just four years as a cowboy, Cato's affinity for cattle and his leadership qualities vaulted him into a successful career as a ranch manager. Serving ably for several ranches, Cato took time in 1881 to marry Julia Jourdan in Austin. Cato and Julia became parents of three daughters and a son: Ethel, Myrtle,

Branding on the XIT.
Photo by Evelyn Cameron, courtesy of Prairie County Museum, Terry, Montana.

John Ozella, and Leo. Deciding to make his home in Miles City, Cato erected a spacious residence at Pleasant Street and Prairie Avenue. The Cato children were sent to local schools, and the family home became a lively social center. O.C. Cato was a stockholder and second vice president of the State National Bank, and he was a member of the Elk and Masonic lodges. In 1891 Cato was elected sheriff of Custer County, and later he served two terms in the Montana State Senate. A devastating family loss struck in 1907, when Leo, the only son, died of heart failure at the age of fourteen.[7]

During his first winter in Montana, Bob Fudge was the sole cowboy assigned to a lonely line camp on the Yellowstone River, the southern boundary of the XIT range (the northern limit was the Missouri River). The XIT provided winter hands with fur coats, fur caps, and fur chaps. Fudge was therefore protected from the cold, but after a couple of months on his solitary rounds he was badly injured when his horse fell. As a result O.C. Cato initiated a policy of keeping two riders at each line camp throughout the long Montana winters.[8]

Aside from line riding, little work was available during the winters until April, when the horse roundup began seven months of intense activity. The fall beef roundups across the vast open range of the XIT involved five big wagon crews, consisting of a chuckwagon and cook, a bed wagon carrying tents and bedrolls, eight to ten cowboys, and two horse wranglers, a day herder and a night hawk. Each roundup crew made two rail shipments during the fall, with Rufe Morris' wagon and crew often making up three trainloads, the final shipments were dispatched by rail to Chicago by the first of November.[9]

Although most cowboys were laid off until the next spring, they were permitted to pick out a horse from their string to use through the winter. Any man not allowed to keep a winter mount was wise to look for work outside the XIT. The remaining 600 horses were kept at the headquarters ranch during the

XIT cowboys gathered at their chuck wagon with their remuda in the background. *Photo by Evelyn Cameron, courtesy of Prairie County Museum, Terry, Montana.*

Eveleyn Cameron, a native of England who became a Montana rancher and a renowned frontier photographer. *Photo by Evelyn Cameron, courtesy of Prairie County Museum, Terry, Montana*

winter months. Wagon boss Rufe Morris was in charge at headquarters, keeping only a cook and one cowboy. Bob Fudge ran the Hatcher subdivision with a cook and Al Denby.[10]

Most of the laid-off cowboys were allowed to stay in the log bunkhouses on the two XIT ranches and, according to Al Denby, "took in all the dances in the country during the winter." Key figures at each dance were XIT men, Ed and Louis Weisner who rode to the festivities with their fiddles strapped to their backs.[11]

It was customary for every man at a dance to pitch in a dollar, and this collection was presented to the musicians. Cowboys readily rode horseback twenty to sixty miles to attend a dance. If a blizzard struck, the ball might become a three- or four-day party. "But there was always plenty to eat," reminisced cowboy J.K. Marsh, "as all of the married women always brought plenty of cakes."[12]

The most popular married woman was Mrs. H.J. Kramer

of Fallon (near Terry), whose husband assisted the XIT with shipping. She loved to waltz and taught the dance to many eager cowboys. As one of her dance partners recalled, Mrs. Kramer "was a large, strong lady who could steer them around."[13]

A problem faced on the XIT in the Texas Panhandle also had to be dealt with in Montana. Gray wolves, sometimes numbering as many as forty in a pack, killed upwards of several hundred XIT cattle per year in Montana. Handling cattle the same way as a group of cowboys, wolves would run the steers into a draw, then hold the bunch while the biggest lobos would dart in to do the killing. The steers would use their horns to fight off attackers from the front, but a wolf would slip in behind and hamstring the prey. Hungry wolves immediately began tearing flesh from the felled victim.

"I have seen cattle and horses with great holes eaten in their hams and shoulders by the wolves," stated Bob Fudge, "and the poor animals would still be living but were unable to get to their feet."

The XIT company bought a score of dogs, including a pair of expensive English stag hounds, to track the wolves. During the winters XIT cowboy George King used the dogs to chase wolves. With a $5 bounty for each wolf pelt, XIT riders would eagerly break away from their duties to gallop after a wolf.

Wolves that had just gorged on a fresh kill could easily be chased down and shot with revolvers. But many cowboys preferred the challenge of roping and dragging a wolf to death.

"To chase and rope wolves was hard on horses and dangerous for the cowboys," testified Fudge, "but exciting — just what a cowboy liked!"[14]

The primary attraction of the XIT for cowboys was the opportunity to practice the old-fashioned art of open-range cowpunching. The XIT in Texas, divided into eight separate divisions, was tightly fenced and cross-fenced, as were other large and small ranches throughout most of the rest of the West. But in Montana, except for horse pastures, the enormous XIT ranges were unfenced. Young cowboys could live and work in a manner that was largely disappearing in the West.

At the height of XIT operations in Montana, as many as 65,000 XIT steers were on the range along with 1,000 cows brought from Texas to raise beef for the roundup wagons and line camps. Two long creeks, the Redwater and the Big Dry, meandered through the heart of the XIT range. Although XIT steers ranged as far west as the Musselshell River, most of the cattle grazed near the Redwater and the Big Dry River during summer months. A beef roundup usually could gather enough steers near these creeks to drive a herd to the shipping point.[15]

The XIT drove its final herds north from Texas in 1897. After that date settlers and their fences closed the Montana Trail to Miles City, making it necessary to pay railroad rates to move Texas steers to Montana. But the XIT in Texas continued to send large numbers of steers north for double wintering. In 1902, for example, 22,000 head were shipped by rail to Montana.[16]

By this time homesteaders were penetrating the XIT range in Montana and introducing sheep in large numbers. The Capitol Syndicate, which owned the three million acres in Texas, already had begun selling off their Panhandle lands to farmers and ranchers. Reducing the Texas cattle operation meant that the Montana range was no longer essential.

On October 8, 1909, after the XIT terminated its Montana operations, O.C. Cato staged a farewell barbecue at the Hatchet Ranch. The *Terry Tribune* reported the event, concluding with a gloomy prophesy: "The XIT is closing out and by next year will be only a name on the page of Montana history."[17]

As the XIT downsized in Montana, O.C. Cato bought a

herd of XIT cattle as well as saddle horses, and he purchased the Hatchet Ranch from the Capitol Syndicate. Although Cato remained active as a Montana cattleman, his health failed in 1915. Plagued by the same heart condition that had claimed the life of his son, Cato returned to Texas to die. He passed away in Austin at the age of fifty-seven, but his remains were transported back to Miles City for burial beside Leo in the family cemetery plot.[18]

The Cato ranching enterprises were carried on by family members, most notably by O.C.'s granddaughter, Mary Cato Swayne. After graduating from high school in Miles City, Mary attended the Spence School for Young Women in New York City. She was the only child of Percy and Myrtle Cato Williamson. Following the death of her father in 1943, Mary Cato assumed leadership of the big N Bar N and other family ranching interests. Two years later she married George Edwin Swayne, and it was remembered that they "enjoyed traveling and dancing for many wonderful years." Of course she enjoyed traveling and dancing — she was a product of a good time town.[19]

The grave of O.C. Cato in Miles City. He returned to Texas to die, but he asked to be buried with his family in Montana, where he had achieved prominence. *Photo by the author.*

Mary also was a lifelong member of the beautiful Presbyterian Church in Miles City, and she was remembered as a "very kind and generous lady" and "a true friend to many people." And, of course, she was a skilled ranch owner. She died in her sleep in 2004 in Miles City, and in her obituary it was pointedly mentioned that she "was the granddaughter of O.C. and Julia Cato of the famous XIT ranch that was such a part of Miles City

Mary Cato Swayne was born in this house on Pleasant Street in 1910, and it was her home for nearly a century. The house of her grandparents, O.C. and Julia Cato, was down the street. Mary graduated from high school in Miles City, before attending an exclusive school for young ladies in New York City. She later ran the family's ranching properties with a skilled hand. *Photo by the author.*

history." Indeed, Mary was thirty-three years old when she took control of the family ranches, only one year older than her grandfather when he came from Texas to establish the XIT in Montana.[20]

Even though the XIT had operated barely two decades in Montana, old-timers from the area long related tales of the massive cattle ranch and its Texas connections. Texas drover Bob Fudge stayed with the Montana XIT until its liquidation and later collaborated with Jim Russell to produce *Bob Fudge, Texas Trail Driver, Montana-Wyoming Cowboy*. The book is replete with XIT range adventures. Both the Prairie County Museum in Terry and the Ranger Riders Museum in Miles City boast a rich Montana collection of XIT photos and memorabilia.[21]

Contrary to the 1901 journalistic foreboding predicting the XIT would be "only a name" in Montana history, the

XIT has proven to be an unforgettable and colorful part of Montana's past. A more accurate tribute to the Montana XIT may be a favorite gravestone epitaph of the era: "Gone But Not Forgotten."

Chapter Eleven
Urban Pioneers

*"We won incorporation with a somewhat
questionable population of fifteen hundred."*
— Sam Gordon

Mountain men, buffalo hunters, gold prospectors, cowboys riding an open range, and farmers in covered wagons were not the only pioneers in the West. Indeed, the settlement of each successive frontier was concluded by urban pioneers who created towns in a wilderness. Like fur trappers, prospectors, and land-hungry farmers and ranchers, urban pioneers sought opportunity in an undeveloped West while relishing the adventure of a new land.

"The attitudes of urban pioneers differed from those of eastern city dwellers," stated frontier historian Ray Allen Billington. "Most were restless seekers after wealth who . . . deliberately selected a promising frontier community as the site of their next experiment in fortune making. There they built a mill, opened a general store, set up a portable printing press, or hung out a shingle as a lawyer or . . . teacher, confident that the town's rapid growth would bring them affluence and social prominence. When they guessed right and the village did evolve into a city they usually stayed on as prosperous businessmen or community leaders . . . Their mobility and restlessness distinguished them from the more stable souls who filled the eastern cities."[1]

Miles City provided an excellent example of the urban frontier. When it was learned that a large military garrison was going to be placed in an unsettled region of Montana, restless and ambitious urban pioneers hurried to the area to see what opportunities beckoned. Saloons and gambling halls promised steady business. So did hardware stores and general mercantile operations, assuming that the prospective businessman had a little experience as a merchant.

Charlie Brown, who tipped the scales at 220 pounds or more, built a popular saloon, kept a pot of stew simmering for all, erected a livery stable, hired a town crier to walk the streets, brought *Uncle Tom's Cabin* to a makeshift stage in his saloon, operated an ice house, and connected a telephone from his home to his place of business. One observer stated that Brown "served as informal host to all that came to Miles City."[2] And when a drunken Bill Rigney insulted women and other family members at their breakfast table, passerby Brown knocked him senseless with a pickaxe handle.

This elegant brick residence was built in 1886 by the first mayor of Miles City, E.H. "Skew" Johnson. *Photo by the author.*

George M. Miles, nephew of Col. Nelson A. Miles, accompanied the army to their new frontier base as a member of the Quartermaster Corps. He quickly became active in the new town, building a log cabin, opening a hardware store, serving as a U.S. Commissioner, and, along with his wife Helen Strevell, became a stalwart of the new Presbyterian Church. George and Helen spent their lives building and promoting the community of Miles City.

Journalist Sam Gordon edited and operated the *Yellowstone Journal* for thirty-three years. He served as a school trustee, became first secretary of the Miles City Board of Trade, and functioned as a keen and faithful chronicler of the frontier town. A later arrival, O.C. Cato, operated the area's most iconic ranch for nearly two decades, was active in both the Elk and Masonic lodges, served a term as county sheriff, spent two terms as a state senator, and was a stockholder and second vice president of the State National Bank.

Such citizens as these were friends who worked together to

Office of the *Yellowstone Journal*, which was operated for more than three decades by Sam Gordon. *Courtesy Range Riders Museum.*

The Masonic Temple was erected on Main Street in 1912. The Miles City Lodge was organized in 1880 in more modest quarters. *Photo by the author.*

improve their community. They realized that by contributing time and effort to grow their frontier town, they were likely to increase their personal positions and fortunes. Serving together on boards and commissions, they built schools and churches and public utilities. They organized community events and fraternal groups, while their wives formed clubs and conducted fairs in support of churches and other local causes.

Most of the future leaders who arrived during the early years of Miles City were young, frequently in their twenties. Indeed, most frontiersmen, including urban pioneers, were young, filled with energy, ambition, and optimism. Miles City's urban pioneers were progressive and confident in the future of their new community.

Schools were an early concern in Miles City. "Frontiersmen

believed that schools were the salvation of democracy and ladders to personal advancement," explained historian Ray Allen Billington. "The principal hope of all pioneers was self-betterment, and this meant equipping the children to rise in the social circle."[3] "Professors" — the universal term for male teachers — and "school ma'rms" were among the most important of urban pioneers.

Nannie Alderson was a ranch wife in the general vicinity of Miles City, but there were no rural schools near enough for her four children. The lack of education weighed heavily on Mrs. Alderson, who could only utilize the Montgomery Ward catalogs — "the wish book" — which the family began to receive in 1885. "All they knew," admitted Mrs. Alderson, "was reading, as taught by Montgomery Ward, and printing block letters, which I taught them." When her oldest child was almost ten, Nannie insisted on moving into town so that the children could attend Miles City schools. Indeed, one of her daughters eventually became a school teacher.[4]

From the early days of Old Milestown there was a determined effort to organize a school. On June 4, 1878, the Custer County Board of Commissioners established School District No. 1, which corresponded with Township No. 1 and which constituted the entirety of Custer County in its original size. Judge Alexander Carmichael was appointed superintendent. But Judge Carmichael died at thirty-seven of consumption in 1880, leaving a widow and four children — and vacant leadership of the new school district. The first classes were held for six weeks beginning on July 18, 1878. School ma'rm, Mary F. Shyrack taught seven pupils in Old Milestown in a makeshift structure. The next year, from January 6, 1879, to April 23, 1879, Miss Nettie Rogan conducted classes in Miles City in a frame building near the Grand Central Hotel. There were seventeen

In 1910, a red brick public high school was erected. Soon outgrown, it was sold a decade later to the Catholics. In 1921, Custer County High School opened, a much larger facility, but the red brick school served the Catholics well for decades. *Author's collection.*

students.[5]

Businessman C.W. Savage soon took over the superintendency, and three teachers were certified to teach: "Professor" W.B. Givens, Miss Anne Alling, and Miss Ella Sheridan. Miss Sheridan was present at a rented building on Main Street when the next session commenced. A bell from the wrecked steamboat *Yellowstone* was set up as the school bell.[6]

The money raised by a county school tax was $711.76. A vote to build a school passed by a razor thin margin: forty-three to forty-two. With a growing student population, an experienced educator, "Prof. A.C. Logan," was employed at $100 per month in 1882. Three female teachers would be paid $75 each per month. By 1882 there were 453 children of school age in the district, and an army wagon now was bringing young scholars from Fort Keogh. The new school, a two-story brick structure costing $15,000 was erected in 1884. Built to accommodate 200 pupils, the main floor held four classrooms, while there was a basement and a second floor utilized as "an exhibition hall and a library." Soon it was necessary to expand, and this center of learning became known as the "First Ward School" and as the "Washington School."

In 1886 classes opened with 130 pupils, with three single school ma'rms teaching, respectively, first and second grades, third and fourth, and fifth and sixth, while Professor T.J. Porter taught seventh and eighth graders, as well as "young businessmen" who wanted to take night classes.[6]

Within a few years, however, classrooms had to be added to the building, and it was arranged to teach classes to ninth-, tenth-, and eleventh-graders as Miles City joined the secondary movement in American education. In 1860 there were merely 311 public high schools in the United States, but the secondary movement grew after the Civil War. By 1890 there were 2,500 public high schools in America, 6,000 by 1900, and by 1910 there were 14,000 high schools across the nation.

In 1893, Miss Sallie Holt was deemed to have completed the requisite eleven years of coursework at the Washington School. Graduation exercises were celebrated for her at the Presbyterian Church in June 1893, and Sallie Holt became the first student to complete high school in Miles City.

The next year there were five graduates, one young lady and four boys. A class of six graduated in 1895, four in 1896, and four again in 1897. No graduates were listed for 1898 — the year of the Spanish-American War — but in 1899 four young men graduated. Elmer Holt, Class of '99 became a politician, serving in both houses of the Montana Legislature before succeeding to the governorship as a Democrat from 1935-1937. Also from the Class of '99, James Ulio was the son of a Civil War veteran and a U.S. Army officer. In 1900 James enlisted in the army, and by

1904, he earned a commission. Following service in World War I, Ulio worked in the Department of the Adjutant General of the U.S. Army. Shortly after U.S. entry into World War II, Ulio was promoted to Adjutant General with the rank of Major General. General Ulio provided exemplary service in a demanding role throughout the war.[7]

Back in Miles City, the high school student body expanded, and in 1910, a handsome red brick high school was built, two stories tall with a full basement. Almost immediately, however, this school was found to be too small. By 1921, a larger Custer County High School opened northeast of downtown, a block south of Main Street. CCHS has been expanded and modernized regularly, and today it is the sole high school in Custer County. Members of the young women's athletic squads are known as the "Cowgirls," while young men who wear the Blue and Gold are of course the "Cowboys."

Simultaneously with the movement to establish schools for the children of Miles City and Fort Keogh, adults in town asked for "reading rooms" (common in communities of the nineteenth century) or even a public library. As described in Chapter Four, Colonel Miles established a library of more than 1,200 volumes early in the existence of Fort Keogh. An average of ninety-five patrons visited the library each day, which probably intensified the desire for a similar facility in town. During the 1880s and the 1890s the Sanborn Fire Maps label "Reading Rooms" on the second floor of various commercial buildings. In 1886 J. Basinski and Bros. general store on Main Street announced a "circulating library of about 600 vols., plus newspapers, magazines and books for sale." In 1886, the Miles City Reading Room Association was organized around two rooms own Basinksi's store, "to be open and free to all."[8]

Women of Miles City called for a public library as early

The Carnegie Library of Miles City was the first in Montana, built across from the courthouse in 1902. *Courtesy Range Riders Museum.*

as 1882, and in 1901, Miles City women's groups prompted attorney and educator T.J. Porter to ask Andrew Carnegie to bestow one of his library grants to the community. Within a month Carnegie approved a $10,000 gift to Miles City, which was the first of his library grants to be awarded to a Montana community. The Miles City Library would be located on Main Street, just south of the courthouse. Designed by Charles S. Haire in the Renaissance Revival Style, the library featured an impressive entry, round arched windows, and deep bracketed eaves. The impressive structure opened on April 1, 1903. Laura Manderscheid Brown Zook directed the Miles City Library for the next forty years. Arriving in Miles City with her family in 1871, aboard a riverboat, she became a teacher, married, returned to teaching after her husband's death, and supervised the library. A needed expansion in 1965 doubled the library's space, but covered up most of the handsome exterior.[10]

For the urban pioneers of Miles City, religious institutions ranked close to educational organizations in establishing tranquility and order in a frontier community. In the midst of saloons and dance halls and brothels, churches came into existence as though providing an antidote for drinking and fighting and whoring. There were far fewer churches than bars and parlor houses, but wives and children could attend the churches, often with improvement to their character.

In November 1877, Rev. E.A. Bridger appeared in Miles City and delivered one of the first sermons in the frontier town. Reverend Bridger was a Methodist preacher, and Methodists long had been known for missionary activity on the American frontier. During 1879, Rev. F.A. Riggin preached on occasion, and Brother W. Van Ordgel also offered sermons from time to time. By 1881, local Methodists petitioned the Methodist Church to incorporate the Methodist Episcopal Church of Miles City. Sunday School began to be held at 2 p.m., with church services at 7:30 p.m.. The Northern Pacific donated a "choice" corner lot on Pleasant Street between Tenth and Eleventh. Under the leadership of Rev. W.J. Hunter, the Methodist-Episcopal Church

The stately Methodist church was built in 1912.
Photo courtesy First Methodist Church.

was built in 1883.[11]

By the early twentieth century the growth of Miles City rendered the 1883 frame structure inadequate. In 1910, the congregation hired a New York City fundraising firm, and soon the Methodists raised $14,000. Furthermore, neighbor C.J. Wagenbreth donated capital needed to complete the project, on condition that no bell be hung in the belfry (he did not want to be awakened by early morning bell-ringing). By 1912, construction featured such eclectic architectural influences as Romanesque Revival windows and crenellated Gothic battlements, as well as round-arched Romanesque openings.[12] The stately structure now has entered its second century of use, and today it remains an impressive place of worship.

In October 1880, the Episcopalian Bishop of Montana Territory, Rev. Leigh Richmond Brewer, ventured to Miles City

The Episcopal Church was built in 1886 and is the oldest religious sanctuary still standing in Miles City. The steeple/bell tower had to be removed. *Photo by the author.*

to conduct religious services. In 1882, Rev. William Horsfall was appointed pastor of St. Paul's Episcopal Mission in Miles City, and a temporary meeting hall was established on the second floor of J.J. Graham's Main Street Grocery Store. Measuring about twenty-five by fifty feet, the hall was lit by a dozen oil lamps. There were thirty wooden chairs, plus barrels supporting planks which provided benches. In all there was room for about seventy-five people at this mission.

In 1886 the stone and brick Emmanuel Episcopal Church was erected, thirty-two feet by sixty-two feet. Designer Byron Vreeland blended Romanesque, Gothic, and Queen Anne architectural styles, while the interior featured a barrel-vaulted wood ceiling trimmed in California redwood. The original bell tower has been removed, but the exterior otherwise remains unchanged since 1886. A walnut altar was created from wood salvaged from a wrecked steamboat. The 1886 Emmanuel Episcopal Church remains the oldest religious structure in constant use in Miles City.[13]

Presbyterians proved to be determined Christian missionaries at Miles City, and they produced a superb house of worship which continues to grace Main Street. In January 1879, Rev. J.D. Hewitt, pastor of the Presbyterian Church of Helena, made a week-long trip in wagons and a stagecoach in sub-zero temperatures to conduct the first services of his denomination in Miles City. About twenty-five people sat on makeshift benches in the upper story of Borchardt's store to listen to Reverend Hewitt. Soon another service was held in the log courthouse on Main Street. A congregation was organized with thirteen members. A Sunday School also was established with George M. Miles as Superintendent and, at first, seven pupils with four teachers. Various locations were utilized until 1883, when a frame church building with a steeple was erected

The frame Presbyterian Church was built in 1882. *Courtesy Range Riders Museum.*

When the old Presbyterian Church was razed, workmen dropped off the steeple at the Range Riders Museum, where it has been preserved. *Photo by the author.*

In 1917 the current Presbyterian Church was dedicated at the head of Main Street. *Photo by the author.*

on property donated by George and Helen Strevell Miles, who had married the previous year. The new church measured thirty-five by fifty-five feet and was occupied debt-free.[14]

By 1911, the same community growth that caused Methodists to launch a fund-raising drive in 1910 spurred Presbyterian trustees to meet and discuss construction of a new church in the $30,000-$40,000 cost range. Pastor J. Forsythe Smith counseled that a new edifice would "provide better social advantages, better intellectual advantages, and better moral and spiritual advantages."

The little frame church was moved elsewhere on the property, and the new brick and concrete sanctuary would occupy the same prominent location on Main Street. The cornerstone was laid on November 26, 1914. C.N. Strevell donated the primary stained glass window which fronted Montana Avenue. George M. Miles gifted the oak-finished, 871-pipe Etsey organ, which was specially designed to fit the organ chamber. This impressive Gothic Revival church was dedicated in 1917 and still "conveys a sense of stability and permanence."[15]

Baptists were among the pioneers who settled Miles City, but for a time they mostly visited the services of other denominations. Early in 1882, however, Rev. G.W. Huntley,

The splendid pipe organ has graced the Presbyterian Church for more than a century. *Photo by the author.*

the General Missionary for North Dakota from the American Baptist Home Mission Society, visited Miles City and, on February 5, 1882, held services in a log cabin on Main Street. A church charter promptly was set up, and within a few weeks Rev. G.E. Downey of Clifton Park, New York, arrived to become the first Baptist pastor. A building was secured at Ninth and Palmer, and among those who made contributions were Col. Nelson A. Miles, who donated $100 toward a church bell.[16]

Catholics got off to an unusually strong start at Fort Keogh and at Miles City. Father Chrysostom Foffa arrived by stagecoach in 1879, the first priest to visit Miles City. He conducted mass at the home of strong supporters, Mr. and Mrs. A.P. Flanagan and their children. The priest stayed on for several months, and in August 1880, Father Lindesmith arrived to assume the duties of fort chaplain. We already have discussed him and his devotion to his military flock and his efforts to establish a Catholic church in town. Father Lindesmith celebrated mass in Miles City on a regular basis, using the homes of parishioners as well as public buildings, such as the log courthouse on Main Street.[17]

Funds for a church building began to be collected and, as was the case with every church project, donations were received from denizens of the saloons and gambling halls and parlor houses. Indeed, Northern Pacific construction workers donated $1,600 in a single collection. Furthermore, it was announced that "ladies of the Sacred Heart Church, Miles City, will raffle a new Cornish piano during the holidays, proceeds to get a church bell . . ." The new Sacred Heart Church cost $2,000, and it stood at the corner of Main and Tenth, measuring twenty-seven by forty feet. Father Lindesmith taught large catechism classes, and he purchased forty acres of land for Catholic classes and Catholic burials. Burial plots were sold to families and this "Mount Olivet Cemetery" soon paid for itself.[18]

Father Lindesmith introduced Christianity to the Northern

The Sacred Heart Catholic Church was built in 1924. Courtesy Sacred Heart Convent, *Photo by the author.*

Six Ursuline nuns ventured into early Miles City, but departed when their cottonwood log convent/school burned. *Photo courtesy Range Riders Museum.*

Cheyennes nearby, and he endeavored to bring six Ursuline sisters from Toledo, Ohio (Father Lindesmith was a native of Ohio). Thirty nuns volunteered for this frontier mission assignment, and those selected were led by Mother Amadeus Dunne. The black-robed sisters arrived in 1884 to start a Catholic school in Miles City and to work among the Northern Cheyenne at Mission St. Labre. Their first convent was built of heavy cottonwood logs, but after the structure burned down in 1897 the sisters left Miles City. But community leaders raised money to erect a towering brick academy on the corner of Montana Avenue and Leighton Boulevard, and the Ursuline sisters agreed to return. Dedicated in 1902, the building accommodated students in grades one through ten. A number of students came from the surrounding countryside, and they settled in on the building's fourth level, beneath the roof. The six nuns each had

The nuns returned to Miles City after the impressive brick Sacred Heart Convent, completed in 1902, made it possible to greatly expand their school. *Photo by the author.*

a separate bedroom on the third level, opening onto a common room. Classrooms were equipped with desks and with musical instruments. There were strict wardrobe requirements for male and female students ("Boarders should have at least six changes of underwear, three for winter and three for summer;").

The 1910 red brick high school, replaced in 1921 by the much larger Custer County High School, was utilized as the Sacred Heart High School for a number of years. The Sacred Heart School now goes through grade eight. The 1902 Academy/Convent eventually faced demolishment. But it was saved by a community volunteer movement. Today it is open as an excellent museum, and it serves the public through non-profit organizations and rented rooms for conferences.[19]

In 1883, Rev. Herman Glaess of the Lutheran faith delivered a sermon in Miles City. The following year Rev. H.T. Rauh, who spoke German, presented a sermon in the Custer County Courthouse. This denomination was enjoying a surge in church attendance, from 175,000 in 1850 to 7 million in 1910. Rev. J.F.M.

Essig was appointed first resident pastor at Miles City in 1907. In 1916 the old frame Presbyterian church was purchased for $2,000, but soon an impressive brick building was erected, and still is utilized by the Trinity Lutheran Church.[20]

A popular evangelistic singer performed a concert in 1910 for forty-four prospective members of the Christian Church. Inadequate finances caused building delays, but a church home finally was erected in 1928.[21] Indeed, other churches were built, and today more than twenty places of worship are listed in Miles City.

Despite the boisterous beginnings of Miles City, there nevertheless was a surprisingly strong and influential religious presence in the community. Frontier wives and mothers always wanted churches, to satisfy their own spiritual and social needs, and for the moral instruction of their children. There were women and children present in frontier Miles City from the founding days of the community, along with a number of men — generally husbands and fathers — who also supported churches. By the 1880s Miles City churchgoers could choose from half a dozen different types of worship. Miles City churches enriched the community's social life, with ladies' meetings and Christmas tree parties and church socials, as well as the town's cultural life, particularly music, with church hymns and pianos and organs — and the quality musical instruction available at the Catholic academy/convent.

Miles City had more than its share of drinking and brawling and womanizing. But throughout its early years the influence of saloons and gambling halls and bordellos was balanced to some degree by churches and churchgoers. And as Miles City matured, the atmosphere of morality disseminated by churches throughout the community, as well as the values, reinforced by a growing number of churchgoers would help propel Miles

City into a new century as a decent and increasingly virtuous town in which to work and live.

The community leaders who built brick schools and impressive churches certainly did not neglect commercial architecture. Log saloons and stores quickly were replaced by frame buildings, usually with false fronts. (A tall front facing the street provided more space for large, eye-catching business signs.) There were frequent fires in Miles City, but burned buildings were replaced by better structures, usually of brick. Enterprising men developed local brickyards, and by 1881 the Northern Pacific shipped bricks in large quantities.

The business section of Miles City modernized its appearance with the construction of "blocks," buildings which took up not an entire block, but several spaces. In 1885 a fire destroyed the Orschel Brothers' grocery and wholesale liquor and hide trading business, along with adjacent buildings in the 500 block

Following a destructive fire, the Orschel brothers promptly erected a brick "Commercial Block" which soon accommodated other prominent businessmen. *Courtesy Range Riders Museum.*

of north Main Street. Rebuilding promptly took the form of a two-story block in high Victorian style, covering four lots with businesses owned by the Orschel brothers, Miles and Strevell, John Carter, and Julius Basinski and Broker. There were tall doors and windows and a great deal of pane glass. Next door was the Leighton and Jordan block, with many similar ornate features. A corner block of two stories and a full basement was built in 1884 with the Commerce State Bank in the center, facing two streets. There was a tailor shop with a basement entrance, which a hotel on the Main Street side utilized for second-floor rooms. A grand look soon dominated the Miles City business section.

One of the most important structures was the Custer County Courthouse, set back from the north side of Main Street between Tenth and Eleventh streets. By the early 1880s the little log courthouse four blocks down the street was woefully inadequate for bustling Miles City. There was only one room, and the "jail" was an outdoor picket fence where a Crow prisoner committed suicide rather than endure the indignity of arrest by white men. Commissioners launched construction of the new courthouse in 1881 and 1882. There were

Behind the court house was the stockade, a picket fence lockup. But when a Crow brave was arrested, he could not bear the indignity of being imprisoned by white men and he committed suicide. *Post mortem photo courtesy of Range Riders Museum.*

accusations of financial chicanery — that a $35,000 building ultimately cost nearly $100,000 ("quite a rakeoff" was a typical observation").[22]

But the urban pioneers of Miles City shrugged off accusations and plunged ahead with building a proper courthouse. Indeed, at this same time a questionable general election in 1882 decided the incorporation of the new county. Incorporation required a population of 1,500 inhabitants. Election headquarters were in the rear of Charlie Brown's popular saloon. Sam Gordon reported that "many soldiers from Keogh were temporarily equipped in citizens' togs and voted. If memory serves, there were about 1,700 votes cast by a population of a possible 1,200 men, women and children. It took the election officials five days to canvas the vote, which procedure was in progress, off and on, for all of that period, at a faro table in the rear of the

The early cottonwood log court house was replaced in 1884 by a handsome brick court house. *Courtesy Custer County Court Recorder's Office.*

The Leighton and Jordan Block was built nearby on Main Street. Along with other commercial blocks, the downtown business section took on a modern appearance in the ornate Victorian style. *Courtesy Range Riders Museum.*

saloon, frequent adjustments being taken to indulge in the other attractions close at hand." And Gordon never solved one mystery of the election, "the 'Wooley's Ranch' vote, a precinct that returned a hundred and ten odd votes . . . that has never yet been located on the map of Custer county."[23]

Nevertheless, civic leaders in 1882 achieved incorporation, as well as the completion of a tall, imposing brick courthouse. There was an impressive tower entry to the main floor, topped with Victorian spires and chimneys that reached skyward. But it was several blocks back to the town's saloon district, so urban pioneer Louis King built a one-room "Courthouse Saloon" nearby (where the Carnegie Library would be located in 1903). Attorneys and clients thus avoided the "fatiguing journey" back to town for refreshment.[24]

Another institution opened in Miles City in 1894. The previous year the Montana Legislature established the Pine Hills Boys and Girls Industrial School, also known as the State Reform School. Two large brick buildings, along with a few small auxiliary structures, were erected at Miles City on

Eleventh Avenue. Cost of the buildings was just over $20,000. Montana courts could commit boys and girls between the ages of eight and twenty-one to the reform school for any offenses other than murder or manslaughter. A crowd of about 300 attended the dedication in March 1894. Soon the State Reform School began to be called a "prep school for the pen." (Young troublemakers learned criminal ways from the older inmates.) Boys and girls were separated in 1917, with females assigned to the Montana State Vocational School for Girls, located seven miles north of Helena. Today the Miles City facility is called simply the "Pine Hills School."[25]

Throughout the rapid development of Miles City, local civic leaders endeavored to bring the urban improvements of the day to their frontier community. Almost immediately there was an opportunity to connect the isolated town to the outside world by telegraph and by the newly-invented telephone. By April 1878, soldiers completed a telegraph line from Fort Keogh to Bismarck.

By the following September miles of telegraph wire had been collected, along with 650 brackets and 360 insulators, as well as a large number of wooden poles. A sizeable detail of soldiers, supplemented by several skilled civilian workers, began setting up a network of telegraph connections, and by 1879, troops from Fort Keogh had run 650 miles of telegraph lines. There were telegraphic connections with Bismarck, Deadwood, Fort Custer, Helena, Fort Ellis, Fort Shaw, and Fort Assiniboine. The army filled the need for telegraph operators at the military posts and at some civilian centers, including Miles City. Two miles of wire connected the telegraph office at Fort Keogh with Miles City, where a telegraph operator and the necessary equipment were installed. Businessmen regarded the telegraph connection as essential, and townspeople used the connection for personal messages as well.

By 1878, telephones were being sold by the pair for private lines. In 1879, Col. Nelson A. Miles secured a pair of telephones and had them connected from the telegraph office at headquarters to his COQ at the western end of the parade ground. A telephone exchange, or "central" office, was located in Miles City in 1881. W.H. Bullard and W.L. Lansing started the town's first phone company by housing the "central" office in their Bullard and Lansing store at the corner of Main and Sixth. A two-mile line connected "central" with Fort Keogh. Rates were $5 per month for businesses and $4 monthly for residential customers. The Bell Company took over the Miles City Exchange in 1884. There were thirty-two phones in 1885, and by 1910 the exchange served 685 subscribers.[26]

Another important form of communication was the newspaper. Frontier journalists were active in Miles City, with a partnership often being formed by an editor-reporter and a capable printer. There always was curiosity among readers about new businesses or residents in town, and about local politics, as well as military news. At least nine newspapers were founded in Miles City in 1885, with some quickly folding or reorganizing:

1879 *Yellowstone Journal*   first issue, July 24, 1879

1881 *Miles City Chronicle*   July 8, 1881, lasted two weeks

1882 *Miles City Weekly Press* first issue, February 2, 1882
     Became the *Miles City Daily Press* in June 1882

1882 *Daily Rustler*   first issue, April 14, 1882

1883 *Miles City Daily Journal* first issue February 1883
     Died quickly, but reappeared in September 1883

1884 *Stockgrowers Journal*   first issue, 1884

1884 *Miles City Press*   first issue, August 9, 1884

1884 *Miles City Daily Record* first issue, September 15, 1884

1885 *Daily Gazette*   first issue, May 11, 1885

This document from the First National Bank lists urban pioneer G.H. Miles as vice president. *Author's collection.*

In an 1883 issue, the *Yellowstone Journal* announced that *Journal* copies sold for five cents at the following newsstands: Bertrand's Bazaar, Bazinkski's, the IO Hotel, and the post office.[27]

In 1885, two local businessmen traveled to communities in the East to determine the advisability of an electric company and water plant. Capitalists from Miles City as well as the East were encouraged to invest in the Miles City Water and Electric Company. The company was incorporated by Montana Territory on April 10, 1886. There already had been an inadequate attempt to provide electric lights, but now several prominent local businesses subscribed to the effort, and more powerful equipment was installed. Now there were electric lights in town at night, and efforts were begun to provide water more reliably than through the wells scattered through Miles City.[28]

Since its earliest days the community had enjoyed medical service through the Fort Keogh hospital and military doctors.

Physicians were among the urban pioneers who were attracted to the growing community, and in January 1882, Dr. C.B. Lebscher opened the somewhat grandly named "Miles City Hospital" at the northwest corner of Pleasant and Tenth. Doctor Lebscher also was listed as owner of the City Drug Store. Indeed, many physicians were at least part owner of a drug store, maintaining their office in the rear of the store or perhaps upstairs. In 1883, for example, the Miles City Drug Store housed the offices of Dr. R.G. Redd and Dr. A.C. Girard.[29]

A "Business Index" compiled during the 1880s, listed five physicians. There were nine attorneys, two osteopaths, three dentists, two undertakers, seven insurance agents and eight real estate dealers. There was a steam laundry, along with two Chinese laundries. There were three plumbers, three painters, five builders, and contractors, three cement contractors, three lumber yards, one housemover, and one architect (Byron

This ornate brick residence is the oldest two-story home standing in Miles City.
Photo by the author.

Vreeland).

There were five grocery stores, three meat markets, three coal merchants, one gunsmith, three barber shops, six restaurants, three bankers, two milliners, three tailors, one music store and two photographers. Always, of course, there were numerous saloons and gambling halls and houses for "female boarders."

In March 1883 local businessmen — George M. Miles, Sam Gordon, C.W. Savage, attorney-businessman Walter A. Burleigh, John J. Graham, James Baskin, and several other prominent men — met and organized a Board of Trade, which in effect was the Miles City Chamber of Commerce.[30]

These leading urban pioneers installed themselves and their families in comfortable homes in what became called the "Carriage House District." The initial Carriage House District neighborhood was along Pleasant Street, which paralleled Main Street and was one block northwest of Main. Many of these residences boasted carriage houses on the residential lot. This neighborhood was near the commercial district and it was close to the schools and churches. If the church was a little too far to walk in Sunday clothes, the family vehicle would be pulled out of its carriage house.

Within a few years of its founding, therefore, Miles City was a well-rounded community. A boom during the 1880s, thanks to the arrival of the Northern Pacific, brought prosperity and optimism, as well as an even more intense pursuit of fun that always had characterized Miles City.

Chapter Twelve
Good Times in Miles City

"All in all, it was a grand night to be alive and in Miles City."
— W.B. Clarke

*"Rah! Rah! Ree! Can't You See?
Hot Time, All Time! MILES CITY!*
— Yell for First Football Game

On Christmas Eve of 1884, Miss Helen Dunning married Fred Whiteside, who operated a lumber business with his brother Will. This happy wedding occasion was made even merrier the next day. On Christmas Day, C.W. Savage, one of Miles City's leading businessmen, raffled off a "magnificent music box" at his drug store. Fred Whiteside drew the lucky number, and the music box would adorn the new home of the newlyweds on Pleasant Street.[1]

Doors of downtown businesses were "wide open" on Christmas Day as "merchants report that the holiday trade exceeded all expectations." The receipts of a Christmas Charity Ball raised $75. Christmas dinner at the MacQueen House was served to more than 200 guests, while Annie Turner's California Restaurant also fed a large crowd.

It already was the custom at Miles City churches to focus Christmas services on gifts and children and music of the season. The Methodist Church held their Yule entertainment on Christmas Eve, featuring "a richly laden tree for the youngsters to gaze upon," while a musical and literary program was in progress. At the Presbyterian Church a Christmas sociable was held. A festive crowd filled each corner of the Baptist Church as everyone enjoyed the tree "and the real Santa Claus." At the Episcopal Church on Christmas Day there was a choral presentation at eleven o'clock in the morning and a Sunday School Festival at seven in the evening. Father E.W.J. Lindesmith led services at the Catholic Church in town before moving to the chapel at Fort Keogh, where he was chaplain. At the chapel "were assembled all the officers of the post with their wives and children."[2]

A number of troopers celebrated in Miles City saloons, where trouble with cowboys was reported on Christmas night. And at Powderville, an area stagecoach stop, the owner of the saloon was killed. Overall, however, Christmas in the wilderness of eastern Montana in 1884 featured appropriate hymns, decorated Christmas trees, a Charity Ball, gifts, and even a wedding. Of course, Christmas celebrations in Miles City would become more elaborate with every passing year.

"Social life in Miles City was a rather magnificent affair," reminisced Mrs. Josephine Decker, who operated a Main Street millinery shop. But as Miss Josephine Minor in the 1880s she participated eagerly in the social opportunities available in her fun-loving community. "Formal balls were held at the MacQueen hotel, with canvas spread over the beautiful rugs in the dining room for the dancers. Usually the Fifth Infantry orchestra from Fort Keogh . . . furnished the music and the young officers in their resplendent uniforms added color to the scene. The Miles City girls always wore elaborate ball gowns, often with diamonds sparkling on their smooth white throats, and their escorts came in full dress with white kid gloves."

Josephine Minor Decker relished the memory of one especially unforgettable evening. From 1880 until 1892, John Phillip Sousa, renowned as "The March King," conducted the US Marine Band while touring frequently — including to big Fort Keogh via the Northern Pacific line. "Often the Fort Keogh officers who enjoyed Miles City hospitality gave balls in return and sent the fort ambulance down to be loaded with young folks. On one particular night Sousa's band furnished the music," recalled Josephine. "It was a snowy, wintery night, bitter cold, and through some oversight the ambulance did not come . . . However, not at all daunted, the Miles City boys and girls muffled up, put on overshoes and walked the two miles through deep snow, and they danced all night."[3]

The youthful party crowd to which Josephine Minor belonged always was ready to venture beyond Miles City for a dance. The Allerton cattle outfit was on the Rosebud River, west of Miles City. "One evening the Allerton girls gave a dance, inviting the Miles City crowd. We went by train to Rosebud where the Allertons met us with wagons. We intended to return on the early morning train. We danced through the night and then learned that our train, held up by blizzards, would be hours late. And so we danced some more . . ." Mattresses and blankets finally were spread throughout the front rooms, while the boys prepared to bunk on the kitchen floor.

"But sleeping seemed a sheer waste of time to us while we might be dancing," recalled Josephine. "Someone began twanging the banjo and promptly the blankets were piled into a corner and we were at it again . . ." On the third morning word came that the train would arrive by afternoon. The party crowd bundled into wagons and drove to the station, where one of the boys shouted, "Who'll dance?" The "pretty, vivacious Josephine Minor then said, 'I will.' And soon the rough station floor was alive with dancing feet."[4]

Just as the next generation of fun-loving Miles City young people remained in constant readiness to dance and party, they also embraced the growing American passion for sports.

America's first team sport was "base ball," and during the Civil War thousands of soldiers learned the game at hundreds of army camps. After the war these young veterans brought the sport home to a multitude of towns and country villages. The Cincinnati Red Stockings played in 1869 as paid professionals, and in 1876, the National League of Professional Base Ball Players was organized. That year soldiers arrived at the Tongue River Cantonment, and from that time baseball was played on occasion between company nines at the fort. Eventually a team of soldiers would play a baseball squad from Miles City. By the twentieth century there were Miles City town teams with flannel uniforms, short-billed caps, and leather "mitts" for catching the ball. The Miles City club would take on the town team from other communities.

During the fall of 1897 interest grew around Miles City for a football team. On an evening in early November about "twenty enthusiasts of the game" met at Fireman's Hall with the goal of

America's first team sport was "base-ball," probably introduced to Miles City by Fort Keogh players. In this late nineteenth century photo, a Miles City town team poses with the team manager and a batboy. *Courtesy Range Riders Museum.*

"adopting a code of signals and practicing some of the intricate plays of the game, such as the wedge, the double crisscross, catching and throwing the ball, end plays, and interference." A few days later an official "yell" was published in the newspaper"

>"Rah! Rah! Ree! Can't You See!
>Hot Time, All Time! MILES CITY!"

This first Miles City football team was not made up of local schoolboys, but rather from young men who had attended college "or who were naturally athletically inclined." Soon there were only enough young men willing to play to fill the required eleven positions. Inmates of the Reform School were enlisted for the opposing team. Four local men, including two physicians, agreed to officiate the game.

The first football game in Miles City was played on Wednesday afternoon, November 17, 1897, at Athletic Park (the site of today's Miles Community College). Admission was twenty-five cents, with ladies admitted free. The ladies wore colored ribbons and chrysanthemums, while men who had attended college flaunted their alumni colors from coats and canes.

With sensitivity typical of the times, the Reform School players were referred to as "The Reforms." The Reforms kicked off to the Miles City team. Right tackle Levi Schwartz picked up the ball and ran for a touchdown (worth four points during this era). End Wiseham Terrett kicked the extra two points, and the score was Miles City, 6 – Reforms, 0. The ladies continued to scream, "Rah! Rah! Ree!" and Miles City continued to score, winning the game 24-0.[5]

One week later the two teams played again. Several high school players joined the town team, but the Reforms won, 6 to 4. In the last game of the season three Miles City players switched to the Reform School squad. Miles City won, however, 10 to 0 over the Reforms.

The year of the first Miles City football season, 1897, also marked a notable loss for the community. The sprawling frame MacQueen House, the largest hotel in town, burned to the ground. Erected in 1882 and frequently expanded, the MacQueen House offered complete hospitality, "many allurements" and "comforts and pleasures," according to journalist Sam Gordon. "In the pleasant summer days the porch would be thronged with cattlemen discussing the many ramifications of their business, the less sedate members breaking away for cards or billiards... Nearly all the unmarried men in the business houses boarded there and at meal times there would be a gathering of this contingent that added to the general gayety of the premises. Dances and banquets were held in the spacious dining room, a special feature being made each year of the Stockmen's dance given during the session of the Stockgrower's Association." Now there was only a deep hole in the ground where the big cellar had been located. Josephine Minor Decker reported that as the hotel burned, "the young folks who had such good times there, stood around crying as they watched the ravaging flames, feeling as though some of their carefree joyousness was being destroyed with it."[6]

Happily, the community's "carefree joyousness" was not destroyed for very long. As soon as winter arrived horse-drawn sleigh rides became popular, and so did ice skating on frozen rivers. Smaller sleds were brought out for toboggan trails. During the 1880s, as roller skating became popular throughout America, a skating rink was erected at the corner of Pleasant and Eighth. The building was fifty feet wide and 150 feet long. The rear twenty-five feet was "fitted up with a stage and dressing rooms and equipped with curtains and scenery." In addition to roller skating, therefore, the building was used for theatricals and a variety of public gatherings, including meetings of the Montana Stockgrowers Association.[7]

Along with sports and other jolly amusements, one observer pointed out that for those with more rugged tastes, part of the population still bristled with "a superabundance of pure cussedness... Every night is marked by a free fight or something else of a lively nature, and if one night passes without some such occurrence, a sort of funeral sadness is cast over the place." One of the more amusing altercations occurred in a saloon on a Saturday night in 1880, when two court officials, Judge William W. Carland and Judge James H. Garlock, "pitched into one another and attempted to wipe up the floor of the saloon" before friends intervened. A few years later there was a five-mile roller skating race at the rink with heavy betting by the sporting crowd. A skating champion from Butte was brought to Miles City to challenge a local saddlemaker named Goettlich. Goettlich came from behind to win, followed by a ten-mile skating exhibition by the Butte visitor, who raced 200 laps in forty-five minutes and nine seconds, according to the official timekeeper. A foot race was arranged between a sprinter from Miles City and a runner from Glendive. A purse was raised and there were lively side bets. Sam Gordon related that the Miles City runner lost, amid suspicions of cheating, and local sports lost $1,500.[8]

Whether it was all-night dancing and sleigh rides and football games by the dancing and party enthusiasts, or a "free fight" each night in a saloon or a race — skating, horses, or sprinters — with serious betting by the sporting crowd, Miles City rollicked its way into the twentieth century. According to the US Census, there were 627 residents of Miles City in 1880, but by 1890 the population had grown by more than half to 956. As the

At one memorable ball at Fort Keogh, officers, their wives, and invited civilian guests were regaled by the music of "the March King," John Philip Sousa, and his renowned US Marine Band. *Courtesy National Archives.*

century turned, the number of Miles City residents more than doubled to 1,938, and in 1910 the Census recorded a population jump to 4,697. By 1920 there were almost 8,000 residents. But the citizens of growing Miles City remained energetic, ambitious, optimistic and, as always, ready for a good time.

Only a few years into the twentieth century, the citizens of Miles City staged a community-wide celebration that proved to be a colorful, memorable event. George W. Farr, attorney and later mayor of Miles City, came up with the idea, based on the famous "Ak-Sar-Ben" carnival in Nebraska. "Ak-Sar-Ben" is Nebraska spelled backward, and spelling Miles City backward produced "Y-Tic-Se-Lim." W.B. Clarke, born in Miles City in 1885 and reminiscing about "Y-Tic-Se-Lim" when he was seventy-five, was an energetic participant in the festivities at the age of twenty-one in 1906.

"Of course," recalled Clarke, "no legitimate carnival was held in those days without having a queen to preside over it — and when there is a queen in charge, there must be maids of honor, ladies in waiting, a Lord High Chancelor, a Keeper of the Exchecquer, Lord High Constables and other ranking officials doing obeisance to the whims of the queen. We had them all..."[9]

Any young lady of the community over the age of twenty was

eligible to be queen, and there were twenty-eight candidates. Votes cost five cents each, and a person could purchase any number of votes. Ultimately 6,583 votes were cast, including 3,800 for Miss Myrtle Cato, daughter of XIT manager, O.C. Cato. In addition to winning the right to rule over the carnival, Queen Myrtle received gifts from sixteen local merchants. The various attendants were young men and women from the partygoers and dancers of Miles City, and one lady in waiting was her sister, John Ozella Cato (who preferred her first name, "John.").

The Y-Tic-Se-Lim carnival was scheduled for Friday and Saturday, September 20 and 21, 1906. A committee worked for six weeks to organize the event. Three blocks of Main Street – the heart of downtown Miles City — would be set aside for pedestrian only traffic. Lining both sides of the street would be

After the MacQueen House burned, the Olive Hotel at 501 Main became the primary hostelry in Miles City. Built as the Hotel Leighton in 1898, new owners in 1908 renamed it the Olive Hotel, after their daughter. The Olive was expanded, and today the Main Street entry door still features beautiful leaded glass, as well as stained glass in the arched transoms of the lobby windows. *Courtesy Range Riders Museum.*

The Montana Bar on Main Street is famous for its Montana-shaped sign and for its splendid back bar. Built as a one-story brick building in 1893, the structure soon was expanded. Today there is a multi-colored mosaic tile floor, a pressed tin ceiling, wildlife mounts — and a bullet hole in one leaded glass panel. *Photo by the author.*

booths, set up by merchants and dispensers of refreshments. At each end of Main Street stood a massive archway, decorated in the carnival color scheme of red, green, and white. A dancing pavilion was erected in Riverside Park, the shaded area between Fifth Street and the Tongue River. Bunting, flowers, and colored streamers provided decorations everywhere. Barber Jim Sipes set up his "booth" — a Cheyenne tipi on loan from the reservation.

At 1:30 on Friday afternoon, September 20, a happy throng gathered while the opening parade aligned in front of the new Carnegie Library. The Reform School band led the march down Main Street. The royal court followed, with Queen Myrtle Cato riding in a chariot drawn by six black horses. Next came the Children's Parade, with more than a score of baby vehicles, some propelled by older sisters. Marching last, according to W.B. Clarke, "was a disturbance called the Little German Band."

Finally the parade halted and Queen Myrtle was given keys to the city "by the Lord Mayor, W.W. Andrus."[10]

After the coronation ceremony, most of the crowd strolled among the refreshment and merchandise booths or made their way to Riverside Park, where there was a vaudeville tent show with black-faced comedians and a trained dog. There also was a high diver and a "Peek-a-Boo" tent — "the best thing offered for the price." Everywhere confetti was thrown. (At medieval fairs candy or coins or fruit or flowers long had been tossed at revelers, but in 1875, just three decades prior to Y-Tic-Se-Lim, a Milan businessman began manufacturing colored paper confetti for the *Carnevale di Milano*. In Miles City, Montanans bought and threw it by the bale.)[11]

At eight o'clock in the evening, Queen Myrtle appeared with her attendants at the park dance pavilion and opened the ball. "All in all," remarked W.B. Clarke, "it was a grand night to be alive and in Miles City." And he added pointedly, "there was not one case of intoxication recorded. Just think of it! Two days with the bridle off in wild and woolly Milestown and not a case of 'booze.' . . . It was more fun to deluge the pretty girls with confetti while making the rounds of the Midway and the booths than to coop oneself up indoors and drink."[12]

By any measure Y-Tic-Se-Lim was a roaring success, demonstrating that Miles City could stage a good-time event that could stand up to a similar activity anywhere. The *Stockgrower's Journal* thought so, and stated their comparison on the front page:

> *Old Rome Is A "Has Been"*
> *And It's Skidoo for Venice,*
> *New Orleans, and The White City*
> *Since Miles City Has Taken Her Flight*
> *Into Realms of Carnival and Pageant —*
> *Gorgeous in Color, Vibrant with Mirth,*
> *The Cow Town Celebrates Its Y-Tic-Se-Lim.*[13]

Chapter Thirteen
From Remount Station to the Range Riders Museum

"When we walked into a dance hall, the girls would whisper, 'The C.B.C. Cowboys!' They would drop the neighbor farm boys like a steer in the road, and we would damn sure give them a whirl!"

— Claire Boyce, CBC Cowboy

A second railroad reached Miles City in 1908. In 1850, construction had commenced on the Milwaukee and Mississippi Railroad, and this incorporated line was all of five miles in length. But railway extensions followed rapidly. There were several name changes, but the railroad became known as the "Milwaukee Road." By the twentieth century the board of directors decided that to be competitive their railroad needed to extend to the Pacific Northwest. A 2,300-mile Pacific Extension was approved at a cost of $60 million. The line now was named the Chicago, Milwaukee and Puget Sound Railway Company, and the next charter called for construction from the Missouri River to Seattle and Tacoma. The Pacific Extension would cross two mountain ranges, the Rockies and the Cascades, and the scenery of this route was exceptional.[1]

Construction of the Pacific Extension began in 1906 and was completed in 1909. The Chicago, Milwaukee and Puget Sound Railway built into Miles City in 1908. Miles City had been designated as a division point, and the big rail yard boasted machine shops and a roundhouse. A large roster of solid-paying jobs bolstered the Miles City economy. Within two years the population jumped to nearly 4,700, according to the US Census, and by 1920 there were almost 8,000 residents.

The Chicago, Milwaukee & Puget Sound division point rail yards brought a substantial payroll to Miles City. The rail yards included machine shops and a round house. *Courtesy Range Riders Museum.*

In 1929 Hollywood filmed *Danger Lights*, a railroad movie which included scenes lensed in the rail yards of Miles City. The principal label on the rolling stock used in the movie was "The Milwaukee Road." *Danger Lights* was a melodrama starring Louis Wolheim, Robert Armstrong, and Jean Arthur (who in 1952 would be featured as the female lead in the Western classic *Shane*). Released in 1930, *Danger Lights* ran for seventy-four minutes, although later it was shortened to fifty-five minutes for television. There were interior and exterior scenes filmed in the Miles City rail yards, as well as a good view of the passenger depot in its prime. Granted, the 1930 movie is set years after the cattle town period of Miles City, but it nevertheless offers a valuable visual record. [2]

Another important development of 1908 involved Fort Keogh and the future of Miles City. There was no longer any dangerous activity by Native Americans in the area after the Ghost Dance disturbances of 1890-91. In 1894 there was a suggestion that Fort Keogh should provide remounts for the US Cavalry, because of good grazing land in the area and the fort's proximity to a major railroad (the Northern Pacific). Although a good idea, for the time being Fort Keogh remained a military base with a steadily shrinking garrison.

But in 1907 the remaining troops at Fort Keogh were assigned to list and check property that would be shipped to other posts. On September 2, 1907, Troops L and M of the Sixth Cavalry were sent to duty in the Philippines. The last detachment of soldiers departed Fort Keogh on October 27, 1908, leaving a small caretaking outfit to maintain the buildings and grounds. Also in 1908 the graves of those buried at the decommissioned post were removed, with most being reinterred at the Custer Battlefield National Cemetery.[3]

Within a year, however, the army decided to utilize old Fort Keogh as a remount station. The conversion began in 1901, as electric lights and steam heat were installed in the aging buildings, which also were painted and otherwise modernized.

The countryside in the vicinity of Miles City teemed with horses, which encouraged the establishment of Fort Keogh as a remount depot. *From a large historical marker in Riverside Park.*

Soon there were 1,661 horses on the Fort Keogh reservation, which encompassed 100 square miles on almost 64,000 acres (minus the acreage for the Miles City townsite). After war broke out in Europe in 1914, horses were brought by the thousands from all over the West to the remount station for training and sales to European armies. "This is Uncle Sam's horse ranch," went one description. "The employees are all civilians and the wranglers are cowpunchers and expert riders. The eastern tourist looking for real western atmosphere can find it here to his heart's content, for the latter day cowboy or buckeroo [sic] is a very picturesque individual in his colored chaps, his big Stetson and his fancy rigging."[4]

At the height of operations, the remount station employed over 100 riders to break "an endless supply" of horses purchased by the Army. From 1910 to 1918, the Fort Keogh Remount Depot processed more than 100,000 head of horses as replacement animals. Sales peaked at the Miles City stockyards in June 1916, when 4,000 horses were auctioned off in four days. It was estimated that the federal government spent $20 million in Miles City for livestock during the war, and that the Allies spent a similar sum.[5]

But after the war ended it was realized that mechanized vehicles would dominate future conflicts. In 1922 the remount depot was converted into a livestock and range management station under the direction of the US Department of Agriculture. Most of the employees lived in the old officers' quarters. The facility was developed and used methodically. As described by the *Great Falls Tribune* in 1968:

> *The entire station is fenced into 52 pastures of 30 to nearly 4,000 acres as range for each season and for research work with cattle. The station breeds more than 1,000 cows in nearly 50 herds, using individual sires and artificial insemination.*[6]

But the loss of the Fort Keogh garrison hurt business in downtown Miles City. In 1917 a drought hamstrung homesteaders who were hoping to grow wheat. The previously ever-expanding population of Miles City dropped for the first time during the 1920s — from 7,937 in 1920 to 7,174 in 1930, nearly a ten percent loss.

The Old West spirit of Miles City nevertheless remained undimmed. There were numerous echoes from the colorful past that still resonated powerfully in the one-time frontier community. Only a decade into the twentieth century, "when the rising tide of immigration was surely and rapidly submerging the early-day residents,' more than 120 signatures were collected for an "Old-Timers association."[6] In 1908 a mock western town, featuring log structures and false fronts and stagecoach rides, was erected as "Elkville" to share the pioneer

During his final visit to Miles City, former president (and rancher) Theodore Roosevelt wore a mourning band to honor his youngest son, Quentin, who was killed in air combat over France. *Courtesy Range Riders Museum.*

origins of Miles City with an Elks Convention. And, since it was Miles City, inevitably there was a huge Main Street parade. There were parades celebrating every Miles City Roundup. On December 20, 1923, a score of rugged-looking frontiersmen attended an Old Time Buffalo Hunters Banquet at a Miles City café. A decade later, on October 14, 1933, a large banquet crowd, including George M. Miles and Leo Orschel, celebrated together as the Half Century Club of Miles City.[7]

An exciting echo from the past arrived by train in 1918. Theodore Roosevelt, as a young rancher in the mid-1880s, was in Miles City during the founding period of the Montana Stockgrowers Association. He was one of the ranchers who wanted to pursue a war against rustlers. But within a few years he divested himself of his ranching interests, focusing on a political career. In 1898 he won fame as Colonel Roosevelt, leader of the Rough Rider victory at San Juan Hill during the War with Spain. Soon he was vaulted to the presidency, serving nearly two terms. Later he led a major exploratory expedition into the jungles of Brazil, incurring illnesses which undermined his health. When the United States entered the Great War, the former Rough Rider chafed that he was not permitted to raise a division of troops. All four of his sons served, and the youngest, Quentin, was killed in action while flying a combat plane.[8]

Roosevelt bravely carried on, and when he arrived in Miles City in 1918, he happily agreed to speak in the cattle town of his adventurous youth, and he was greeted by men who had donned wooly chaps and creased hats and other cowboy attire. Miles City happily welcomed the vigorous and colorful former president and Rough Rider. But within a few months, on the night of January 6, 1919, Roosevelt died of a coronary embolism at the age of sixty. At least Miles City could find solace that there had been a final visit by the immensely popular cowboy

A cowboy riding a bucking bronc at an early Miles City Roundup. *Courtesy Range Riders Museum.*

president.

Another reminder of Miles City as a frontier cowboy town came every year with the local rodeo. The Miles City Roundup was an occasion for mounted parades, bronc riding, bulldogging, Native American activities, street dances, and other cowboy — and cowgirl — fun. Distinguishing the Miles City Roundup from other small rodeos was the presence of Skyrocket, an exceptional bucking horse. A whirling tornado in the rodeo arena, *Skyrocket* from Miles City won the hearts of Montanans.[9]

The official beginning of the Miles City Roundup was in 1913. A dominant rodeo champ of that early era was tall, athletic Yakima Canutt from Oregon. Canutt presumably was attracted to the Miles City Roundup by *Skyrocket*. Canutt joined the US Navy in 1918, then resumed his rodeo career after the war. His exceptional riding skills led inevitably to Western movies, where he became a close friend of John Wayne, and where he markedly advanced the exciting but dangerous profession of stuntman.[10]

Rodeo champion Yakima Canutt visited the Miles City Roundup to challenge the spectacular bronc *Skyrocket*. Canutt began appearing in Western movies, and soon he became the pre-eminent stuntman in the motion picture world. *Author's collection.*

The Miles City Roundup of 1914 showcased Fannie Sperry Steele, who earned honors as Woman Saddle Bronc Champion of the World in 1912 and again in 1913. In 1914, Fannie, who was raised on a ranch north of Helena, won the Miles City Cowbelles bucking horse event. Seated in the crowd was famed cowboy artist Charles Russell from Great Falls. In later years Alice and Margie Greenough, who were champion riders from Red Lodge, also bucked broncs at the Miles City Roundup.[11]

With the end of the constant horse roundups for the remount depot, horses began to multiply on the nutritious ranges of eastern Montana. Drought-ridden wheat farmers deserted their homesteads, often leaving behind their draft animals. By the late 1920s the horse market collapsed, with animals worth only pennies per pound — and no place to ship them.

But opportunity — an opportunity that would be headquartered in Miles City — was developed by the Chappel Brothers Corporation (CBC) of Rockford, Illinois. The Chappel brothers — Philip Mitchell (P.M.), Earl, and Ernst — founded the CBC during the Great War, shipping horse meat to Europe for human consumption. The CBC horse meat packing plant grew to be the world's largest, and in 1922, P.M. Chappel introduced Ken-L-Ration, the first canned dog food produced in

Cowgirls at the 1914 Miles City Roundup parade.
Courtesy Range Riders Museum.

the United States. Five years later, while on a horse-buying trip to eastern and central Montana, P.M. noted the great numbers of unclaimed horses ranging free.

In February 1929, the CBC was incorporated in Montana. Corporate offices were established on Main Street in Miles City, and Miles City was named center of one of the four CBC operational divisions. The CBC was whimsically nicknamed "Corned Beef and Cabbage" or "Coffee, Biscuits, Colts" or "Chappel Brothers Cannery." Whatever it was called, the CBC intended to conduct large-scale horse roundups for its canned meat industry.[12]

The CBC began purchasing or leasing big tracts of land under terms that gave the Corporation ownership of all the unbranded horses ranging on these tracts. At the peak of operations, the CBC owned or leased 1.6 million acres in Montana, Wyoming, and South Dakota. An estimated 60,000 horses grazed on CBC lands in Montana. Cowboys were hired, young men who could withstand long — very long — days in the saddle. Their work would be seasonal, four or five months of rising as early as three a.m. and not bedding down until eight or nine p.m.. And they would be in the saddle seven days a week.

CBC cowboys rounded up large herds, branding the animals at the sites where they were gathered. Area ranches sent "reps" to these roundups, as they had during the earlier days of large cattle roundups on the open range. Also like the big cattle roundups, there was a roundup crew and wagon with each herd of horses. A wagon boss was in charge of the roundup and crew. The cook handled the chuck wagon and meals. Each member of the crew was assigned a specific job. The horse wrangler tended the mounts, and the nighthawk herded the remuda during the nights. After the roundups and branding, the cowboys sorted and trailed horses to railheads for shipment to Rockford. Once shipped to the cannery in Rockford, the horses became chicken feed, dog and cat food, fertilizer, and glue. The Russian government signed a contract to purchase tons of horse meat for food. Meanwhile, CBC cowboys finished their season by breaking saddle horses for the remuda, gelding two-year-old stallions, and branding colts.

Also visiting the Miles City Roundup was famed cowboy artist Charles Russell, from Great Falls. *Author's collection.*

CBC cowboys were paid $40-$45 per month, excellent wages for the Great Depression years of the 1930s. "The C.B.C. was prestigious in that if you had a job there, you were automatically considered a top hand by your peers," reminisced former CBC rider Claire Boyce. "It really never stopped there, either. When we walked into a dance hall, the girls would whisper, 'The CBC cowboys!' They would drop the neighbor farmer boys like a steer in the road, and we would damn sure give them a whirl!"[13]

Prices on the horse market rebounded in 1934, and the CBC sold animals by the boxcar load. With most of the range horses gathered and shipped, the CBC discontinued its Montana operations after 1937, although area cowboys were paid $5 per head to gather stragglers. In 1942 the CBC company in Rockford sold out to Quaker Oats.

CBC cowboys had participated in the last old-time roundup, branding and driving-to-railheads experience of any size in the West. It was like the 1880s, and CBC reunions were held at Wolf Point in 1975, 1977, and 1987. In attendance were former CBC cowboys and their families, along with members of the Chappel Family. Appropriately, the final roundup of CBC cowboys was held at Miles City in 1994.

By the time the Chappel Brothers Corporation was concluding its 1880s-style horse roundup operation in the late 1930s, another plan was being developed to honor the Wild West past of Miles City. In 1939 a group of cowboys and ranchers formed the Range Riders Association with the aim of preserving the memory of the "pioneer range rider." A reunion of these pioneer range riders was held in 1940, with membership open to anyone who had ridden the open range before 1940.[13]

The group decided that the best way to preserve the rich memories of Miles City and Fort Keogh and the surrounding countryside was to erect a museum "with the focus on the western heritage and history of events that occurred within a 150-mile radius of Miles City."[14] No funding was available; indeed, the Range Riders Museum to this day receives no city, county, or state tax. Furthermore, the museum does not purchase artifacts: the entire collection is made of items that have been donated or that are on loan.

It was deemed appropriate to construct a log museum

The Range Riders Museum began to be organized in 1939, and opened its doors to the public two years later. *Photo by the author.*

building on the site of the original 1876 Fort Keogh cantonment. Citizens began to contribute the logs, and five cowboys and a newspaperman volunteered to provide the labor. In order to pay for necessary professional help, cowboys and ranchers paid $25 to put their brand on the logs. To date more than 500 brands are on display in the original log building. The log structure opened as the Range Riders Museum in 1942. Since then a dozen buildings have been added, and the museum area has expanded to 38,000 square feet of display space.

One of the surviving officers quarters, although badly dilapidated, was moved a couple of miles from the old parade ground to the museum complex. The duplex was carefully rebuilt through grants and donations, and it is furnished with period artifacts. A local gun collector provided more than 400 firearms, which are on display in the Bert Clark Gun Room. There are fine dioramas of Fort Keogh and the LO Ranch. Among the thousands of items on display include pioneer possessions, Native American items, and an eye-popping collection of saddles that were produced locally. A large

The Waterworks Art Museum is a unique art gallery housed in a 1910 concrete building, which was erected as the centerpiece of the Miles City water system. *Photo by the author.*

wagon barn houses a superb collection of pioneer and military vehicles. The Range Riders Museum is a splendid repository of the historic community's frontier past.

Located only a short distance from the Range Riders Museum is another outstanding museum. The WaterWorks Art Museum housed a varied and impressive art collection in the concrete and brick structure that was built in 1910 as the centerpiece of the Miles City drinking water system. Because the primary building of the city water supply was erected on the military reservation, an act of Congress was required in 1911 for final permission. As the system was modernized, the 1910 water treatment facility was turned over to the community for use as a museum in 1977.

First known as the Custer County Art Center, the museum acquired a permanent collection of arts and photographs. There are outstanding photo displays from pioneer photographers L.A. Huffman and Evelyn Cameron. Adult and children's classes are offered throughout each year, and the museum vans transport artworks and art supplies to rural schools in the county. The Montana Arts Council and the National Endowment for the Arts provide important support for these and other museum activities. And anyone who visits the galleries in the 1910 treatment facility is exposed to a unique historical structure, and venerable buildings truly are our most tangible reminders of the past.

Chapter Fourteen
The World Famous Miles City Bucking Horse Sale

"The past is never dead. It is not even past."
— William Faulkner

The World Famous Miles City Bucking Horse Sale — a truly ambitious title for a livestock event in an Old West town with a population of only about 8,500. This annual event also is called "The Cowboy Mardi Gras" — another florid label. But despite a somewhat inauspicious beginning, the World Famous Miles City Bucking Horse Sale has evolved into a colorful, fun-filled celebration that measures up to the liveliest and most nostalgic traditions its sponsors could hope to invoke. For four days each May, the Cowboy Mardis Gras transforms Miles City into a center of the Old West excitement that made it a famous community of the once-wild frontier.

The *Stockgrowers Journal* of Miles City seemed to take a peek into the future as early as 1885: "With the demand from cattlemen for cow ponies, Miles City is likely to become quite a horse market." Horses thrived on the rangelands surrounding Miles City. Indeed, by the late 1880s breeders in the vicinity were producing cow ponies, saddle horses, cavalry mounts, carriage horses, draft animals for farming and freighting, race horses and even polo ponies.[1]

In 1890 the Miles City Horse Sales and Fair Association began holding auctions for local stock. Between 1895 and 1907, a local stockman, A.B. Clark, conducted the sales of thousands of Montana horses. As we already have seen, during the heyday of the Fort Keogh remount depot, more than 100 civilian horsemen endured daily "rodeos" while breaking horses at the depot. Even after the close of the remount station, horses rapidly restocked their favorite ranges. "There were horses on every knoll and hill in sight," it was observed. The Chappel Brothers Corporation paid area cowboys good wages to round up horses during the 1930s, but the horses always rebounded strongly. And young buckaroos happily accepted pay for the pleasure of riding horseback, western-style.[2]

But despite the proliferation of horses in the vicinity, as well as the deeply ingrained love of forking a saddle by young men and women raised in ranch country, the Miles City Bucking Horse Sale got off to an unpromising start. In 1950 Les Boe, owner of the Miles City Livestock Commission, purchased some yearling steers from a dealer known as Heavy Lester. Lester headquartered at Ekalaka, a small county seat town located southeast of Miles City. When Les Boe and his son-in-law, Bob Pauley, collected the steers, they found that Lester had thrown in thirty-five unwanted — untrained, untamed, "spoiled" — bucking horses. Not knowing what else to do, Boe and Pauley decided to offer these horses for sale, hiring riders to buck out these animals for "mount money" — five dollars a head for bareback (smaller) horses, and ten dollars each for the larger saddle broncs.

The idea, adapted in part from the old remount depot methods, was that each horse would be auctioned for sale immediately after the ride. With the transaction completed, the next ride would promptly commence. Boe and Pauley spread the word, and when the sale riding began, a number of old cowboys and ranchers showed up simply to watch the action.

Les Boe understood the appeal of non-stop bucking horse rides. The next year, 1951, Boe and Pauley gathered more

Built in 1914, the "new" sales yard in Miles City staged the largest horse sale in the world. *Courtesy Range Riders Museum.*

than 1,000 horses from area ranchers. The plan was to buck out and sell 350 horses each day for three days in May. Mount money again was offered to riders, while Paddy Ryan and Bob Askin were hired as pickup men. Once more a large number of spectators attended not to buy horses but to watch the rides. It was decided to charge one dollar admission. It also was announced that the Miles City Bucking Horse Sale would become an annual event, and the official starting date has been recorded as 1951.

The next year Gene Autry, the famous "Singing Cowboy" of movies, television, and recordings, was present in one of his business roles. Autry was an influential rodeo producer, and at Miles City he purchased several promising bucking horses. Numerous other rodeo stock contractors became regulars at the Miles City Bucking Horse Sale. Famous bucking horses that came out of the early sales included *Big John, Dark Journey, Crazy One, Mexico Kid, High Roll,* and *Lemon Drop.* By 1956 local Jaycees were providing refreshments to visitors. In 1962 a match bronc race between noted cowboys was organized to showcase such horses as *General Custer*, *Sage Hen*, and *Trail's End*. Other events and activities were added to keep the spectators entertained.[3]

After a long day at the rodeo arena, sales attendees converted Miles City's Main Street into a big dance floor. Street dance crowds became so large that beer was served in tubs or troughs, as it had been at the Cottage Saloon on Fort Keogh paydays.[4] Sometimes a happy cowboy would ride his horse into a bar, as in the old days. Extra policemen were hired, and jail cells were filled. There were half-hearted clampdowns, but Miles City remained at its core a party town, with music and laughter, dancing and drinking.

The population of Miles City exceeded 9,000 during this period, and in 1975 13,000 visitors came to enjoy the World Famous Bucking Horse Sale. Even though the town population leveled back to about 8,500, visitors to Miles City during the three or four days each May regularly total 10,000 or more, with an annual economic impact of $10 to $12 million.

While the World Famous Miles City Bucking Horse Sale was reaching iconic status as a western entertainment event, the one-time frontier town finally received cultural recognition. Dodge City, Tombstone, and Abilene often were utilized in film and fiction as the setting for Wild West towns challenged by outlawry and gunplay. Miles City, however, was almost never even mentioned in a Western movie or television series, and therefore was not well known to the public. But if Miles City was scarcely ever the backdrop of Old West drama, it does have the distinction of being the site of a climactic fictional event, of powerful drama between the two stars of one of the most popular of all Western novels and films.

Lonesome Dove was the masterpiece of Texas author Larry McMurtry. The tale of two former Texas Rangers, Captains Augustus McCrea and Woodrow Call, *Lonesome Dove* colorfully recounts the epic adventures of their cattle drive from Texas to Montana. *Lonesome Dove* won the 1986 Pulitzer Prize for fiction. Filmed as a television mini-series starring Robert Duvall and Tommy Lee Jones, *Lonesome Dove* dominated the 1989 Emmy Awards with eighteen nominations and seven wins, including Best Mini-Series and Best Actor in a Mini-Series (Duvall).

In episode four, after at last reaching Montana, Gus makes it to Miles City suffering from mortal wounds. The single muddy street, flanked by log buildings with false fronts, closely resembles Main Street of early Miles City. Woodrow finds his friend and partner in a doctor's office, having endured the amputation of one leg and resisting with a drawn pistol the removal of his remaining leg. A moving death scene occurs that night, with dramatic consequences to follow. If Miles City had only one appearance in a Western novel and film, *Lonesome Dove* provided a singular pinnacle.

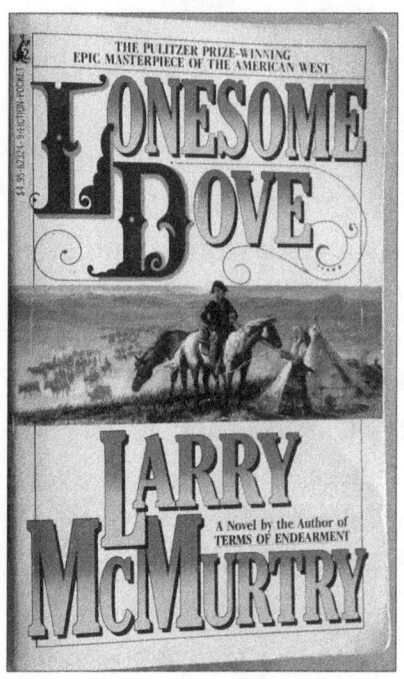

Miles City was featured in the climax of the award-winning novel and TV mini-series, Lonesome Dove. *Photo by the author.*

While Miles City finally achieved a long-deserved place in the fiction of the Old West, the town's modern entrepreneurs continued to shape and improve "The Cowboy Mardi Gras." Just as the early settlers of frontier Miles City boldly seized every opportunity to improve their business or community, the modern generation of businessmen and businesswomen, of community leaders male and female, focuses on the opportunities made possible by their unique western event. The town rallied enthusiastically behind every promising idea, and one activity after another — either in the arena or in town — received strong support.

As of this writing, the most current Bucking Horse Sale took place in 2024. The "three-day" event — Friday, Saturday, Sunday — now begins on Thursday evening with a Kick-Off Concert. At 6 p.m. Kalyn Beasley and his Honky Tonk Arcade led off, and one hour later Chancey Williams, son of an area rancher who became a singer – songwriter, took over the concert with music that included his hit, "She Loves Me Anyway." At eight o'clock the popular headliner, Josh Turner, a Grammy winner and a member of Grand Ole Opry, came on to electrify the crowd in the arena.[5]

The next three days were packed with bucking and racing events. On Friday and Saturday three-man teams (the Montana Team, the Team Young Guns, the Texas Team, etc.) competed in wild horse races in which it often takes several minutes just to throw a saddle on an untamed bronc. Finally there is a race around the arena, and of sixteen teams, eight qualify for the Sunday Finals.

There is a rodeo grand entry on Friday, Saturday, and Sunday. A trade show, featuring over 100 vendors, is open throughout the BHS, and the shopping is a constant delight. On Saturday at 6 .m., the Range Riders Museum offers a Cowboy Breakfast in the museum's Memorial Hall. Later in the morning the Waterworks Art Museum stages a Quick Draw Art Contest (thirty minutes is allotted to each artist). On Saturday morning a Main Street parade showcases floats and horseback riders and the Seventh Cavalry Drum and Bugle Corps from American Legion Post 7 in Sheridan, Wyoming.

Attired in 1870s cavalry uniforms and led by a Custer figure in a buckskin jacket, the group leads off with "When the Saints Go Marchin' In" and later closes with the "Garryowen" battle song, a favorite of Custer's. During the evenings the group marches into one bar after another playing their rousing martial music. Each night "after parties" are staged late in the Montana Bar or the Bison Bar or Hole in the Wall or the historic Olive Hotel. The Olive Hotel starts serving breakfast at 2 a.m., with the tempting reminder that "Bloody Marys & Caesar's [are] served daily."[6]

At 10 a.m. on Sundays, Cowboy Church services are held. Prior to the BHS weekend, Derby Days races are staged with the Churchill Downs simulcast of the Kentucky Derby (in 2024 on May 4 and 5). The following Sunday, May 12, offers a slate of Mother's Day races and, appropriately, mothers are admitted free.

Throughout the three days of the BHS there are bucking bronc and bull riding exhibitions, along with almost every variety of horse racing (Wild Horse Races, of course, Match Bronc Riding Calcutta, PRCA Xtreme Broncs Match, with $57,000 in prize money added.) Other race variations include Mutton Bustin', in which children try to stay aboard big wooly sheep.

"This has always been horse country," insists John L. Moore, rancher, journalist, author, and historian of the World Famous Miles City Bucking Horse Sale. Moore points out that Miles City was "the horse capital of the world for decades." The BHS event vaulted to popularity originally "because it was so wild. There wasn't anything like it for pure wildness." And John Morford, President of the Board of Governors of the World Famous Miles City Bucking Horse Sale, states emphatically that "Miles City is a bastion of the cowboy heritage."[7]

Indeed, it is easy to imagine today's participants in the BHS riding their mounts in impromptu races up and down Main

The 7th Cavalry Drum and Bugle Corps of the Sheridan, Wyoming, American Legion, is a colorful addition to the parade which opens the Bucking Horse Sale — and to the downtown celebration each evening. *Photo provided by the 7th Cavalry Drum and Bugle Corps, American Legion Post No. 7, courtesy of Ron Schaal of Sheridan, Wyo.*

Street during the 1880s. And the same fun-loving cowboys who dipped their beer mugs into an open trough at one of today's Main Street bars would have done the same at a beer-filled tub at the Cottage Saloon during the 1870s. Furthermore, a reveler from the 1880s would be comfortable eating a 2 a.m. breakfast at the Olive Hotel, especially if he were served a Bloody Mary. The young ladies who danced all night at an 1880s Miles City event would readily join a modern street dance. And the parades which featured western-clad horsemen and horsewomen, along with festive floats, would attract the same participants and onlookers whether it was the 1880s, the 1920s, the 1950s, the 1990s, or the 2020s. For those who want to experience tangible elements of early Miles City, there are such buildings as the 1886 Episcopal Church, the towering Sacred Heart Convent, early residences along Pleasant Street, venerable downtown commercial structures, and from Fort

Keogh, an 1870s furnished officers' duplex at the Range Riders Museum — which is a repository for thousands of artifacts large and small from frontier Miles City and from old Fort Keogh. It is easy to feel the ghosts at historic Miles City.

One can almost see the fun-loving, high-spirited citizen of today's Miles City fitting comfortably into Old Milestown. Or the citizens of frontier Miles City quickly adapting to the modern community. The spirit of Miles City seems irrepressible, so that the citizens of the old frontier town probably would thrive in the modern town. As the literary giant William Faulkner mused, "The past is never dead. It's not even past."[8]

Endnotes

Chapter One: *Introduction to a Frontier Town*

1. Abbott, *We Painted Them North*, 89.

Chapter Two: *Birth of a Frontier Town*

1. Often overlooked is the Battle of the Wabash, also called St. Clair's Defeat or the Battle of a Thousand Slain. A 1791 campaign in the Old Northwest between a Native American confederacy and an army led by Major General Arthur St. Clair climaxed on November 4, 1791, at the U.S. Army camp near the headquarters of the Wabash River. A dawn attack by about 1,100 Shawnees, Miamis, and Delawares routed St. Clair's men - only twenty-four soldiers escaped unharmed. The army lost 656 killed or captured and another 279 wounded, adding up to a 97 per cent casualty rate, along with 88 per cent casualties among the 52 officers. St. Clair was one of the few soldiers who survived unscathed. There were about 200 camp followers, and most of these women and children were slain, adding up to 832 dead Americans - three times the number who died alongside Custer at the Little Bighorn. Two years later, when another U.S. Army force marched into the area, the battle site was identified by the piles of unburied skeletons. These remains were buried in a common grave. The Native Americans lost twenty-one warriors KIA and about another forty wounded. "St. Clair's Defeat," Wikipedia; R.D. Evans, "The Battle of the Wabash - Inside the Disastrous First Campaign of the U.S. Army," *Wikipedia*.

2. *Bismarck Tribune, Extra Edition*, July 6, 1876.

3. "Fort Keogh," *Wikipedia*; "Fort Keogh, Montana-Legends of America," www.legendsofamerica.com

4. Miles, *Personal Recollections of General Nelson A. Miles*, 213, 218.

5. Miles, *Personal Recollections*, 213-214; Wooster, *Nelson A. Miles & the Twilight of the Frontier Army*, 77, 79-80.

6. Miles, *Personal Recollections*, 217.

7. Hart, *Old Forts of the Northwest*, 179-181. Herbert M. Hart, who explored the entire American West while compiling a series of books on frontier forts, created a drawing of the Tongue River Cantonment parade ground from data in the National Archives and from the mounds of dirt and rubble which remained when he examined the site of Fort Keogh and the cantonment.

8. Miles, *Personal Recollections*, 232.

9. *Ibid.*

10. Brown and Felton, *The Frontier Years*, 133, 245 note 5.

11. Gordon, *Recollections of Old Milestown*, 14. Sam Gordon was an early settler of "Old Milestown" who spent thirty-three years as editor of *The Daily Yellowstone Journal*, and whose recollections are pure gold to any historian of frontier Miles City.

12. Gordon, *Old Milestown*, 3, 16.

13. Gordon, *Old Milestown*, 4, 21.

14. Gordon, *Old Milestown*, 3-4.

Chapter Three: *General Nelson "Bear Coat" Miles*

1. Miles, *Personal Recollections*, 221.

2. *Ibid.*

3. *Nelson A. Miles & the Twilight of the Frontier Army*, by Robert Wooster, is a superb biography, full of detail and insight. Also useful is DeMontravel, *A Hero to His Fighting Men, Nelson A. Miles, 1839-1925*. Another fine account is *The Unregimented General: A Biography of Nelson A. Miles*, by Virginia Johnson. Not to be overlooked, of course, are the memories of Miles: *Personal Recollections and Observations of General Nelson A. Miles*, published in 1896; and the somewhat ponderous *Serving the Republic: Memories of the Civil and Military Life of Nelson A Miles, Lieutenant-General, United States Army*, 1911.

4. For the story of the attack on the German family, along with the murder of the parents, a brother, and a sister, and the capture of four sisters, see: Olive Dixon, "Rescue of Four German Sisters . . . ," *Fort Worth Star Telegram*, August 14, 1938; Baldwin, Memoirs, 76; Miles, *Personal Recollections*, 175-176, 179-181; Dixon, *"Billy" Dixon*, 233-234; Craine to Miles, January 11, 1875.

5. Miles, *Personal Recollections*, 222, 225.

6. *Ibid.*, 217, 218.

7. *Ibid.*, 218-219.

8. *Ibid*, 219-220.

9. *Ibid.* 226. In addition to the first-person account of Miles in *Personal Recollections*, see the chapter on "The Conquest of the Sioux, 1876-81" in *Frontier Regulars* by Robert M. Utley.

10. Miles, *Personal Recollections*, 227-228.

11. Miles, *Personal Recollections*, 231, 238-239; also see Rickey, "The Battle of Wolf Mountain," *Montana*, Winter 2001.

12. Miles, *Personal Recollections*, 231, 240-243.

13. *Ibid.*, 243.

14. *Ibid.*, 244.

15. *Ibid.*, 248-253.

16. *Ibid.*, 256.

17. Wooster, *Nelson A. Miles*, 94-95.

18. Miles, *Personal Recollections*, 256.

19. *Ibid.*, 259-274. Also see Utley, *Frontier Regulars*, "Nez Perce Bid for

Freedom," 306-330; Greene, "The Army at the Clearwater, Tactical Victory and Defeat in the Nez Perce War," *Montana*, Winter 2000; Whittlesey, "The Nez Perces in the Yellowstone in 1877," *Montana*, Spring 2007.

20. Miles, *Personal Recollections*, 272-273.

21. *Ibid.*, 274-275.

22. *Ibid.*, 275.

23. *Ibid.*, 294-295.

24. *Ibid.*, 295; also see Utley, *Frontier Regulars*, 331-337.

25. Miles, *Personal Recollections*, 296-305.

26. *Ibid.* 132.

27. Wooster, *Nelson A. Miles*, 117-118.

28. *Ibid.*, 119-120.

29. *Ibid.*, 120, 129.

30. *Ibid.*, 130-131; Miles, Personal Recollections, 352.

31. Miles, *Personal Recollections*, 480-532; Wooster, *Nelson A. Miles*, 144-162; Utley, *Frontier Regulars*, 396-402.

32. Wooster, *Nelson A. Miles*, 175.

33. *Ibid.*, 176-194, 204, 210-231, 262.

Chapter Four: *A Tale of Two Cities*

1. *A Tale of Two Cities*, the enormously successful historical novel by Charles Dickens, was published in 1859, just seventeen years before the founding of the Tongue River Cantonment and Milestown. The famous opening paragraph by Dickens begins "It was the best of times, it was the worst of times . . ." *A Tale of Two Cities* refers to Paris and London, with a background of the French Revolution and the Reign of Terror. Although Fort Keogh and Miles City hardly command the stature on the world stage equal to Paris and London, perhaps Native Americans and soldiers and settlers of the 1870s and 1880s experienced elements of their own Reign of Terror and of revolutionary changes of lifestyles on the Montana frontier.

2. Warhank, "Fort Keogh: Cutting Edge of a Culture," pp. 7-8.

3. The Master's Thesis by Josef James Warhank, "Fort Keogh: Cutting Edge of a Culture," is the most thorough study of Fort Keogh. For the early construction details see pp. 6-11.

4. Captain Heintzelman's father was West Point Class of 1826, and the captain's son was Class of 1899. Both the father and the son of Captain Heintzelman reached the rank of major general. Unfortunately the captain fell ill and died at the age of thirty-five in Washington, D.C., in 1881. Thompson, ed. *Fifty Miles and a Fight, Samuel Peter Heintzelman Journal*, 2, 57n.; also see the entry on Captain Heintzelman by Hoopes, *This Last West*, 158.

5. Warhank, "Fort Keogh."

6. *Ibid.*, 103-104.
7. Miles, *Personal Recollections*, 330-333; Warhank, "Fort Keogh," 107.
8. Warhank, "Fort Keogh," 107; Hoopes, *This Last West*, 120, 29.03-204
9. Warhank, "Fort Keogh," 107; Hoopes, *This Last West*, 120, 288-289.
10. Hoopes, *This Last West*, 56-57, 204.
11. *Ibid.*, 56-57, 113, 244, 245, 288, 332-333.
12. Baldwin, Alice Blackwood, *Memoirs of the Late Frank D. Baldwin*; Hoopes, *This Last West*, 11-12.
13. Hoopes, *This Last West*, 173-174, 211-212; Gordon, *Recollections of Old Milestown*, 33; Warhank, "Fort Keogh," 55-56.
14. Hoopes, *This Last West*, 28-29.
15. *Ibid.*, 121-124.
16. *Ibid.*, Warhank, "Fort Keogh," 12, 56-57, 82, 235, 288.
17. Hoopes, *This Last West*, 207.
18. Warhank, "Fort Keogh," 114-115.
19. *Ibid.*, 115.
20. *Yellowstone Journal*, August 14, 1879 and February 16, 1884; Warhank, "Fort Keogh," 115-119.
21. Wilson, F.M. "Miles City," *Avant Courier*, Bozeman, Montana, April 3, 1879. This article may also be found under the heading , "A Word Picture of Miles City, 1879."

Chapter Five: *Frontier Violence*

1. Each of these films is available online or on DVDs.
2. Gordon, *Recollections of Old Milestown*, 19.
3. *Ibid.*
4. *Ibid.*, 5.
5. Warhank, "Fort Keogh," 64.
6. *Ibid.*, 111.
7. Hoopes, *This Last West*, 67, 167, 198, 294.
8. Gordon, *Recollections*, 37.
9. *Ibid.*, 38.
10. Hoopes, *This Last West*, 72, 298; Gordon, *Recollections*, 39.
11. Gordon, *Recollections*, 39.
12. *Ibid.*, 40.
13. *Ibid.*, 41; Hoopes, *This Last West*, 62-63.
14. Gordon, *Recollections*, 41-42.
15. Hoopes, *This Last West*, 62-63.
16. Gordon, *Recollections*, 41-42.
17. *Medal of Honor*; "James Pym," Wikipedia.

Endnotes 217

18. "James Pym," Wikipedia; Hoopes, *This Last West*, 289.
19. Huffman account in Brown and Felton, *The Frontier Years*, 156-157.
20. "James Pym," Wikipedia.
21. *Medal of Honor*; "Henry Hogan," Wikipedia.
22. "James Pym," Wikipedia.
23. Warhank, "Fort Keogh," 112.
24. "Big Nose George," Wikipedia.
25. Brown and Felton, *The Frontier Years*, 156-157.
26. *Ibid.*, 157-158; Hoopes, This Last West, 279; "Big Nose George," Wikipedia.
27. Hoopes, *This Last West*, 375.
28. Brown and Felton, *The Last Frontier*, 155.
29. Hoopes, *This Last West*, 375.

Chapter Six: *Miles City Demimonde*

1. "Demimonde." *Wikipedia*. The terms "demimonde" and "demimondane" went out of fashion early in the twentieth century with the emergence of the "new woman."
2. *Yellowstone Journal*, June 14, 1884, and December 25, 1886.
3. *Yellowstone Journal*, December 25, 1886; Hoopes, *This Last West*, 351.
4. Hoopes, *This Last West*, 351; *Yellowstone Journal*, November 4 and 19, 1882.
5. Hoopes, *This Last West*, 41.
6. Abbott and Smith, *We Pointed Them North*, 103-104.
7. *Ibid.*, 104-105.
8. *Ibid.*, 105, 228-229.
9. Hoopes, *This Last West*, 161-162; Abbott and Smith, *We Pointed Them North*, 111-112.
10. Hoopes, *This Last West*, 161-162, 277.
11. Alderson and Smith, *A Bride Goes West*, 21-22.
12. *Ibid.*, 114-115.
13. *Ibid.*, 116-117.
14. Abbott and Smith, *We Pointed Them North*, 108.
15. Hoopes, *This Last West*, 45, 124-125, 161-162.
16. *Ibid.*, 150, 352.
17. *Ibid.*, 144, 310-311; Abbott and Smith, *We Pointed Them North*, 166.
18. Abbott and Smith, *We Pointed Them North*, 167.
19. *Ibid.*, 101, 107.
20. Hoopes, *This Last West*, 111, 127, 175, 313, 351.
21. Brown and Felton, *The Frontier Years*, 144-145.
22. Abbott and Smith, *We Pointed Them North*, 80-81.
23. Hoopes, *This Last West*, 74, 361.
24. Gordon, *Recollections of Old Milestown*, 21.

25. *Ibid.*, 21-22.
26. Brown and Felton, *The Frontier Years*, 144; Hoopes, *The Last West*, 284.
27. Sanborn maps female bonds
28. McLaird, *Calamity Jane*, 117-119, 122-123, 137, 144, 168-169; Jacovy, *Searching for Calamity*, 92, 137, 146; Abbott and Smith, *We Pointed Them North*, 74-76; Brown and Felton, *The Frontier Years*, 146-148.
29. Abbott and Smith, *We Pointed Them North*, 110.

Chapter 7: *From Fire Boats to Bullwhackers to the Iron Horse*
1. For an illuminating description of the new western riverboats, as well as other craft on the Missouri and Yellowstone rivers, see O'Neil, *The Rivermen*.
2. Miles, *Recollections*, 213.
3. *Ibid.*, 215.
4. *Ibid.*, 325-326.
5. Hanson, *Conquest of the Missouri*. Author Joseph Mills Hanson was a lifelong admirer of Captain Grant Marsh. Hanson put together a biography of Marsh that was reinforced by materials furnished by the captain. Marsh was born in 1838 and Hanson in 1876, and both had homes in Yankton, North Dakota. Also see the biographical article on Captain Marsh in Wikipedia..
6. "Far West (steamship)," Alchetron. This article provides a thorough description of the famous sternwheeler *Far West*. Also see Hoopes, *This Last West*, 109.
7. There are numerous accounts of the record-breaking journey of Captain Marsh and the *Far West* with the wounded troopers from the Little Bighorn Battlefield. See, for example, Hanson, *Conquest of the Missouri*, 215-229; O'Neil, *The Rivermen*, 221-225; Hoopes, *This Last West*, 216-217.
8. Hanson, *Conquest of the Missouri*, 247-248.
9. *Ibid.*, 249-307; Hoopes, *This Last West*, 216-217.
10. Hanson, *Conquest of the Missouri*, 248-249.
11. Warhank, "Fort Keogh: Cutting Edge of a Culture," 48.
12. Hoopes, *This Last West*, 327.
13. *Ibid.*, 93.
14. Sam Gordon related his memories and his reflections of bull trains and the Diamond R corner and, most memorably, the bullwhackers on pages 20 and 21 of *Recollections of Old Milestown*.
15. Warhank, "Fort Keogh: Cutting Edge of a Culture," 49-50
16. *Ibid.*, 50-51; Kelly, "*Yellowstone Kelly*," *Memoirs*, 207; *Yellowstone Journal*, August 28, 1879.
17. Nevin, *The Expressman*, 123-187; Everard H. Smith, III, "stagecoach," in Lamar, ed., *The Reader's Encyclopedia of the American West*, 1138-1140.
18. Twain, *Roughing It*, 33.
19. Clay, *My Life on the Range*, 86-87.

20. See the distance tables and maps in Hoopes, *This Last West*, 398-399 and the unnumbered map section in the center of the book.
21. Twain, *Roughing It*, 36-37.
22. Warhank, "Fort Keogh: Cutting Edge of a Culture," 54.
23. Lubetkin, *Joy Cooke's Gamble, The Northern Pacific Railroad, The Sioux, And The Panic of 1873*.
24. "Northern Pacific Railway," Wikipedia.
25. Gordon, *Recollections*, 37.
26. *Ibid*.
27. Bell, *New Tracks in America*, Vol. 1, 254.
28. Gordon, *Recollections*, 38; Brown and Felton, *The Frontier Years*, 185.
29. Gordon, *Recollections*, 38.
30. Miles City photographer L.A. Huffman received an invitation from the Northern Pacific for Thanksgiving Dinner in 1881, shortly after the NP reached Miles City. Mark H. Brown and W.H. Felton, authors of *The Frontier Years: L.A. Huffman, Photographer of the Plains*, found the invitation in Huffman's papers and reproduced the information in their excellent book.
31. Gordon, *Recollections*, 37.
32. "Northern Pacific Railway," Wikipedia; Taylor, "The Northern Pacific's Last Spike Excursion," *Montana*.

Chapter 8: *Cattle Town*

1. Toole, *Montana*, 142; Stockman Bank, *Miles City Memories*, 45.
2. Abbott and Smith, *We Pointed Them North*, 64-65.
3. Hoopes, *This Last West*, 255; Warhank, "Fort Keogh," 123.
4. Abbott and Smith, *We Pointed Them North*, 100.
5. *Ibid.*, 13.
6. Hoopes, *This Last West*, 266; Abbott and Smith, *We Pointed Them North*, 60, 89-91.
7. Abbott and Smith, *We Pointed Them North*, 94-95.
8. *Ibid.*, 101.
9. *Ibid.*, 102.
10. *Ibid*.
11. Hoopes, *The Last West*, 12, 234, 241, 328.
12. *Ibid.*, 98, 173, 292.
13. *Ibid.*, 173-174, 211
14. Abbott and Smith, *We Pointed Them North*, 219-220.
15. *Ibid.*, 218.
16. *Bozeman Avant-Courier*, July 31, 1879, quoted in Hoopes, *This Last West*, 241.
17. It may be recalled that "shindies" were bar fights, "swaddies" were

soldiers on a night in the saloons, and "coffee coolers" were loafers who hung around offices at Fort Keogh sipping coffee. "Honyockers" were sodbusters who arrived, often unwelcome, in the cattle grazing country of eastern Montana ("Don't plow it under," went the cowman's warming to the newcomer, "the best side is already up.") And Texas cowboys quickly learned that cattle driven into Montana from the West, from Oregon and Idaho, were called "Westerners."

18. "Miles City Saddlery, Original Coggshall Saddles," History.

19. Guy Logsdon, "Rodeo" entry in Lamar, *Reader's Encyclopedia of the American West*, 1027-1031.

20. Stockman Bank, *Miles City Memories, The Early Years*, 112-135. "Miles City Traditions," *Western Horsemen*, August 28, 2007.

Chapter 9: Montana *Stockgrowers Association*

1. *Bozeman Avant Courier*, January 4, 1883; *Bismarck Tribune*, May 4, 1883; Hoopes, *This Last West*, 59-60.

2. Stuart, *Forty Years on the Frontier*, 195.

3. Hoopes, *This Last West*, 256; Stuart, *Forty Years on the Frontier*, Vol. II, 191-193, 195-226; Abbott and Smith, *We Pointed Them North*, 83, 131-134; Roosevelt, *Ranch Life and the Hunting-Trail*, 7 ff.; Clay, "A Call to Order," *Montana*, Autumn 2008; " Montana Stockgrower's Association," Wikipedia.

4. Stuart, *Forty Years on the Frontier*, 195-197.

5. *Ibid.*,196-197.

6. *Ibid*.

7. *Ibid,*. 197

8. Barrows, *U-bet*, 204.

9. Stuart, *Forty Years on the Frontier*, 202-205.

10. *Ibid.*, 205-209

11. Abbott and Smith, *We Pointed Them North*, 135.

12. Stuart, *Forty Years on the Frontier*, 209.

13. Abbott and Smith, *We Pointed Them North*, 135.

14. Roosevelt, *Ranch Life in the Far West*, 14.

15. Wallis Huidekoper, quoted in Brown and Felton, *Before Barbed Wire*, 119.

16. Abbott and Smith, *We Pointed Them North*, 134.

17. Stuart, *Forty Years on the Frontier*, 196, 209.

18. *Ibid.*, 209.

19. Roosevelt, *Ranch Life in the Far West*, 7.

20. Gordon, *Recollections of Old Milestown*, 31; Hoopes, *This Last West*, 242.

21. Gordon, *Recollections of Old Milestown*, 31.

22. For information on the career and personal life of Pierre Wibaux, see: Welsh, *Pierre Wibaux, Cattle King; Wibaux County Diamond Jubilee*, N.p., 1989; Hoopes, *This Last West*, 368-369.

Chapter Ten: *The XIT in Montana*
1. Literature is abundant on the XIT of Texas. See, for example, Miller, *XIT, A Story of Land, Cattle, and Capital in Texas and Montana*; 2020; Haley, *The XIT Ranch of Texas*; Duke and Frant, *6,000 Miles of Fence*.
2. Duke and Frantz, *6,000 Miles of Fence*, 139-140.
3. Haley, *The XIT Ranch of Texas*, 140-141.
4. *Ibid.*, 138-155.
5. Russell, *Bob Fudge*, 81, 89.
6. Duke and Frantz, *6,000 Miles of Fence*, 145.
7. O.C. Cato, obituary, *Miles City Star*, May 13, 1915.
8. Russell, *Bob Fudge*, 76-77.
9. Duke and Frantz, *6,000 Miles of Fence*, 146-150.
10. *Ibid.*, 149-150.
11. *Ibid.*, 187-188.
12. Duke and Frantz, *6,000 Miles of Fence*, 187-189.
13. *Ibid.*, 189.
14. Russell, *Bob Fudge*, 90, 92, 108-111.
15. *Ibid.*, 55-63.
16. Haley, *The XIT Ranch of Texas*, 130.
17. *Terry Tribune*, October 9, 1909.
18. O.C. Cato, obituary. *Miles City Star*, May 13, 1915.
19. Mary Cato Swayne, obituary, August 19, 2004.
20. *Ibid*.
21. Russell, *Bob Fudge*; visits by the author to the Prairie County Museum in Terry and to the Range Riders Museum in Miles City.

Chapter Eleven: *Urban Pioneers*
1. Billington, *Westward Expansion*, 6-7.
2. Hoopes, *This Last West*, "Brown, Charlie," 37.
3. Billington, *America's Frontier Heritage*, 78, 88.
4. Alderson and Smith, *A Bride Goes West*, 231-232.
5. Hoopes, *This Last West*, "Carmichael, Judge Alexander," 53-54; "Logan, Prof. Arthur C., 266-267; "Miles City Schools," 243-244.
6. Hoopes, *This Last West*, "Miles City Schools," 243-244; "Porter, Prof. Thomas Jefferson," 285.
7. Clarke, *Dusting Off the Old Ones*, "Miles City High School Graduates."
8. Hoopes, *This Last West*, "Reading Room Association," 243.
9. Sanborn Fire Maps for Miles City; Hoopes; *This Last West*, "Basinki, J. Store," 15, and "Miles City Reading Room Association," 243.
10. Captions on photo study of Miles City Library.
11. Hoopes, *This Last West*, "Methodist-Episcopal Church," 235.

12. "Methodist Church" historical marker on display at the church.

13. Hoopes, *This Last West*, "Episcopal Church," 106; Horsfall, Rev. William, 164; "St. Paul Church (Episcopal)," 326; "Graham, John," 141-142; "Emmanuel Episcopal Church" historical marker, located beside the front entrance.

14. Hoopes, *This Last West*, "Presbyterian Church," 288; "Rev. W.L. Austin," 9; "Rev. J.D. Hewitt," 159; "Miles, George M." 244-245; "Mrs. George M. Miles," 245; "Linnell, Rev. Edward Payson," 205.

15. "First Presbyterian Church" historical marker.

16. Hoopes, *This Last West*, "Baptist Church," 12; and "Downey, Reverend George D." 97.

17. Hoopes, *This Last West*, "Catholic Church," 56-57; "Lindesmith, Rev. Eli Washington John," 203-204; Flanagan, Augustus P.," and "Flanagan, Mrs. Augustus P., 114.

18. Hoopes, *This Last West*, "Catholic Church," 57.

19. Sacred Heart Parish Website, "History, Sacred Heart Church," sacredheart.com. A tour of the building was given to the author by Executive Director Sharon Moore.

20. Website: Trinity Lutheran Church of Miles City, "Our Lutheran Church History."

21. Christian Church historical marker.

22. Gordon, *Recollections of Old Milestown*, 30, 43; Hoopes, *This Last West*, "Courthouse (Old)", "Courthouse (New)", 77.

23. Gordon, *Recollections*, 5, 30.

24. Hoopes, *This Last West*, "Courthouse Saloon", 77-78; "Louis King", 189.

25. www.mtmemory.org, Montana History Portal, Reform School.

26. Hoopes, *This Last West*, "Montana's First Telephone Exchange"; Warhawk, Fort Keogh, "Wire Communication," 55-57.

27. Hoopes, *This Last West*, "Miles City Newspapers" and "Miles City Newsstands", 242-243.

28. Hoopes, *This Last West*, "Electric Company (Miles City)," 103-104.

29. Hoopes, *This Last West*, "Miles City Hospital," and "Miles City Drug Store," 242; and "Lebscher, Dr. Chester B." and "Lebscher's Drug Store", 198-199.

30. Clarke, *Dusting Off the Old Ones*, "A Business Index" and "Miles City's First Chamber of Commerce."

Chapter 12: *Good Times in Miles City*

1. Hoopes, *This Last West*, "Whiteside Fred" and "Whiteside and Brother", 367; Clarke, *Dusting Off the Old Ones*, "Shade Tree Bill's First Christmas."

2. Clarke, *Dusting Off the Old Ones*, "Shade Tree Bill's First Christmas."

3. *Ibid.* "Social Life in Miles City in the Eighties"; and Hoopes, *This Last West*, "Decker, Mrs. Josephine," 90.

4. Clarke, *Dusting Off the Old Ones*, "Early Day Country Dance"; Hoopes, *This Last West*, "Allerton, George A.," and "Allerton H.P.", 4.

5. Clarke, *Dusting Off the Old Ones*, "Miles City's First Football Game."

6. Gordon, *Recollections of Old Milestown*, 33-34; Clarke, *Dusting Off the Old Ones*, "Social Life in Miles City in the Eighties."

7. Clarke, *Dusting Off the Old Ones*, "The 10 Mile Race in Miles City."

8. *Ibid.* "Our Undersheriff Holds a News Conference", "Reporting in 1880", and "The 10-Mile Race in Miles City"; Gordon, *Recollections of Old Milestown*. 35-36.

9. Clarke, *Dusting Off the Old Ones*, "Y-Tic-Se-Lim."

10. *Ibid.*

11. "confetti", Wikipedia.

12. Clarke, *Dusting Off the Old Ones*, "Oh! We're All Right."

13. *Stockgrowers Journal* quoted by Clarke in *Dusting Off the Old Ones*, "Y-Tic-Se-Lim."

Chapter 13: *From Remount Station to the Range Riders Museum*

1. "Milwaukee Road," Wikipedia.

2. "Danger Lights," Wikipedia. The movie, in its original form, in its shortened length, and in its colorized version, may be googled under, *Danger Lights* (1930).

3. Warhawk, *Fort Keogh: Cutting Edge of a Culture*, 124.

4. *Ibid.*, also see Clarke, *Dusting Off the Old Ones*, "The Remount Depot — Fort Keogh."

5. Historical marker at Riverside Park in Miles City.

6. Warhank, *Fort Keogh; Cutting Edge of a Culture*, 124; and *Great Falls Tribune*, Great Falls, MT, April 14, 1968.

7. Gordon, *Recollections of Old Milestown*, "Roster of Old Timers," 44-45; *Miles City Memories*, 17, 90-91, 108.

8. Literature on Theodore Roosevelt is prolific. Doris Kearns Goodwin earned the Pulitzer Prize for *The Bully Pulpit*, which features meticulous research on Roosevelt and William Howard Taft.

9. "Miles City Traditions," *Western Horsemen*, August 28, 2007; "Who Was Steamboat the Unrideable? The STory of a Wyoming Legend." Wyoming PBS. Steamboat was the star bronc of Cheyenne's Frontier Days, and was held in even higher regard than Skyrocket.

10. "Yakima Canutt," Wikipedia.

11. Collard, *The World Famous Miles City Bucking Horse Sale*, 26-27; "Fannie Sperry Steele," National Rodeo Hall of Fame.

12. "Chapel Brothers Corporation (Inc. 1929)," Montana Cowboy Hall of

Fame; Historical Markers at Riverside Park; Eiffel, "Rounding Up Canners for the 'Corned Beef and Cabbage." Montana, Autumn 1986.

13. Unpublished writing of former CBC cowboy Claire Boyce.

14. *Range Riders Museum*. Pamphlet published and distributed by the museum.

15. *Ibid*. I was enlightened about the Range Riders Museum in a series of interviews with Curator Bunny Miller during my visit to Miles City in September 2023. Bunny has been part of the museum staff all of her life — her parents directed the Range Riders Museum for twenty-five years.

Chapter 14: *The World Famous Miles City Bucking Horse Sale*

1. *Stockgrowers Journal of Miles City*, March 7, 1885; historical marker at Riverside Park.

2. Historical markers at Riverside Park.

3. "World Famous Miles City Bucking Horse Sale," Montana Cowboy Hall of Fame; Carlson, "The Rowdy History of Miles City's Bucking Horse Sale," *Distinctly Montana*, May 16, 2024; "Miles City Bucking Horse Sale," Wikipedia.

4. Sam Gordon recalled that on military paydays "there was no time wasted on drawing beer. It was emptied into a couple of wash-tubs behind the bar, and dipped up in the beer glasses in a continuous service; one shift filling the tubs and another emptying them." Gordon, *Recollections*, 5. A similar process was used decades later to serve thirsty customers during the Bucking Horse Sale.

5. "Kalyn Beasley & the Honky Tonk Arcade," Chancey Williams and the Younger Brothers Band," and "Josh Turner," Wikipedia.

6. The Bucking Horse Sale schedule is available online.

7. *Ranch It Up, with Tigger & Becca*, Season 4, Episode 182, John L. Moore interview, www.ranchitup.com; *Montana This Morning; Miles City Bucking Horse Sale*, John Morford, interview.

8. The quote is from Faulkner's 1951 novel, *Requiem for a Nun*, which also was made into a play.

Bibliography
Books

Abbott, E.C. "Teddy Blue," and Helena Huntington Smith. *We Pointed Them North, Recollections of a Cowpuncher*. Norman: University of Oklahoma Press, 1955 [1939].

Adams, Andy. *The Log of a Cowboy, A Narrative of the Old Trail Days*. Garden City, NY: Doubleday and Company, Inc, 1903.

Alderson, Nannie T., and Helena Huntington Smith. *A Bride Goes West*. Lincoln: University of Nebraska Press, 1969 [1942],

Ambrose, Stephen E. *Undaunted Courage: Meriwether Lewis, Thomas Jefferson, and the Opening of the American West*. New York: Simon & Schuster, 1996.

Baldwin, Alice Blackwood. *Memoirs of the Late Frank D. Baldwin, Major General, U.S.A.* Los Angeles: Wetzel Publishing Co., 1929.

Barrows, John R. *U-bet*. Caldwell, Idaho: The Caxton Printers, 1947.

Bell, William A. New Tracks in North America, Vol. 1. Longon: Chapman and Hall, 1869.

Bobinski, George S. *Carnegie Libraries: Their History and Impact on American Public Library Development*. Chicago: American Library Association, 1969.

Brown, Mark H. *The Plainsmen of the Yellowstone, A History of the Yellowstone Basin*. Lincoln: University of Nebraska Press, 1969.

Brown, Mark H. and W.R. Felton. *Before Barbed Wire: LA Huffman, Photographer on Horseback*. New York. Bramhall House, 1956.

Brown, Mark H. and W.R. Felton. *The Frontier Years: L.A. Huffman, Photographer of the Plains*. New York: Bramhall House, 1955.

Clarke, W.B. *Dusting Off the Old Ones*. Miles City: Privately Published, 1961.

Clarke, Norm, Wynona Breen, and June Frank. *Tracing Terry Trails, A Chronological History*. Terry Country Centennial Celebration, 1982.

Clay, John. My Life on the Range. New York: Antiquarian Press, Ltd., 1961 [1924].

Collard, Sneed B. III. *The World Famous Miles City Bucking Horse Sale*. Missoula, Montana: Bucking Horse Books, 2010.

Cushman, Dan. *The Great North Trail*. New York: McGraw-Hill Book Company, 1965.

DeMontravel, Peter R. *A Hero to His Fighting Men, Nelson A. Miles, 1839-1925*. Kent, OH: The Kent State University Press, 1998.

Dresden, Donald. *The Marquis de Mores, Emperor of the Bad Lands*. Norman: University of Oklahoma Press, 1970.

Duke, Cordia Duke, and Joe B. Frantz. *6000 Miles of Fence, Life on the ZIT Ranch of Texas*. Austin: University of Texas Press, 1961.

Dykstra, Robert R. *The Cattle Towns*. New York: Atheneum, 1970.

Frink, Maurice, with Casey Barthelmess. *Photographs on an Army Mule*. Norman: University of Oklahoma Press, 1965.

Frost, Lawrence A. *The Custer Album, A Pictorial Biography of General George A Custer*. Seattle, Washington: Superior Publishing Company, 1964.

Goff, John V. *Miles City, Montana: An Architectural History*. Custer County Society for the Presentation of Local Folklore, Legend, History and Tradition, 1987.

Gordon, Samuel. *Recollections of Old Milestown*. Miles City: Privately Printed, 1918.

Haley, J. Evetts. *The XIT Ranch of Texas and the Early Days of the Llano Estacado*. Norman: University of Oklahoma Press, 1929.

Hanson, Joseph Mills. *The Conquest of the Missouri, Being the Story of the Life and Exploits of Captain Grant Marsh*. Chicago: A.C. McClurg & Co. 1909 {Softcover edition by Big Byte Books, 2018],

Herda, D.J. *Calamity Jane: The Life and Legend of Martha Jane Cannary*. Latham, Maryland: The Rowman & Littlefield Publishing Group, Inc., 2018

Hoopes, Lorman L., M.D. *This Last West: Miles City, Montana Territory, and Environs, 1876-1886, The People, The Geography, The Incredible History*. Miles City: SkyHouse Publishers, 1990.

Hunter, Louis C. *Steamboats on the Western Rivers: An Economic and Technological History*. Dover Maritime Publications, 1949.

Johnson, Virginia W. *The Unregimented General, A Biography of Nelson A. Miles*. Boston: Houghton Mifflin, 1962.

Jucovy, Linda. *Searching for Calamity, The Life and Times of Calamity Jane*. Philadelphia: Stampede Books, 2012.

Kelly, Luther S. *"Yellowstone Kelly": Memoirs of Luther S. Kelly*. New Haven, Conn: Yale University Press, 1926.

Kolp, Monsignor James R. *The Amazing Father Lindesmith: Chaplain in Indian Country*. St Raphael Custer, Inc., 2004.

Lamar, Howard R. ed. *The Reader's Encyclopedia of the American West*. New York: Thomas Y. Crowell Co., 1977.

Lubetkin, M. John. *Jay Cooke's Gamble: The Northern Pacific Railroad, The Sioux, and the Panic of 1873*. Noman: University of Oklahoma Press, 2006.

Lucey, Donna M. *Photography Montana, 1894-1928: The World of Evelyn Cameron*. Helena: Montana Historical Society, 1991.

Majors, Alexander. *Seventy Years on the Frontier. Alexander Majors' Memoirs of a Lifetime on the Border*. Minneapolis: Ross & Haines, Inc. 1965.

McChristian, Douglas C. *Regular Army O! Soldiering on the Western Frontier, 1865-1891*. Norman: University of Oklahoma Press, 2017.

McElrath, Frances. *The Rustler: A Tale of Love and War in Wyoming*. New York: Funk & Wagnalls Company, 1902.

McLaird, James D. *Calamity Jane: The Woman and the Legend*. Norman: University of Oklahoma Press, 2005.

The Medal of Honor. Washington, D.C.: United States Government Printing Office, 1948.

Miles, Nelson A. *Personal Recollections and Observations of General Nelson A. Miles*. 1896; rpt. New York: DaCapo Press, 1969.

Miles, Nelson A. *Serving the Republic: Memoirs of the Civil and Military Life of Nelson A. Miles*. New York: Harper, 1911.

Miller, Bunny. *Miles City Memories, The Early Years*. The Billings Gazette and Stockman Bank, 2017.

Miller, Michael M. *XIT: A Story of Land, Cattle, and Capital in Texas and Montana*. Norman: University of Oklahoma Press, 2020.

Minton, Gretchen E. *Shakespeare in Montana: Big Sky Country's Love Affair with the World's Most Famous Writer*. Albuquerque: University of New Mexico Press, 2020.

O'Neil, Paul. *The Rivermen*. New York: Time-Life Books, 1975.

Paul, Virginia. *This was Cattle Ranching, Yesterday and Today*. Seattle, Wash.: Superior Publishing Company, 1973.

Rickey, Don, Jr. *Forty Miles a Day on Beans and Hay, The Enlisted Soldier Fighting the Indian Wars*. NormanL University of Oklahoma Press, 1963.

Roosevelt, Theodore. *Ranch Life and The Hunting-Trail*. New York: The Century Co.: 1888.

Russell, Jim. *Bob Fudge: Texas Trail Driver, Montana-Wyoming Cowboy, 1862-1933*. Aberdeen, S.D.: North Plains Press, 1981.

Shields, George O. *Rustlings in the Rockies*. Chicago: n.p., 1883.

Stiles, T.J. *Custer's Trials, A Life on the Frontier of New America*. New York: Alfred A. Knopf, 2015.

Stuart, Granville, and Paul C. Phillips, ed. *Forty Years on the Frontier, as seen in the Journals and Reminiscences of Granville Stuart, Gold-Miner, Trader, Merchant, Rancher and Politician*. 2 Vols. Cleveland: The Arthur H. Clark Company, 1925.

Thompson, Jerry, ed. *Fifty Miles and a Fight, Major Samuel Peter Heintzelman's Journal of Texas and the Cortina War*. Austin: Texas State Historical Association, 1998.

Toole, K. Ross. *Montana, An Uncommon Land*. Norman: University of Oklahoma Press, 1984.

Twain, Mark. *Life on the Mississippi*. James R. Osgood and Company, 1883. [New York: A Signet Classic, 1961]

Van Slyck, Abigail. *Free to All: Carnegie Libraries & American Culture, 1890-1910*. Chicago: University of Chicago Press, 1996.

Webb, Walter Prescott. *The Texas Rangers*. Austin: University of Texas Press, 1935.

Welsh, Donald H. *Pierre Wibanx, Cattle King*. Bismarck, N.D.: The State Historical Society of North Dakota, 1953.

Wibaux County Diamond Jubilee and Montana Centennial, 1989.

Articles

Arguimbau, Ellen. "From Party Lines and Barbed Wire, A History of Telephones in Montana." *Montana, The Magazine of Western History*, Autumn 2013, Volume 63, No. 3, 34-45.

Beyrais, David. "'If you had fought bravely I would have sung for you." *Montana, The Magazine of Western History*, Spring 2019, Vol, 69, No. 1, 3-20.

Booth, Ryan W. "Fort Keogh's Commissary: A Global Market on the Great Plains from 1876 to 1900." *Montana, The Magazine of Western History*, Spring 2020, Vol. 70, No. 1, 44-66.

Brust, James S. "Photojournalism, 1877: John H. Fouch, Fort Keogh's First Post Photographer," *Montana, The Magazine of Western History*, Winter 2000, Vol. 50, No. 4, 32-39.

"Chappel Brothers Corporation (Inc. 1929)." Montana Cowboy Hall of Fame.

Corbett, Peter. "Miles City, Montana." *True West*. September 2023, 68-71.

Dixon, Olive King. "Rescue of Four German Sisters . . . Incident Miles Expedition Against Plains Indians in 1874 and 1875." *Fort Worth Sunday Star Telegram*, March 16, 1936.

Dunning, Shane. "The Geddes Murder Trials: Gender, Race, and Murder-for-Hire in Eastern Montana's Criminal Justice System." *Montana, The Magazine of Western History*, Winter 2022, Vol. 72, No. 4, 25-42.

Eiffel, Robert W. "Ike." "Rounding up 'Campers' for the 'Corned Beef and Cabbage." *Montana: The Magazine of Western History*. Autumn 1986.

Gordon, Greg. "The Shopkeeper's Frontier: How the General Store Transformed Montana Territory, 1850-1885." *Montana, The Magazine of Western History*, Winter 2019, Vol. 69, No. 4, 37-55.

Greene, Jerome A. "The Army at the Clearwater, Tactical Victory and Strategic Defeat in the Nez Perce War." *Montana, The Magazine of Western History*, Winter 2000, Vol. 50, No.4, 18-31.

Hanshew, Tracey. "Here she comes, wearin' them britches!" Saddles, Riding Skirts, and Social Reform in the Turn-of-the-Century Rural West." *Montana, The Magazine of Western History*, Winter 2020, Vol. 70, No. 4, 39-53.

Hawthorne, Lloyd. "Captain Henry Miller Shreve, Master of the Red." *North Louisiana History*, Vol. 2, No. 1 (Fall 1970), 1-6.

Hoehne, Patrick T. "Apostles of Disorder: Montana Merchants, Vigilantes, and the Interconnectivity of Extralegal Violence." *Montana, The Magazine of Western History.* Autumn 2022, Vol. 72, No. 3, 3-21.

"Miles City Traditions," *Western Horseman,* August 28, 2007.

Miller, Michael M. "Cowboys and Capitalists, The XIT Ranch in Texas and Montana, 1885-1912." *Montana, The Magazine of Western History.* Vol. 65, Number 2, Winter 2015, 3-28.

Minckler, Thomas E. "Yellowstone Cowboy, The Real Story of Teddy Blue." *True West.* September 2023, 22-27.

Minton, Gretchen E. "Shakespeare in Frontier and Territorial Montana, 1820-1889." *Montana, The Magazine of Western History.* Summer 2020, Vol. 70, No. 2, 24-44.

Monaghan, Leila. "Cheyenne and Lakota Women at the Battle of the Little Bighorn." *Montana, The Magazine of Western History,* Vol. 67, No. 3, 3-21.

Niedringhaus, Lee I. "The N Bar N Ranch." *Montana, The Magazine of Western History.* Vol. 60, Number 1. Spring 2010, 3-23.

O'Neal, Bill. "When the Vast Texas XIT Expanded to Montana." *Ranch Record,* Spring 2021, 38-43.

Pearson, Jeffrey V. "Nelson A. Miles, Crazy Horse, and the Battle of Wolf Mountains." *Montana, The Magazine of Western History,* Winter 2001, Vol. 51, No. 4, 52-67.

Predelli, Maria Bendinelli. "Working on the Railroad: A Memoir by Immigrant Labor Poet."

Antonio Andreoni." *Montana, The Magazine of Western History,* Spring 2017, Vol. 67, No. 1, 46-70.

Rickey, Don, Jr. "The Battle of Wolf Mountain," *Montana,* 13, No, 2 (April 1963), 44-54.

Robinson, Ken. "Captain Grant Marsh: King of Montana River Navigation." *Historical Fort Benton,* Blog, August 11, 2008. Overholser Historical Research Center in Fort Benton.

Rosebrook, Stuart. "Eyewitness to History." *True West.* Jan. 30, 2020.

Schwantes, Carlos A. "The Steamboat and Stagecoach Era in Montana and the Northern West." *Montana.*

Taylor, Jan. "Marketing the Northwest: The Northern Pacific Railroad's Last Spike Excursion." *Montana, The Magazine of Western History,* Winter 2010: Vol 60, No. 4, 16-35.

Welch, Bob. "Leading the Charge." *Ranch Record,* Ranching Heritage Association, Vol. 53, No. 4, Fall 2023, 16-17.

Whittlesey, Lee. "The Nez Perces in Yellowstone in 1877." *Montana, The Magazine of Western History,* Spring 2007, Vol. 57, No. 1, 48-55.

Internet Articles

"Big Nose George." *Wikipedia, The Free Encyclopedia.*

"Buffalo Soldiers in Montana (1888-1898)," Blackpast. www.blackpast.org

"Far West (steamship)." *Wikipedia, The Free Encyclopedia.*

"Fort Keogh – Historic District." List of Historic Markers at Fort Keogh and in Miles City. Internet.

"Fort Keogh." FortWiki Historic U.S. and Canadian Forts. www.fortwiki.com.

"Fort Keogh, Montana." *Wikipedia.* En.wikipedia.org.

Fort Keogh Post Commissary Records, Archives West. archiveswest.orbiscascade.org

Fort Keogh (Mont.) Collection. Archives and Special Collections, Maureen and Mike Mansfield Library, The University of Montana, Missoula. library.archives@umontana.edu.

"Fort Tours/Fort Keogh." Miles City Chamber of Commerce article. www.forttours.org.

Fouch, John H., Fort Keogh, Montana. yellowstonestereoviews.com

Gray, Warren. "Guns and Bravery: Is This What Really Happened at the Little Bighorn?" *Gunpowder Magazine,* December 29, 2019.

"Henry, Hogan." *Wikipedia, The Free Encyclopedia.*

"Historical Perspective." Livestock and Range Research Laboratory, Miles City, MT. USDA ARS Fort Keogh Livestock and Range Research Laboratory.

"Lindesmith, Eli Washington John (1827-1927)." *WikiTree.*

Livestock and Range Research Laboratory. USDA ARS. www.usda.gov.

Livestock and Range Research Laboratory, Miles City, Montana. "Historical Perspective." Stanley J. Morrow Stereograph collection. Archiveswest.orbiscascade.org.

"Montana Stockgrower's Association." *Wikipedia, The Free Encyclopedia.*

"Pym, James." *Military Wikipedia.* Military-history.fandom.com/wiki/James_Pym.

"Miles City." Montana Historical Society. Montana.gov.

"Northern Pacific Railway." *Wikipedia, The Free Encyclopedia.*

USDA ARS, Fort Keogh. www.ers.usda.gov.

Vermere, Dr. Lance, Livestock and Range Research Library. "Introduction to Fort Keogh."

"Wichita Mountains, Oklahoma." *Wikipedia, The Free Encyclopedia.*

"World's Largest Snowflake Fallas, January 28, 1887." www.historyandheadlines.com

Miscellaneous

Ball, Larry, to the author, July 20, 2023.

Cottonwood Springs, Texas, Historical Marker on State Highway 199, 9 miles southeast of Olney. Placed in 1974.

Cottonwood Springs Topo Map in Young County, Texas. www.anyplaceamerica.com.

Crain, Newford, U.S. Consul to Gen. N.A. Miles, Fort Leavenworth, Kansas. March 1, 1875.

Sanborn Fire Insurance Maps from Miles City, Custer County, Montana. Nov. 1884 (2 sheets); Nov. 1886 (2 sheets); Dec. 1888 (5 sheets); Sept. 1893 (8 sheets); Dec. 1904 (10 sheets); Nov. 1910 (19 sheets)

Warhank, Josef James. "Fort Keogh: Cutting Edge of a Culture." Master's Thesis. Long Beach: California State University, 1984. USDA ARS, Abstract. www.ars.gov. *Wibaux County Diamond Jubilee and Montana Centennial, 1989.* N.p., 1989.

Index

A

Abbott-Downing Company 96
Abbott, J. Stephen 96
Abbott, Teddy Blue 1, 4, 70, 72-73, 75-77, 81-82, 106, 108, 113, 128-129
Abilene, Kan. 3, 106, 207, 234
Ak-Sar-Ben 186
Alaska (state of) 34, 57
Albuquerque, N.M. 123, 227
Alderson, Nannie 73, 155
Allegheny River 88
Alling, Anne 156
American Bankers Insurance Co. 136
American Baptist Home Mission Society 165
American Legion Post 7 209
American Revolution 18
Andrus, W.W. 189
Appomattox, Va. 19
Arapaho (Native American tribe) 56
Arizona (state of) 120
Arlington National Cemetery 36, 48
Armstrong, C.O. 132
Armstrong, Robert 191
A.R. Nininger & Co. 110
Arthur, Jean 191
Askin, Bob 206
Athletic Park 183
Austin, Texas 138, 142
Autry, Gene 206

B

Bad Route Creek 23
Baldwin, Alice 48
Baldwin, Capt. Frank 19, 47-48, 95
Bannock (Native American tribe) 31-32
Barthelmess, Christian 44
Basinski, Julius 171
Baskin, James 178
Batchelor (riverboat) 47, 90
Battle of Big Dry River 23
Battle of Cedar Creek 67
Battle of Shiloh 88
Battle of the Little Bighorn 6, 66, 86, 229
Battle of Vicksburg 88
Battle of Wolf Mountain 25, 214, 229
Bazinkski's 176
Bear Paw Mountain 28, 67
Beasley, Kalyn 209, 224
Beaver Valley 133, 136
Bell Company 175
Bell, William 102
Bennett, Capt. Andrew 32
Bert Clark Gun Room 201
Bertrand's Bazaar 176
Bibulous Babylon of the Plains (Dodge City, Kan.) 106
Big Crow 24
Big Dry Creek 23, 140, 147
Bighorn River 7, 41, 66, 89
Big Muddy Creek 26
Billington, Ray Allen 151, 155
Bismarck, N.D. 6, 43, 52, 60, 84, 89, 95, 97-98, 100-101, 174, 213, 220, 228
Bismarck Tribune 6, 213, 220
Bison Bar 210
Bob Fudge, Texas Trail Driver, Montana-Wyoming Cowboy 149
Boe, Les 205
Boer War 118
Boice, Henry 135
Boot Hill 3, 106
Borchardt, Maj. Paul 49
Boston, Mass. 18, 67
Boulder Pass, Mont. 31
Boyce, Claire 190, 199, 224
Bozeman Avant-Courier 114, 219
Bozeman, Mont. 52, 95, 97, 107, 114, 216, 219-220
Bozeman Trail 107
Brage, Private 68
Brazil 195
Brazos River 142
Brewer, Rev. Leigh Richmond 161
Bridger, Rev. E.A. 160
Brisbin, Maj. James 51
Broadwater, Hubbel and Co. 53, 55

Brown, Charlie 62,-64, 73, 78, 152, 172
Brown, Hallett and Co. 122
Brown's Park Cattle Assn. 123
Bruce, Harry 79
Buffalo Rapids 91
Buford, Mont. 92
Bullard, Bill 71
Bullard, W.H. 175
Burleigh, Walter A. 178
Burns, Maggie 2, 71-72, 75, 82
Burris, Charlie 68
Butte, Mont. 104, 185

C

Cahn, Morris 68
Cahn's Coulee 68
Calamity Jane (Martha Jane Cannary) 2, 80-82, 218, 226-227
Caldwell, Kan. (Border Queen) 3, 106, 120
California Ed 127
California Restaurant 71, 76, 179
California (state of) 71, 76, 99, 116, 118, 127, 162, 179, 231
Call, Capt. Woodrow 207
Cameron, Evelyn 7, 141-145, 202, 226
Campbell, Bob 63
Campbell, Gracie 63
Canada 25, 28-29, 30-31, 134
Cannary, Martha Jane (Calamity Jane) 2, 80-82, , 218, 226-227
Canutt, Yakima 196, 197, 223
Capitol Syndicate Ranch (XIT) 138-139, 147-148
Carland, Judge William W. 185
Carlton, Minn. 100
Carmichael, Judge Alexander 155
Carnegie, Andrew 159
Carnegie Library of Miles City 159
Carnevale di Milano 189
Carriage House District 178
Carson City, Nev. 96
Carter, John 171
Casey, Lt. Edward 51
Catholic Church 166, 180, 222
Cato, Ethel 142
Cato, John Ozella 143, 187

Cato, Julia (Jourdan) 142
Cato, Leo 143
Cato, Myrtle (Williamson) 142, 148, 187-188
Cato, Osceola C. (O.C.) 4, 138, 142-144, 147-149, 153, 187, 221
Cato, Percy 148
Cattle Raisers Assn. of Texas 123
Cattle Theft Assn. 123
Cedar Creek, Va. 22, 59, 67, 139, 140
Central City, S.D. 110
Central New Mexico Cattlegrowers Assn. 123
Central Pacific Railroad 99
Chancellorsville, Va. 19
Chappel Brothers Corporation 190, 197-200, 205, 224, 228
Chappel, Earl 197
Chappel, Ernst 197
Chappel, Philip Mitchell (P.M. 197-198
Charlie Brown's Livery 73
Cheyenne Club 124
Cheyenne (Native American tribe) 6, 9, 20, 23-24, 48, 56, 81, 87, 89, 167, 188, 223, 229
Cheyenne, Wyo. 38, 111, 116, 124
Chicago, Ill. 35, 132, 137, 144, 190-191, 225-228
Chicago, Milwaukee and Puget Sound Railway Co. 190
Chief Joseph 27-31
Chinnick, John 64-65
Chinnick, Nell 66
Chisholm Trail 106, 142
Christian Church 169
Christmas Charity Ball 71, 179
Churchill Downs 210
Church's Livery Stable 48
Cincinnati Red Stockings 182
Circle Bar 47
City Drug Store 177, 222
Civil War 1, 9, 19, 26, 31, 48-49, 51, 65, 88, 98-99, 105, 157, 182
Clark, A.B. 204
Clarke, W.B. 179, 186, 188-189
Clark, Lt. William 7-8, 83
Clark's Fork Pass 31
Clay, John 83, 96

Clemens, Samuel 88
Clifton, Clara 60
Clifton Park, N.Y. 165
Cody, William F. "Buffalo Bill" 11, 90
Coggshall, Charles E. 117
Cold Harbor, Va. 19
Colorado Cattle Growers Assn. 123
Colorado (state of) 48, 123
Comanche (horse) 14-15
Comanche (Native American tribe) 9
Commerce State Bank 171
Concord Coach 97-98
Concord, N.H. 96
Congressional Medal of Honor 1, 19, 35, 48, 59, 66-67, 95, 216-217, 227
Conley, Jim 63
Connie the Cowboy Queen 2, 73-75
Continental Divide 88
Cooke and Co. 100
Cooke, Jay 100, 226
Coonrod, Sgt. Aquille 59
Cooper, Mary Ellen "Nelly" (Wibaux) 132, 134
Corps of Discovery 7
Corps of Engineers 39
Cosmopolitan Theater 63-64
Cosmopolitan Theatre and Saloon 78-79
Cottage Saloon 32, 47, 58-59, 62, 92, 111, 207, 211
Coulson, CDRE Sanford B. 88
Coulson Packet Company 88, 90
Courthouse Saloon 173, 222
Cowboy Church 210
Cowboy Mardi Gras 204, 208
Crazy Horse 8, 24-25, 229
Crook, Gen. George R. 20, 23, 27, 34
Crow (Native American tribe) 24, 171
Custer Battlefield 41, 192
Custer Battlefield National Cemetery 192
Custer County Art Center 202
Custer County Board of Commissioners 47, 155
Custer County Cemetery 67
Custer County Courthouse 6, 168, 171
Custer County Court House 65
Custer County High School 6, 156, 158, 168

Custer County, Mont. 6, 47, 54, 65, 67, 71, 107, 139, 143, 155-156, 158, 168, 171-172, 202, 226, 231
Custer, Gen. George Armstrong 6-10, 13-15, 20, 29, 33, 38, 41, 47-49, 54, 65-67, 71, 86, 89, 94-95, 97, 107, 139, 143, 155-156, 158, 168, 171-174, 192, 202, 207, 209-210, 213, 226-227, 231
Custer, Libbie 9-10
Custer Massacre 6

D

Daily Gazette 175
Daily Rustler 175
Dakota Territory 7, 10, 110, 125
Dance, Jimmy 91
Danger Lights 191, 223
Davis, Jefferson 19
Deadwood, S.D. 1, 5, 73, 81-82, 92, 95, 110, 137, 174
Decker, Mrs. Josephine (Minor) 180, 184
demimonde 70-71, 73, 75-76, 82, 217
Denby, Al 142, 145
Denver, Colo. 48
Derby Days 210
DHS Ranch 122, 126-127
Diamond R Corral 94
Diamond R Overland Freight Co. 92
Dodge City 57
Dodge City, Kan. 3, 5, 57, 106, 207
Dover, England 133
Downey, Rev. G.E. 165
Downing, Lewis 96
Downs, Billy 127
Duluth, Minn. 100
Dumas, Alexandre 70
Dunne, Mother Amadeus 167
Duvall, Robert 208

E

Eastern Montana Protective Assn. 124
Eastern Montana State Veterans Cemetery 68
Eastern Montana Stockgrowers Assn. 124
Ekalaka, Mont. 205

Elk Lodge 153
Elk River 37
Elk River Fort 37
Elks Convention 195
Emmanuel Episcopal Church 162, 222
Emmy Awards 208
England 132
Episcopal Church 160-162, 180, 211, 221-222
Essig, Rev. J.F.M 168
Europe 95, 132, 193, 197

F

Fallon, Mont. 146
Fallon, Rattlesnake Jake 127
Farr, George W. 186
Farwell, John V. 139
Far West 84, 88-90, 218, 220, 230
Faulkner, William 204, 212
Fields, Eva 76
Fifth Infantry 9-10, 20, 25-26, 29, 42, 46, 54, 95, 180
Fireman's Hall 182
First Methodist Church 160
First National Bank of Miles City 47, 51, 110-111, 136, 176
First Presbyterian Church 6, 47, 222
Flanagan, Mr. A.P. 165
Flanagan, Mrs. A.P. 165
Flynn, Ed 46
Flynn, Errol 57
Foffa, Father Chrysostom 165
Forbush Memorial Library 54
Fort Abraham Lincoln, N.D. 10, 89, 97, 100
Fort Assiniboine, Mont. 174
Fort Benton, Mont. 88, 229
Fort Buford, N.D. 17, 87, 92
Fort Custer, Mont. 38, 41, 95, 97, 174
Fort D.A. Russell, Wyo. 38
Fort Ellis, Mont. 31, 174
Fort Fetterman, Wyo. 124
Fort Harker, Kan. 20
Fort Hays, Kan. 9, 20, 48
Fort Keogh Band 44
Fort Keogh, Mont. 1, 3, 5, 13, 15,-16, 20, 28, 30, 32-35, 37-60, 66, 68-69, 83, 88-89, 91-92, 94-95, 97-98, 101, 103-104, 108-109, 116, 118, 124, 156, 158, 165, 174-176, 180-182, 186, 191-194, 200-201, 205, 207, 211-213, 215-220, 222-223, 228, 230-231
Fort Keogh Road 95, 97-98
Fort Keogh String Band 45, 51
Fort Leavenworth, Kan. 9-10, 20, 71, 87, 231
Fort Pease, Mont. 49
Fort Shaw, Mont. 174
Fort Worth, Texas 3, 214, 228
Forty-Four House 71
Fredericksburg, Va. 19
French Dragoons 132
French, Fanny 76
Freuen Cattle Co. 122
Fudge, Bob 4, 138, 141, 143, 145-146, 149, 221, 227
Furstnow, Al 116
Furstnow's Saddle Shop 117
F.Y. Batchelor 90

G

Gall 8
Gallagher, Brocky 127
Garlock, Judge James H. 185
Ghost Dance 35, 45, 191
Gibson, Col. George 60
Girard, Dr. A.C. 177
Givens, W.B. 156
Glaess, Rev. Herman 168
Glendive, Mont. 92, 101, 132, 185
Goettlich Harness & Saddlery Shop 116
Gold Creek, Mont. 104-105
Golden Spike 99
Goose Creek 122
Gordon, Sam 6, 13-14, 58, 62, 65, 78, 80, 92-94, 101-102, 104, 130, 151, 153, 172, 178, 184-185, 214, 218, 224
Gracie. Campbell 63
Graham, John J. 54, 162, 178
Graham, Texas 123
Grammy Awards 209

Grand Central Hotel 155
Grand Ole Opry 209
Great Depression 199
Great Falls, Mont. 193, 197, 199, 223
Great Falls Tribune 193, 223
Greenough, Alice 197
Greenough, Margie 197
Grinnel, L.S. 122
Grisy, Gus 133, 135

H

Haire, Charles S. 159
Hardiman, Kitty 75-76, 82
Hardy, Alexander 110
Hart, Herbert M. 15, 39, 213
Hartle, Paul J. 39
Hatchet Ranch 139, 140, 147, 148
H. Durfee 46
Heflin, Van 57
Heintzelman, Capt. Charles Stuart 38, 40, 215
Helena, Mont. 32, 124-125, 162, 174, 197, 225-226
Hewitt, Rev. J.D. 162, 222
Hickok, Wild Bill 69, 81, 82
Hoffman, Connie (Cowboy Queen) 2, 73-75, 82
Hogan, Sgt. Henry 67, 217
Hogg, Dr. A.J. 60
Hole in the Wall 210
Holt, Elmer 157
Holt, Sallie 157
Homelund, Kurt 68
Honky Tonk Arcade 209, 224
Hoopes, Dr. Lorman L. 70
Horsfall, Rev. William 162
Hotel Leighton 187
Howard, Gen. O.O. 28, 31
Huffman, L.A. 61, 67, 69, 202, 219, 225
Hunter, Rev. W.J. 160
Huntley, Rev. G.W. 164

I

Idaho (state of) 31, 107, 220, 225
Illinois (state of) 33, 197
Inter Ocean Hotel 48, 111, 176

Iron Star 26
Italian Orchestra 71

J

J. Basinski and Bros. 158
Jerome, Lt. Lovell H. 30
Johnson, E.H. "Skew" 152
Johnson, Willie 76
Jones, Tommy Lee 208
Josephine 8
Judith Mountains 122

K

Kansas (state of) 3, 9, 20, 48, 106, 120, 231
Kellogg, Mark 6
Kelly, Luther "Yellowstone" 11, 19, 23-24, 95, 218, 226
Ken-L-Ration 197
Kentucky Derby 210
Kentucky (state of) 134, 210
Keogh, Capt. Myles 13
Key West 8
King, George 146
King, Louis 173, 222
King Philip's War 18
Kitty Hardiman Dance Hall and Saloon 75
Kramer, Mrs. H.J. 145

L

Ladd, Alan 57
Lame Deer 25
Lansing, W.L. 175
Latham, Clem 118
Lebscher, Dr. C.B. 177
Lebscher, Dr. Chester B. 60
Le Demi-Monde 70
Leighton, Joe 111
Leighton - Jordan Co. 90
Lester, Heavy 205
Lewis and Clark Expedition 7
Lewis, Capt. Meriweather 7, 83
Lewistown, Mont. 127
Life on the Mississippi 88, 227
Liggitt, Lt. Hunter 51

Lincoln, Neb. 108
Lincoln, Pres. Abraham 99
Lindesmith, Eli Washington John 42-43, 45-46, 165-167, 180, 226
Little Bighorn (battle of) 1, 6, 7, 15, 66, 84, 86, 89, 213, 218, 229-230
Little Bighorn River 7, 66
Little Chief 25
Little German Band 188
Logan, A.C. 156
Logan, Maj. T.H. 50-51
Logan, Mrs. Jennie 42
Lonesome Dove 207, 208
Louella 88

M

Mackenzie, Col. Ranald 20
MacQueen Hotel 49, 74, 111-112, 131
MacQueen House 46, 49, 75, 111-112, 113, 131, 179, 184, 187
MacQueen, Maj. William N. 48, 111
Maguie, Lt. Edward 39
Marquis de Mores 7, 125, 133, 225
Marsh, Capt. 88-89, 218, 226, 229
Marsh, J.K. 145
Masonic Lodge 50, 143, 153-154
Masonic Temple 154
Massachusetts Agricultural College 46
Match Bronc Riding Calcutta 210
McCrary, George W. 33
McCrea, Capt. Agustus 207
McKay, George W. 63
McKenzie, Sam 127
McMurtry, Larry 207
Memorial Hall 209
Merchants & Drovers Bank 110
Methodist Church 6, 160, 179, 222
Methodist Episcopal Church of Miles City 160
Milan, Italy 189
Miles, Cecilia 27, 33
Miles City Bank 110
Miles City Board of Trade 153, 178
Miles City Brewery 71
Miles City Bucking Horse Sale "World Famous" 3, 4, 121, 204-205, 207, 209- 211, 223-225

Miles City Chamber of Commerce 178, 230
Miles City Chronicle 175
Miles City Club 130, 131
Miles City Daily Journal 175
Miles City Daily Press 175
Miles City Daily Record 175
Miles City Drug Store 177, 222
Miles City Exchange 175
Miles City Horse Sales and Fair Assn. 204
Miles City Hospital 177, 222
Miles City Library 159, 221
Miles City Livestock Commission 205
Miles City, Mont.
    Early Settlement 1-6,
    Military 7-12, 23-24, 27, 35
    Vice & Violence 37-41, 47-51, 58, 65-69, 73, 77-80, 84, 86, 88-92, 94-98, 100-106,
    Cattle & Ranching 107,-110, 115, 118-121, 128-132, 134, 136-137, 139-140, 142-144, 146,
    Education & Churches 162, 164-179
    Recreation & Entertainment 180-183, 186-190, 194-195, 198-200
    Bucking Horses & Rodeo 202, 204-208, 210-211
Miles City Preservation Committee 54
Miles City Press 122, 175
Miles City Reading Room Assn. 158, 221
Miles City Roundup 3, 8, 120-121, 195-199
Miles City Saddlery 118-220
Miles City Water and Electric Co. 176
Miles City Weekly Press 175
Miles Community College 183
Miles, Gen. Nelson A. 1-10, 12-38, 40-52, 54-58, 60-62, 64-84, 86-92, 94-98, 100-122, 124-126, 128-134, 136-137, 139-140, 142-144, 146-162, 164--200, 202, 204-231
Miles, George H. 48, 111
Miles, George M. 46, 153, 162, 164, 178, 195, 222

Miles, Helen (Strevell) 47, 153, 164
Miles, Mary (Sherman) 9, 19, 27, 33
Miles, Sherman 27, 33-34
Milestown (Miles City) 5, 13-16, 37, 49, 52, 61, 64, 71, 82, 89, 101, 155, 189, 212, 214-218, 220, 222-223, 226
Milwaukee and Mississippi Railroad 190
Minnesota (state of) 67, 100
Mission St. Labre 167
Mississippi River 84-85
Missoula, Mont. 104, 225, 230
Missouri River 7, 17, 22, 84-85, 87-89, 127, 139-140, 143, 190
Missouri (state of) 6-7, 17, 22, 35, 80, 84-85, 87- 89, 92, 96, 127, 139-140, 143, 190, 218, 226
Montana Arts Council 203
Montana Bar 188, 210
Montana Saddle Tree 117
Montana (state of) 2, 4-5, 8-10, 12, 14, 16, 18, 20, 22, 24-26, 28, 30, 32-34, 36-38, 40, 42, 44, 46, 48-50, 52, 54, 58, 60, 62, 64, 66, 68, 72, 74, 76, 78, 80, 82-84, 86, 88, 90, 92, 94, 96, 98, 100, 102, 104-110, 112-118, 120-150, 152, 154, 156-162, 164, 166-168, 170, 172-174, 176, 178, 180, 182, 184-186, 188, 192, 194-198, 200, 202-204, 206-210, 212-216, 218-231
Montana State Senate 4, 143
Montana State Vocational School for Girls 174
Montana Stockgrowers Assn. 4, 49, 112, 122-131, 133, 135, 137, 185, 195, 220
Montana Stock Growers Assn. 124, 129
Montana Team 209
Montana Territory 32, 37, 46, 74, 107, 161, 176, 226
Montgomery Ward 155
Moore, John L. 210, 224
Moreno, Al 117
Morford, John 210, 224
Morphy, M.H. 122
Morris, Rufe 144-145
Murphy, W.A. 122
Museum of the American Indian 21
Musselshell River 127-128, 140, 147

N

National Anthem 36
National Archives 8-9, 13-14, 17, 19, 24, 28, 33-35, 41, 53, 89, 115, 186, 213
National Endowment for the Arts 203
National League of Professional Base Ball Players 182
National Register of Historic Buildings 47
National Register of Historic Places 136
N Bar N Ranch 148, 229
N Bar Ranch 72-73, 109, 148, 229
Nebraska (state of) 106, 108, 186, 225
New Mexico (state of) 123, 138, 227
Newton, Kan. 106
New York City, N.Y. 33, 44, 88, 95, 131, 148-149, 161, 165, 225-227
Nez Perce (Native American tribe) 27-30, 67, 214-215, 228
Nininger, A.R. 110
Niobrara Cattle Company (N Bar Ranch) 109
Nome, Alaska 57
North Dakota (state of) 133, 165, 218, 228
Northern Cheyenne (Native American tribe) 166
Northern New Mexico Stock Growers Assn. 123
Northern Pacific Depot 111
Northern Pacific Railroad 8, 48, 60, 78, 100, 133, 219, 226, 229
North to Alaska 57

O

Ogallala, Neb. 106
Ohio (state of) 19, 43, 46, 167
Old Forts of the Northwest 15, 39, 213
Old Time Buffalo Hunters Banquet 195

Olive Hotel 187, 210-211
Omaha, Neb. 99, 116
Ordgel, W. Van 160
Oregon (state of) 28, 100, 106, 196, 220
Orschel Brothers 170-171
Orschel, Leo 195
Otis, Lt. Col. E.S. 94
Owen, Red 127

P

Pacific Ocean 99-100
Pacific Railroad Act 99
Paget, Sid 73
Parrot, Big Nose George 68
Pauley, Bob 205
Paul McCormick and Company 53
Payson, Ariz. 120
Pease, Maj. F.D. 13
Pecos, Texas 120
Petersburg, Va. 19
Philadelphia, Pa. 33, 95, 226
Philippines 48, 192
Pine Hills Boys and Girls Industrial School 173
Pine Hills School 174
Pope, Gen. John 17
Pope Leo XIII 43
Porter, T.J. 157, 159
Potts, Gov. Benjamin F. 32
Powder River 97, 122
Powderville, Mont. 180
Prairie County Museum 7, 141-145, 149, 221
PRCA Xtreme Broncs Match 210
Presbyterian Church 6, 47, 148, 153, 157, 162-165, 179, 222
Presbyterian Church of Helena 162
Prescott Frontier Days 120
Price, Kenneth 44
Puerto Rico 35
Puget Sound 100, 190, 191
Pym, Pvt. James 66, 68, 216, 217

R

Rain-in-the-Face 8
Ranchman's Hotel 111
Range Riders Association 200

Range Riders Museum 2-3, 5, 30, 39, 42, 44-45, 50- 51, 58-59, 62-65, 80, 81, 91-93, 100, 111, 117-120, 131, 153, 159, 163, 167, 170-171, 173, 182, 187, 190-191, 193-203, 206, 209, 212, 221, 223-224
Rauh, Rev. H.T. 168
Rawlins, Wyo. 69
Redd, Dr. R.G. 177
Red Lodge, Mont. 197
Red Mike 127
Red River War 9, 20, 48
Red Ward's Opera House 77
Redwater Creek 140, 147
Reece, Bill 60
Reece's Dance Hall and Sampling Room 60
Reforms 183-184
Reform School 173-174, 183-184, 188, 222
Regimental Band 44
Remount Depot 4, 191, 193, 195, 197, 199, 201, 203, 223
Riggin, Rev. F.A. 160
Rigney, Bill 63, 152
Ringer, D.W. 49
Ringling Brothers Circus 36
Riverside Park 54, 188, 189, 192, 223, 224
Robaix, France 132, 133
Robbins and Lenoir Saddlery 117
Rockford, Ill. 197, 199
Rock Island, Ill. 33
Rocky Mountains 190, 227
Rogan, Nettie 155
Roller Skating Rink 71
Rome, Italy 43, 189
Romeyn, Lt. Henry 29, 67
Roosevelt Nature and History Assn. 126
Roosevelt, Pres. Theodore 4, 122, 125-126, 128, 130, 194-195, 223
Roosevelt, Quentin 194-195
Rosebud Creek 32, 181
Rosebud, Mont. 32, 181
Rough Riders 195
Russell, Charles 197, 199
Ryan, Paddy 206

S

Sacramento, Calif. 99
Sacred Heart Catholic Church 166
Sacred Heart Church 46, 166, 222
Sacred Heart Convent 46, 166, 168, 211
Sacred Heart High School 168
Sacred Heart School 168
Sanborn Fire Insurance 79, 112, 231
Sanborn Fire Map 112
San Juan Hill 195
Saunders, Ed 68
Savage, C.W. 60, 110, 156, 178-179
Schaal, Ron 211
Schmalsie, Fred 69
Schwartz, Levi 183
Scott, Randolph 57
Seattle, Wash. 190, 226-227
Second Cavalry 25, 29
Seventh Cavalry 7-10, 14-15, 29, 66, 89, 100, 209
Seventh Cavalry Drum and Bugle Corps 209
Shane 57
Sheridan, Ella 156
Sheridan, Gen. Phil 1, 6-8, 34
Sheridan, Wyo. 209, 211
Sherman, Elizabeth 27
Sherman, Gen. William Tecumseh 19, 27, 33-34
Sherman, Mary (Miles) 19, 27, 33
Sherman, Sen. John 19
Shyrack, Mary F. 155
Sierra County Cattle and Horse Protection Assn. 123
Sierra Nevada Mountains 99
Silver City, N.M. 123
Sioux (native American tribe) 6, 8-9, 22-23, 26, 28, 30, 56, 87, 89, 214, 219, 226
Siringo, Charles 120
Sitting Bull 8, 20-23, 25, 28-31
Sixth Cavalry 192
Skyrocket 196, 197, 223
Smith, J. Forsythe 164
Soap Suds Row 41
Sousa, John Phillip 180
Southwestern Stockman's Assn. 123

Spanish-American War 35, 48, 157
Spearfish, S.D. 110
Spence School for Young Women 148
Spottsylvania, Va. 19
Stanley, Col. David S. 8
State National Bank 143, 153
Stebbins-Post-Mund Bank 110
Steele, Fannie Sperry 197, 223
Stieffel, Pvt. Hermann 54
St. Joseph, Mo. 96
St. Louis, Mo. 7, 48, 88, 109
Stock Growers Assn. 123, 124, 129
Stockgrowers Journal 175, 204, 223-224
Stockgrowers National Bank 110
Stockmen's Dance 131
Stock-Raisers Assn. of Northwest Texas 123
Story, Nelson 107
St. Paul's Episcopal Mission 162
Strader's Saloon 69
Strevell, Charlie 47
Strevell, C.N. 164
Strevell, Helen (Miles) 47, 153, 164
Strevell, Jason 47
Stringer, John 128
Stuart, Granville 4, 122, 124-125, 129, 227
Stuart's Stranglers. 4, 125-126
Stubbins-Mund & Co. 110
Suds Row 41, 42
Swayne, George Edwin 148
Swayne, Mary Cato 148-149, 221

T

Tacoma, Wash. 190
Tascosa, Texas 3
Taylor, Dogg 77
Team Young Guns 209
Terrett, Wiseham 183
Terry, Gen. Alfred 27, 90
Terry, Mont. 7, 139, 141-145
Terry Tribune 147, 221
Texas and Southwestern Cattle Raisers Assn. 124
Texas (state of) 1, 3-4, 9, 21, 74, 106-108, 115-116, 120, 123-125, 134, 138-139, 141-142, 146-149, 207-209, 220-221, 226-229, 231, 234

Texas Team 209
The Spoilers 57
This Last West 39, 70, 215-223, 226
Thompson, Bill 126
Tilton, Miles Alford 67
Toledo, Ohio 167
Tombstone, Ariz. 3, 5, 207
Tongue River 3, 7-8, 10-13, 15-17, 20, 23, 25, 34, 37, 46, 49-52, 54-55, 58, 64, 71-72, 89, 103, 108, 182, 188, 213, 215
Tongue River Barracks 11, 13
Tongue River Cantonment 10-12, 15, 16, 20, 23, 37, 46, 49, 89, 182, 213, 215
Total Abstinence Society 44
Trinity Lutheran Church 169, 222
Tub Town 41
Turner, Cowboy Annie 2, 71,-73, 76, 82, 179
Turner, Josh 209, 224
Twain, Mark (Samuel Clemens) 88, 96, 98
Twenty-second Infantry 10, 23, 25
Twenty-second Massachusetts Volunteers 18

U

Ulio, James 157
Uncle Tom's Cabin 78, 152
Union Pacific Railroad 99, 102
United States Centennial 7
United States Military Academy (West Point) 20, 34, 38, 215
US Cavalry 67, 191
US Census 185, 190
US Depart. of Agriculture 107, 193
US Marine Band 180
US Navy 196

V

Vancouver Barracks, Wash. 34
Villard, Henry 101, 104
Vreeland, Byron 178

W

Waco, Texas 142
Wagenbreth, C.J. 161
Wallowa Valley, Ore. 27
Warhank, Josef James 52, 215
Washington, D.C. 33, 35, 215, 227
Washington. Eli 42, 222, 230
Washington School 157
Washington (state of) 100
WaterWorks Art Museum 5, 202
Wayne, John 57, 196
W-Bar Ranch 132-136
Weisner, Ed 145
Weisner, Louis 145
Wells, J.A. 126
Western Trail 106, 109
Westminster, Mass. 18, 46, 54
West Point (United States Military Academy) 20, 34, 38, 215
Whipple, Maj. Charles D. 59
Whistler, Lt. Col. J.N.G. 10
White Bird 31
Whiteside, Fred 179
Whiteside, Helen (Dunning) 179
Whitney, Dr. C.S. 130
Wibaux, Cyril 134
Wibaux, Mont. 135
Wibaux Park 137
Wibaux, Pierre 7, 132, 135-137, 220
Wichita, Kan. 106, 230
Wild Horse Races 210
Williams, Chancey 209, 224
Williamson, Mary Cato 148
Williams River Cattle and Horse Growers Assn. 123
Wilson, F.M. 37, 52, 54-55
Wilson, Lem 69
Wolf Mountain 24-25, 214, 229
Wolf Point, Mont. 200
Wolheim, Louis 191
World War I 36, 48, 158
World War II 158
Wormwood, Hank 69

Y

Yankton, S.D. 10, 87, 218
Yellowstone Expedition 8-9
Yellowstone 91
Yellowstone (steamboat) 156
Yellowstone Journal 52, 56, 70, 153, 175-176, 214, 216-218
Yellowstone Lake 88
Yellowstone National Park 88
Yellowstone Park 31
Yellowstone River 1, 3-4, 7-9, 11, 17, 19, 22-25, 27, 31-34, 37, 40, 46, 52, 55-56, 70, 84-85, 8-89, 91-93, 95, 97, 101, 103, 108-109, 114, 139-140, 143, 153, 156, 175-176, 214-218, 225-226, 229
Yellowstone Valley 93
Y-Tic-Se-Lim 186-187, 189, 223

Z

Zook, Laura Manderscheid Brown 159

Author Bio

Bill O'Neal was appointed State Historian of Texas by Governor Rick Perry, and during his six-year tenure he traveled tens of thousands of miles across the Lone Star State as an ambassador for Texas history. He is a past president and fellow of both the East Texas Historical Association and the West Texas Historical Association, and he has been a member of the Texas State Historical Association for over half a century.

Bill is the author of more than fifty books. He was awarded the A.C. Greene Literary Award at the 2015 West Texas Book Festival in Abilene. In 2012 Bill received the Lifetime Achievement Award of the Wild West Historical Association, and in 2007 he was named *True West Magazine's* Best Living Non-Fiction Writer. His account of Wyoming's *Johnson County War* won a book of the year award.

Bill has appeared on TV documentaries on TBS, The History Channel, The Learning Channel, CMT, A&E, and the American Heroes Channel. During a long career at Panola College in Carthage, Texas, his most prestigious teaching award was a Piper Professorship, presented in 2000.

In 2013 Panola's new dormitory was named Bill O'Neal Hall, and in that same year he received an honorary Doctor of Letters degree from his alma mater, Texas A&M University-Commerce. Bill's four daughters all have entered the field of education, and he is the proud grandfather of seven grandchildren.

Bill O'Neal Books From Eakin Press

The American Association: A Baseball History 1902-1991
Paperback • 400 pages • ISBN 978-0890158128 • $26.99

The Arizona Rangers
Paperback • 234 pages • ISBN 978-0-89015-610-0 • $22.99

Billy and Olive Dixon: The Plainsman and His Lady
Paperback • 270 pages • ISBN 978-1-68179-145-6 • $19.75

The Bloody Legacy of Pink Higgins: A Half Century of Violence in Texas
Paperback • 186 pages • ISBN 978-1-57168-304-5 • $19.75

Border Queen Caldwell: Toughest Town on the Chisholm Trail
Paperback • 254 pages • ISBN 978-1-934645-66-6 • $24.95

Captain Harry Wheeler, Arizona Lawman
Paperback. •. 198 pages • ISBN 978-1-57168-064-8 • $21.95

Cassity Jones: The Man, The Corporation
Paperback • 168 pages • ISBN 978-1934645420 • $19.99

Cattlemen vs Sheepherders: Five Decades of Violence in the West
Paperback • 236 pages • ISBN 978-1934645420 • $24.99

Cheyenne: 1867 to 1903: A Biography of the Magic City of the Plains
Paperback • 398 Pages • ISBN 978-1934645420 • $29.95

Doris Miller — Hero of Pearl Harbor
Paperback • 64 pages • ISBN 978-1-934645-01-7 • $9.99

Great Gunfighters of the Old West
Paperback • 98 pages • ISBN 978-1-68179-059-6 • $12.95

Historic Ranches of the Old West
Paperback • 378 pages • ISBN 978-0-9789150-9-4 • $26.95

International League: 125 Years of Baseball
Paperback • 263 pages • ISBN 978-1934645567 • $24.99

John Chisum: Frontier Cattle King
Paperback • 174 pages • ISBN 978-1-68179-113-5 • $19.95

John S. "Rip Ford: Texian Hero
Paperback • 312 pages • ISBN. 978-1-68179-352-8 • $26.99

Johnson County War
Paperback • 306 pages • ISBN 978-1-57168-876-7 • $27.95

Lampasas 1855-1895: Biography of a Frontier City
Paperback • 262 pages • ISBN 978-1-940130-63-7 • $24.95

Long Before the Pilgrims — The First Thanksgiving
Paperback • 42 pages • ISBN 978-1-57168-498-1 • $12.95

Miles City: Rollicking Cow Capital of the Montana Frontier
Paperback • 252 pages • ISBN 978-1-68179-388-7 • $24.99

The Pacific Coast League – 1903-1988
Paperback • 378 pages • ISBN 978-1-68179-116-6 •. $26.99

Reel Rangers: Texas Rangers in Movies, TV, Radio & Other Popular Culture
Paperback. •. 216 pages. •. ISBN 978-1-57168-840-8. •. $19.95

Sam Houston: A Study in Leadership
Paperback. •. 270 pages. •. ISBN 978-1-68179-037-4. •. $24.99

Sam Houston Slept Here: Homes of the Chief Executives of Texas
Paperback. •. 180 pages. •. ISBN 978-1-57168-584-1. •. $19.95

Sons of the Pioneers
Paperback. •. 258 pages. •. ISBN. 978-1-57168-644-2. •. $24.95

The Southern League: Baseball in Dixie, 1885-1984
Paperback. •. 292 pages. •. ISBN 978-0-89015-952-1. •. $24.99

Texas Country Music Hall of Fame
By Bill O'Neal and Tommie Ritter Smith
Paperback. •. 160 pages. •. ISBN 978-1-68179-263-7. •. $19.99

The Texas League: A Century of Baseball
Paperback • 408 pages • ISBN 978-0-89015-609-4 • $29.99

Tex Ritter: America's Most Beloved Cowboy
Paperback • 160 pages • ISBN 978-1-57168-249-9 • $22.99

Wild Horse Media Group
Eakin Press • NorTex Press • Wild Horse Press
P.O. Box 331779 • Fort Worth, Texas 76163 • www.WildHorseMedia.com

www.ingramcontent.com/pod-product-compliance
Lightning Source LLC
Chambersburg PA
CBHW021146160426
43194CB00007B/714